DIRECTOR

CLASSIC
RACING
MOTORCYCLES

Brian Woolley

Aston Publications

Sole distributors for the USA
Motorbooks International
Publishers & Wholesalers Inc.
Osceola, Wisconsin 54020, USA

Published in 1988 by Aston Publications Limited,
Bourne End House, Harvest Hill, Bourne End,
Bucks. SL8 5JJ.

ISBN 0 946627 47 9

Designed by Chris Hand

Photoset and printed in England by
Redwood Burn Limited
Trowbridge, Wiltshire

Sole distributors to the UK book trade,
Springfield Books Ltd.,
Norman Road,
Denby Dale, Huddersfield,
West Yorkshire, HD8 8TH.

Sole distributors for the USA,
Motorbooks International,
PO Box 2,
729 Prospect Avenue,
Osceola,
Wisconsin 54020,
United States.

Contents

Title Page: *Flat out round the first turn at the steeply banked Fisco track near Tokyo goes the field at the opening meeting in 1965 of this Japanese circuit*

Front cover: *Mike Hailwood (AJS 7R) in 1962. The machine was painted red because private entrant Tom Kirby always raced in that colour.* (Nick Nicholls)

3

Acknowledgements

I first encountered racing motorcycles as a small boy when I was taken by my father to an early meeting at Donington Park. The passion that began then has not abated after something like fifty-five years. I fell in love with the Isle of Man when I was stationed there in the RAF during the war, and I made my first voluntary trip there (the first of many) to watch the Manx Grand Prix in 1946. I saw most of the Classic era at first hand, riding myself in a modest way and later becoming quite seriously involved in racing motorcycle development. During those years I had the good fortune to make many friends, all too many of whom, alas, are now gone, but I try to keep in touch with most of those who remain. I must say that in those days I never thought that at the age of sixty I would begin a new 'career' as a writer, but then along came *Classic Bike* and later its companion quarterly *Classic Racer*, and thanks to the encouragement of the editor, Mike Nicks, I soon became a regular contributor, a role that led to my employment as archivist and researcher for the various Classic titles published by EMAP Ltd. In this capacity, not only did I renew a lot of old friendships but made many new ones.

So many people have been helpful during the writing of this Directory that I can only thank a few of them here: notably Tony Pritchard, who commissioned the book and has been patiently supportive whilst it was being written, and Tim Parker in America, who has read the manuscript (and corrected some silly mistakes) and encouraged me at long distance. I have had help too from that paragon of motorcycling journalists Vic Willoughby, and from fellow writers Mick Walker, Raymond Ainscoe, Phil Heath and Alan Cathcart in settling various points of fact. I was assisted too by Herman Meier (now retired to Majorca) and by Obering Siegfried Rauch, for so long associated with the DKW company. Dr Helmut Krackowizer, organizer of the Austrian Old Timers Grand Prix was tremendously helpful, as also was ex-Guzzi rider and TT winner Maurice Cann. Arch NSU enthusiast and expert Emlyn Evans saved me from perpetrating a couple of gross errors that had crept into the accepted NSU story, and Ing. Giulio Carcano kindly confirmed certain obscure points in the history of Moto Guzzi. So did veteran Guzzi designer Antonio Micucci who, to my surprise, I discovered to be living in Mandello dell Lario and at 79 years of age still enthusiastic over his involvement in Moto Guzzi's post-war racing. There were many other helpful contributors. Above all I will remember the enthusiasm of almost everyone I approached; typical was the long telephone conversation I had with Alan Shepherd.

In a voice that rang with sincerity, he said to me, 'If you've been involved with motorcycle racing, you never forget it, do you? You'll go back to it and back again. Once you're into motorcycle racing, it's something that stays with you until you die.'

Alan, you never spoke a truer word!

Introduction

When I was first asked to compile this directory, I had a very real problem in deciding which motorcycles to include and which to leave out. The time span was decided for me by the Classic Racing Motorcycle Club's ruling that a Classic racer was one built and raced between – in the case of a four-stroke – 1946 and 1972. For two-strokes, the CRMC stipulate the earlier cut-off date of 1967. After a lot of debate, I decided that the other major qualification for inclusion would be an association with the TT races in the Isle of Man. During the Classic years, the TT, which counted towards both riders' and constructors' Championships, was of tremendous importance. No European manufacturer with sporting pretensions ignored the series, and to win a TT counted with the public quite as much if not more than a World Championship!

Rather reluctantly, I next decided that I could not do justice to the multitude of 'specials' – some of them of great interest, and built to the highest of engineering standards – that raced during the Classic years. I am sorry about this, but to have included even just the best of such machines would have increased the length of the directory by 50 per cent!

For similar reasons, I was forced to ignore the peculiarly Italian phenomenon of long-distance road races on public roads, the Clubman's TT series of 1946–56 and the Formula 750 TT of 1971–74. Many machines that took part in these events are of great interest, and deserve a book or books of their own, but most of them were really 'motorcycles that were raced' rather than racing motorcycles.

Let me emphasize that this directory is not at all about the Classic racing scene of today. It is about the machines (and, inevitably, some of the men) of an era and how they compared in their day. I am sure that some readers will feel that I have devoted far too much space to some makes and nothing like enough to others. I can only plead that as far as I could I have let results speak for themselves.

As someone who had the wonderful good fortune to be there during the Classic era, and to have played a modest but active part in some of the events, I have seen with mixed feelings how in the last few years some makes and models have been elevated to an importance that they scarcely enjoyed in their day. There are often good reasons for this late-flowering popularity, which in itself is harmless enough, but one ought not to lose sight of history. Fortunately, the very popular magazines *Classic Bike* and *Classic Racer* have always, in my opinion, presented balanced and well-researched articles about racing motorcycles of both Vintage and Classic times. Long may they continue to do so.

And what of Classic racing today? I have said that this directory is not concerned with it and nor is it, but it is after all the reason for worldwide interest in the Classic era, and it is itself a growing and changing movement. I myself go to as many meetings as I can, though I have to be truthful and say that I prefer the parades to the races, because the machines are almost always more authentic. Classic racing's remarkable growth in popularity has had two inevitable effects. One is the rise in value of authentic machinery, until it becomes unthinkable that such bikes should be raced in anger and possibly be blown up or crashed. The other is the subtle (and sometimes not so subtle) modernization of those machines that *are* raced in earnest. Both the VMCC and the CRMC have shown an awareness that whilst racing what I can only describe as 'Classic bangers' can be good and reasonably cheap fun for the owners it has precious little spectator appeal. I for one cannot persuade myself that a stripped down Honda road bike of 1970 is either Classic or a racing motorcycle!

Then we come to a very vexed question indeed, that of authenticity. So long as a Classic racer is neat and tidy and does not display silly anachronisms, I am afraid that I cannot get worked up about the fact that either, on the one hand, it is 'original' or, on the other, that it is built up from the assorted remains of half a dozen incomplete machines plus some castings and sheet metal work of modern origin. Almost all racing motorcycles are modified and rebuilt continuously to such an extent that a claim that such and such a machine is the one on which so and so won the TT, especially when applied to a bike that is thirty or forty years old, is almost bound to be highly suspect. I will leave it to others to argue about this subject, but suffice it to say that even those machines that are shown in factory museums are usually built up from assorted parts, some of them re- manufactured.

Speaking of museums and collections, some of which are open to the public, do not take it for granted that they are open permanently. It is always advisable to make sure of the actual opening dates and hours in plenty of time before making a visit.

If you want to see Classic racing motorcycles in action, then in England the VMCC and CRMCC (and various other clubs) serve you well. Both *Classic Bike* and *Classic Racer* publish and update calendars of such events. At the time of writing, the Classic Manx Grand Prix appears to be well established, but the same cannot, alas, be said of Classic involvement with the TT. This has varied from year to year and has been generally ill-organized and disappointing, though it is hard to know who to blame for this. Once again, things alter, and there are now hopeful signs that the situation may be improved in the future.

The two major events that have become established in Europe are the Historic Motorcycle Grand Prix held at Misano, Italy, in June and the Old Timers' Grand Prix held at the Salzburgring, Austria, in September. These are both two-day events, and not so much races as high-speed parades.

They are enormously popular and many 'works' machines emerge from factory and other museums for these events. In America every March there is Vintage and Classic racing at the famous circuit at Daytona, Florida, run under the rules of the American Historic Racing Motorcycle Association (AHRMA).

Classic racing in Europe is controlled by the International Historic Racing Organization (IHRO), whose rules, differently framed to those of the CRMC, encourage – indeed demand – the racing of machines of genuinely Classic specification and exclude anachronisms and 'banger racers'.

Finally, a word of warning to anyone contemplating acquiring a Classic racing motorcycle, especially if the eventual intention is to race it. Join the VMCC, CRMC or the IHRO as appropriate, before, rather than after, spending what these days has got to be a lot of money, and make 100 per cent sure that you fully understand the eligibility rules of the club. Quite a few people have had a nasty surprise when they have joined a club, turned up for a meeting and only then discovered that some feature or other renders their pride and joy ineligible to race. They have only themselves to blame.

But to return to this directory. Dealing as I have done with over thirty makes, not to mention different models, has sometimes called for a certain amount of elision and omission of details. I sincerely hope that this has not distorted history or led to any glaring inaccuracies! If it has, I am sure that my readers will let me know!

Thank you for reading this directory and I sincerely hope that you enjoy it.

AJS
The Porcupine

It is hard today to credit the sensation created when, for the 1947 Senior TT, Associated Motor Cycles (AMC) revealed their new E90 parallel twin. It was totally new, strikingly original and the specification was a formidable one. At a stroke it made such rivals as the Manx Norton and the Velocette appear positively archaic. How could it fail to be a winner? The engine lay nearly horizontally in the cradle frame, which itself embodied many advanced features. Bore and stroke were all but 'square' at 68 × 68.5mm, 498cc. The pistons rose and fell together, firing at 360 degrees. Twin overhead camshafts and bucket tappets operated the valves, which were controlled by hairpin springs. The whole of the valve gear was enclosed and driven by a train of spur gears, the first of which also drove the Lucas racing magneto. Spur gears also drove the unit construction four-speed gearbox, which was of conventional British style, with clutch and final drive sprocket coaxial. The engine, therefore, ran 'backwards'. The clutch itself was massive and ran dry in the open air.

There were twin Amal racing carburettors, which at first were carried on straight flexibly mounted inlet pipes so that the mixing chambers were horizontal. This was soon changed, and curved inlet pipes carried the carburettors more nearly vertical.

Inside the engine, the massive three-bearing crankshaft ran in a plain centre bearing and two ball races, and the light alloy connecting rods used plain white metal bearings for the big ends. High-pressure oil was supplied to the crankshaft and valve gear by a large gear pump, and was returned to the 1.5-gallon oil tank by a scavenge pump in the dry sump. Another pump, driven from the exhaust camshaft, scavenged the valve gear. Externally the light alloy cylinders with pressed-in steel sleeves were cooled by generous longitudinal fins, but most noticeable was the feature for which the E90 was nicknamed, the peculiar spiky finning of the light alloy cylinder heads. The heavy emphasis on cooling reflected the fact that originally the Porcupine had been designed for supercharging, permitted before the war, but banned by the FICM for 1947.

The E90 parallel twin 'Porcupine' with curved inlet pipes. This machine was 500cc World Champion in 1949.

Bill Doran in the 1951 Senior TT on the E90 Porcupine. He finished in a well-earned second place. The 'Porcupine' fins on the cylinder head can just be seen in this photograph.

The original genesis of the Porcupine sprang from Norton race chief Joe Craig's urgent wish in the late nineteenth-thirties to develop a 'blown' multi with which to compete against the supercharged machines from Gilera and BMW. Frustrated by Norton's unwillingness to comply, and by their withdrawal from racing in 1939, Craig went first to BSA, then to AMC.

In retrospect, it is curious how, in contrast to some more highly regarded firms, the Collier Brothers' rather ramshackle seeming Matchless Empire always appeared to have money to spare for 'adventures'. Their road going Silver Arrow and Silver Hawk multis were commercial failures and must have cost the company dearly in the depressed early 1930s but then they designed the astonishingly bold Vee-four AJS first proposed as a road bike, then with the addition of a supercharger as a Grand Prix racer. An unsuccessful outing at the 1936 Senior TT did not discourage the Collier brothers – instead they called in development engineer Matt Wright to redesign the bike completely and it was raced in 1938 and 1939 with water cooling – but with no very great success. Its enduring claim to a place in history is Walter Rusk's 100mph lap in the 1939 Ulster Grand Prix before one of the links in the girder front forks snapped.

That the Collier Brothers were willing to consider abandoning the Vee-four is a startling proof of their open mindedness, because its potential was considerable. But they were receptive to Craig's ideas and made him chief of the racing department. Then Craig, ever a disciple of the simple approach, had second thoughts. Would a twin not serve as well as a four? Within a short time he had convinced himself that such was the case, and had produced rough sketches of the machine he envisaged.

Although not himself a draughtsman, he had no difficulty in having designers Vic Webb and Phil Irving turn his concept into reality. The cycle parts were

Reg Armstrong at Ballaugh in the 1951 Senior TT.

equally as advanced as the engine, with a robust wide-spaced twin-cradled welded frame, modified AMC Teledraulic front forks and swinging arm rear suspension controlled by spring and damper units of AMC's own make. Notably advanced was the use of two leading-shoe brakes front and rear. Unfortunately for AJS, Joe Craig left to return to Norton on more advantageous terms before the FICM ban on superchargers. Had he stayed to develop the unblown E90 as he did the Norton singles, history might have been very different! As it was, AJS development engineer Mat Wright did well to make the Porcupine competitive in the short time he had.

Riders in the 1947 Senior were Les Graham and veteran Jock West, AMC sales manager, who in 1939 had finished second in the Senior race on a blown BMW. In practice they had their share of problems; the bikes had never been ridden until their arrival in the Isle of Man, and they found the oil drag of the plain bearings making starting difficult and disliked the engines' lack of flywheel effect. The supercharger's rotating inertia had been calculated into the total rotating inertia of the engine and its loss made the engine only too easy to stall riding away from a slow corner. Though it was not realized at the time, this characteristic was responsible for the infuriating tendency of the magneto shaft to shear, which happened more than once, although the most notorious occasion was in 1949, when poor Les Graham was robbed of a Senior TT victory only two minutes from the chequered flag.

The 1947 race was no fairy tale debut. West's first lap was quite disastrously slowed by a slipping clutch, taking a heartbreaking 1 hour 24 mins as against his fastest lap, his fourth, in 26 mins 59 secs, which compared well with the fastest lap of the race of 26 mins 56 secs.

Graham, not so fast, at least had a consistent ride into ninth place, though having to push in from Governor's Bridge with a rear chain that had jumped the sprocket. At the Ulster Grand Prix, West was a good third and Ted Frend was fifth.

For the 1948 TT Graham, West and Frend were entered and started well, Graham being second and West fifth at the end of the first lap. But Frend retired on lap two, Graham on lap three and West on lap six, with, of all things, a broken

The E95 – ridden here in the 1952 TT by New Zealander Rod Coleman.

throttle cable. At the Ulster Grand Prix, West was third and Frend fifth. Les Graham was by now emerging as a star, and, in 1949, though he retired at the Belgian Grand Prix, which Bill Doran won for AJS, and after leading the Senior TT virtually throughout he had to push in from Hillberry to finish tenth, his performances were enough to win him the 500cc World Championship and the constructor's title for AJS.

Gradually some of the problems with the E90 were resolved: fitting a larger sump and doing away with the remote oil tank reduced bearing drag when cold; and heavier full-circle flywheels replaced the original bob-weights. Some fine riders were associated with the Porcupine after Les Graham's departure in 1951, Reg Armstrong, Bill Doran (who finished second in the 1951 TT), Bob McIntyre, Bill Lomas and Rod Coleman all spring to mind, but results remained uncertain and largely disappointing.

Strangely, rather than continue to develop the E90, AMC management had H. J. Hatch design a completely new machine for 1952 with the engine canted at 45 degrees in the frame to improve cooling of the exhaust port area. But the new E95 model was no more successful than the E90, and at the end of 1954 AJS retired from racing. Four E90s and four E95s had been built with perhaps half a dozen spare engine units and many spare forgings and castings. The 1954 season was not quite the end of the Porcupine, however, for in late 1963, after the AJS racing department was disbanded, veteran entrant Tom Arter acquired one of the E95s for Canadian rider Mike Duff. The ten-year-old bike proved uncompetitive, and spares were in short supply. Although he rode the Porcupine several times in 1964 and 1965, Duff pursued his career as a Yamaha rider.

At the time of writing, it is thought that one, possibly two, E90 models still exist, and of the three, possibly four, E95s believed to survive, at least two are built up from a hodge-podge of bits, old, new and re-manufactured. The Porcupine was a failure, yet it still exercises a strange fascination!

The 7R

In February 1948, at a time when in England good news was conspicuous only by its absence, many a racing motorcyclist's spirits were lifted by the announcement that AJS were to make a new 350cc model for sale to the private owner. Given the pre-war designation of 7R, the new machine shared nothing with its forebear, except for its capacity and the use of a single overhead camshaft driven by a Weller-tensioned chain. The 7R frame was in effect a copy of that of the 'works' E90 Porcupine twins, a robust wide-spaced double cradle of welded steel tube. Modified AMC Teledraulic forks, oil-damped spring units controlling a swinging arm rear suspension, and conical hubs with twin leading-shoe front and rear brakes all resembled those of the E90. The brand new 74 × 81mm 348cc single-cylinder engine made extensive use of magnesium castings, which were treated with a distinctive gold-coloured corrosion-inhibiting paint. The heavily finned light alloy cylinder barrel had a pressed-in iron liner, and iron valve seats were shrunk fit into the light alloy cylinder head, the whole assembly being rigidly attached to the crankcase by four long bolts.

The single overhead camshaft, rockers and hairpin valve springs were enclosed and access for adjustment of the eccentric rocker spindles was by way of detachable covers. Spur gears drove the Lucas racing magneto situated behind the cylinder, and an Amal racing carburettor was fitted at a fairly steep downdraught angle. Primary transmission was by an open single-row chain to a conventional separate Burman racing gearbox with four close ratios.

The design of the AJS 7R was nominally ascribed to the long-serving Philip Walker, but there is no doubt at all that credit for the concept and many of the details should go to AMC Sales Director Jock West, himself a road racer of considerable repute. A very thorough pre-launch testing programme ensured that the machines delivered in time for the 1948 TT were remarkably reliable. No fewer than 23 7Rs were entered in the Junior race, with the factory machinery ridden by Les Graham, Jock West and Ted Frend. In view of the enforced use of 75-octane petrol, the speed of the winner, Freddie Frith on his Mk VIII Velocette, was remarkably high at 81.5 mph.

Bob Foster on another works Velocette was second, followed by the factory

Jock West airs the 7R AJS for the very first time at Brands Hatch when it was still a grass track.

1948 – the original 7R AJS as sold – this one to Fergus Anderson.

Nortons of Artie Bell and Johnny Lockett. Private 7R owner Maurice Cann came home in a truly remarkable fifth place, but perhaps indicative of the effort that AMC were devoting to the 500cc E90 Porcupine at this time, the factory 7Rs could do no better than for Les Graham to finish seventh and Jock West 13th. No fewer than ten 7Rs finished within replica time, a most gratifying debut for a virtually untried motorcycle. But the sensation of the 1948 TT series was in the Senior race, when Geoff Murdoch (who had experienced every trouble imaginable in the Junior) finished in an astonishing fourth place!

Both Norton and Velocette were slow to resume full production of 'over the counter' racing machinery, and the 7R AJS sold freely. Twenty-six were entered for the 1948 Manx Grand Prix, and on one of them Phil Heath finished a very close second to Denis Parkinson's Norton. Ten other 7R riders won replicas. The 7R never did win a TT, but Don Crossley finished third in the Manx Grand Prix in 1949 and was victorious the following year at record speed.

Thereafter, the AJS 7R made up a very large part of the starting grid at events in Britain, on the Continent and in the Isle of Man, and some very famous names were

The AJS 7R in its last 'short-stroke' version in 1961.

associated with its success. The factory's own efforts by contrast were curiously lacklustre. However, in 1952, veteran designer H. J. Hatch joined AMC and (for the works team only) he devised the 7R3, an entirely new engine with bore and stroke of 75.5 × 78mm and with twin exhaust valves. A chain-driven camshaft operated the inlet valve direct, and another camshaft, bevel-driven from the inlet camshaft, ran fore and aft, operating the exhaust valves by rockers. A strange concept – but it worked. The bike brought AJS their one and only post-war TT win in the 1954 Junior, Rod Coleman coming home at a record speed of 91.51 mph ahead of team-mate Derek Farrant on another 7R3. At the end of the year a team of riders led by Rod Coleman used the 7R3 to take thirteen world records at Montl-héry. Thereafter, AJS as a factory withdrew from road racing. However, de-velopment of the 7R continued in the capable hands of Jack Williams, who had replaced Matt Wright as development engineer in 1953.

The production engine was given the 75.5 × 78mm dimensions of the three-valve engine, and a stiffer crankshaft assembly. Over the next few years, Williams, by patient attention to the new engine's breathing, raised its power from 37 hp at 7500 rpm to 42 hp at 7800 rpm and this improvement, in conjunction with reduction of weight over the years, kept the 7R competitive at national racing levels. Though AMC abruptly decided to end production of racing motorcycles in 1962, the 7R was still raceworthy well into the middle, even the late sixties, though as time wore on it began to lose ground to the 350cc Aermacchis and to the Bultaco two-strokes, a process which was completed by the appearance of the TR Yamahas. The sheer number of 7Rs made between 1948 and 1962 meant that a good number survived, and it is very prominent today in Classic racing. At least one of the factory 7R3 models also survives.

The three-valve AJS 7R3 engine with transverse and fore and aft camshafts.

Adler

After World War II the very old-established German firm of Adler reentered motorcycle manufacturing with a series of small two-stroke machines that culminated in 1953 with the 54 × 54mm 247cc twin-cylinder M250. Of very advanced specification, it had air-cooled iron cylinders with light alloy cylinder heads, a pressed-up crankshaft that had its two halves united by machined 'dogs' and a high-tensile bolt tightened with a special key through the hollow mainshaft. The crankshaft ran in four ball-bearing races and the big end bearings were crowded needle rollers. The four-speed gearbox was in unit, driven by primary gears and the clutch was on the end of the drive side mainshaft of the crankshaft. The very nicely styled engine was fitted into a stout tubular frame of double-loope cradle pattern with plunger box rear suspension. At the front there were bottom link forks that bore a passing resemblance to those used on the racing Moto Guzzis.

Soon after the appearance of the M250, which for its day had a brilliant performance, a stripped and mildly tuned version was raced in German Club events by Walter Vogel, whose modest results led factory development engineer Kurt Grassman to create a genuine 'over the counter' racing machine for sale for 1954. For this, the RS250, 26 hp at 7500 rpm was claimed, but, alas, this was a wild exaggeration! The RS250 had twin racing carburettors, a raised compression ratio, slightly larger ports and characteristic racing exhaust pipes with parabolic reverse sections and short tail-pipes. On such a model, rider Helmut Hallmeier won the 250cc race on the RS250's first appearance at a speed meeting at Diedburg early in 1954. The RS250 was not cheap at approximately £400, or at 1988 prices near enough £5,000!

Unfortunately, the Adler factory did little or no development, almost certainly because of the rapidly worsening domestic market for motorcycles in Germany that caused many factories, including Adler, to close their doors in 1957–58. But in 1955, Helmut Hallmeier, backed by his father's engineering business, was offering

Greg Volichenko's beautiful drawing of the Adler RS250 with full Hallmeier conversion.

many special parts for RS250s, including special pistons, larger carburettors and full conversions for water-cooling. So 'professional' were some of the machines that were built by German enthusiasts over the next few years that it has often been assumed that these were factory products and that Adler ran a works team. Not so. And though Adler riders did well enough in domestic events, the two-stroke twins were always overshadowed by the NSU Rennmaxes and DKWs in National and International events, and had no notable success at a more ambitious level. Except, that is, in 1958 in the Isle of Man! In that year, in the 250cc Lightweight class of the TT, run on the Clypse circuit, Dieter Falk did remarkably well to finish fifth, only 3.1 mph slower than winner Tarquinio Provini's MV, and otherwise beaten only by Carlo Ubbiali on the other works MV and Mike Hailwood and Bob Brown on Sportmax NSUs. Behind Dieter, finishing on the same lap, came Sammy Miller on a works CZ and Eric Hinton, Tommy Robb and Fron Purslow on Sportmax NSUs. A very creditable result for man and machine. Alas, in 1959 when there were four Adler entries, Gunter Beer did not start, Hans Scheifel and Arnold Jones both retired and Siegfried Lohman finished a poor tenth. No Adlers ran in 1960. One of the water-cooled Adlers ridden by John Dixon did quite well in British events in the very early 1960s, but was soon put in its place by the Ariel 'Arrow' racer (said to be derived from the Adler) developed by Herman Meier. Perhaps the RS250, Adler's greatest claim to fame, was the starting point for the development of the racing Yamahas!

Quite a few of the water-cooled RS250s survive and are a welcome feature of Classic meetings on the Continent.

Aermacchi

The classic Aermacchi four-stroke, with near horizontal cylinder, push-rod and rocker operation of the valves and unit construction gearbox evolved from an unlikely forebear, the strikingly styled all enclosed 172cc 'Chimera' that was the sensation of the Milan Show in 1956. From this engine, designer Alfredo Bianchi developed a 66 × 72mm 246cc unit to power a much more sporting road machine, the Ala Verda, and from this, in the nature of things Italian, a genuine racing model emerged, at almost the same time that America's Harley-Davidson acquired a half-share in the Varese concern. This was a mutually profitable arrangement that worked well, Harley-Davidson importing Aermacchi singles in large numbers for many years as credible lightweight machines to supplement their own big Vee twins. In time, H-D were wholly to own Aermacchi. The first Aermacchi to appear and race in England was one of the Ala Verda sports models, imported by that ubiquitous entrepreneur Arnold Jones for the 1960 Thruxton 500-mile race for production machines.

Prepared and entered by dealer Peter Doncaster, and ridden by Jones and Horace Crowder, the Aermacchi was sensationally fast, but, alas, when Crowder was two clear laps ahead, the primary drive gears broke, forcing him to retire. Nevertheless, so impressed was one spectator, veteran rider, entrant and enthusiast for Italian machinery Bill Webster, that he immediately made contact with the factory, and in September 1960 announced that for 1961 he would import 250cc Aermacchis, and that the consignment would include ten genuine racing machines. In appearance, the Aermacchi altered little in a dozen years – the early Webster imports had the classic large-diameter spine frame tube, with swinging arm rear suspension, Ceriani front forks and drum brakes fore and aft that were to be a familiar sight in paddocks throughout the Classic era. Painted Italian fire engine red, the Aermacchis set many pulses racing, and if the factory's claims for power

The typical Aermacchi engine-gearbox layout, unaltered for so many years.

output had been truthful, the bikes would have trampled all over the feeble competition in British racing. Unfortunately an unsatisfactory oiling system, poor materials and even worse quality control meant that these early long-stroke, four-speed racers were terribly unreliable.

Factory-entered riders Alberto Pagani and Gilberto Milani raced on the Continent with moderate success, but in an era dominated by multi-cylinder Grand Prix machines from Japan could scarcely hope for high placings in the Classics. In Britain, the bikes were regarded as fast – but fragile. This was realized by the factory, and resulted in a major redesign of the engine for the 1963 season, with bore and stroke of 72 × 61mm and with a five-speed gearbox. In April 1963 Bill Webster died suddenly, and the Aermacchi concession was taken over by another dealer, Southampton-based ex-Norton team rider Syd Lawton. The new short-stroke two-fifty was considerably improved over the years through Lawton's no-nonsense approach, and it was he who persuaded the factory to take the 350cc class seriously, with the result that from 1965 the larger Aermacchi became an ever-growing force in British short circuit racing.

The 350cc Aermacchi of 1965 that led on to fortune.

Bob Farmer makes his mark, winning the 1966 Manx Grand Prix 250cc race on an Aermacchi.

Aermacchi never won a TT or a World Championship in the Classic era, and indeed their TT record was a poor one, the best performance until Brian Steenson's second place to Agostini's Junior MV in 1969 being Pagani's fifth in the 1962 Lightweight event.

The Lightweight Manx Grand Prix was a happier story. Reintroduced after a long lapse, the 1964 event was won by Gordon Keith on a Greeves two-stroke, but Rex Butcher, Terry Grotefeld and John Blanchard, all on Aermacchis, finished second, third and fourth. In 1966, taking advantage of the Aermacchi's frugal petrol consumption, Bob Farmer made a non-stop run to win the three-lap race.

The 250 model was, however, now beginning to be overshadowed by the rising tide of Yamahas, and development of the 350cc machine took first place. This was very apparent by 1969, in which year, in the Junior TT, not only did Steenson finished second, but Jack Findley was third; in all, another eleven Aermacchi riders won replicas. In the Lightweight race, only one Aermacchi finished, in twelfth place. In the Manx Grand Prix that year, Aermacchi-mounted Robin Duffy won, and five other riders took replicas in the Junior event, whereas in the Lightweight class only four Aermacchi riders finished, the highest placed being 17th. The following year a similar pattern emerged. There were no Aermacchi finishers in the 250cc class at the TT, but Alan Barnett finished second to Agostini's Junior MV, Peter Berwick finished sixth and ten other Aermacchi riders won replicas.

At the Manx, the best, indeed the *only*, Aermacchi finisher in the Lightweight was 19th, whereas the Junior race was won by Charlie Brown with eight other Aermacchi riders winning replicas. In the last year of the Classic era, an Aermacchi ridden by Ken Hugget again won the Junior Manx Grand Prix. After that, even the Manx Grand Prix was overwhelmed by the Japanese two-strokes. So complete was the eclipse, even at club racing level, of 250cc and 350cc four-strokes that the abiding wonder is that, over the next few years, so many survived! Fortunately, sentiment and affection for the Aermacchi's qualities meant that very few were scrapped.

Since the formation of the CRMC, the Aermacchi has come back into its own, well served with new, even improved, spare parts, and a body of knowledge derived from experience that ensures that a well prepared and serviced bike is actually faster than it was when new, and certainly more reliable. Survival rate is high, and in Classic racing a good Aermacchi is hard to beat. Considering its push-rod and rocker valve gear, the Aermacchi was, and is, astonishingly quick.

BMW

Many people take it for granted that the famous firm of BMW moved into road racing only in the late 1930s and certainly they gained startling prominence when in 1938 they won the 500cc European Championship – previously regarded as almost the property of Norton – and then capped this by winning the 1939 Senior TT. But, of course, BMW had raced in Germany and elsewhere (admittedly in a modest way) almost since the company's inception in 1923. Their late flowering was due to the National Socialist Party's use of motor sport success as propaganda and their financial incentives to that end. The 500cc supercharged BMWs raced in the last three years of peace were superb examples of racing design free from commercial considerations. But after the war, BMW were slow to come back. Though Germany was readmitted to the FIM at the end of 1950, not until 1953 did BMW re-enter serious international racing. When they did so, it was with a motorcycle that, though unsupercharged, closely resembled its pre-war ancestor. The bore and stroke remained the same at 66 × 72mm, giving a capacity for the flat-twin engine of 493cc. The two valves per cyclinder set at an included angle of 82 degrees were operated by twin overhead camshafts and rockers driven by shafts and bevels.

There was a pressed-up two main bearing crankshaft, and although it turned in caged roller and ball bearing racers, the big ends consisted of crowded rollers (later, dural cages were used). Allegedly safe to 9,000 rpm, the Rennsport (RS) engine with its Bing racing carburettors, engine speed clutch and unit construction four-speed gearbox was claimed to produce 58 hp, though in early solo form this sounds unlikely on the results obtained. The transverse-mounted engine and gearbox with shaft final drive to the rear wheel were mounted for 1953 in a frame that had more than a passing resemblance to Norton's 'Featherbed', but one leg of the rear swinging fork doubled as housing for the shaft drive. What was a real surprise to everyone was that BMW, originators in 1935 of the universally copied oil-damped telescopic front fork, had chosen to use a controversial (not to say suspect) front suspension system based on Ernie Earles' patents.

The BMW RS was announced shortly before the 1953 TT, in which, alas, rider Walter Zeller completed only one lap, but he won the German Grand Prix at

Walter Zeller's BMW, late in the 1953 season with crude fuel injection system.

Zeller's BMW of 1957 with direct fuel injection. Almost the end of the line!

Schotten, where his machine was now fitted with fuel injection into the bellmouths of the inlet tracts.

This victory was a hollow one, for the event was comprehensively boycotted – on the grounds of safety – by the other factory riders, nor did BMWs feature on the leaderboards of any other major meetings during the 1953 season. The RS was originally conceived as being sold, like the Manx Norton, to top-ranking private owners, and because the price was heavily subsidized by the factory, only 50 were to be made. Even so, nothing like this number were ever sold for use as solo racers. At this time, BMW were in desperate financial difficulties due to the near-insolvency of the car side of their business, and there were no TT entries in 1954 and 1955 and little or no solo racing success elsewhere. To a great degree this was because of the RS 500's immediate and successful acceptance for sidecar racing, where its astonishing record of winning 18 World Championships in 19 successive years (no championship was awarded in 1954) is tribute enough to the engine, which was successfully uprated year by year and, from an early date, fitted with fuel injection directly into the cylinder head. Some of the lessons learned contributed to a surprisingly effective comeback by Walter Zeller on the solo in 1956.

One of the highlights was his performance in the Senior TT, which that year was run in winds so strong that Zeller elected to remove the full fairing with which he had practised. The loss of streamlining upset his gearing – it was too late in the day for it to be altered – and so he was limited to using only four of his five gears, but he rode a brilliant race to finish fourth at 94.69 mph behind John Surtees on the four-cylinder MV, who won at 96.57 mph, and the factory-supported Nortons of John Hartle and Jack Brett. Zeller went on to finish second in the Dutch and Belgian events, in each case second only to Surtees' MV. Disappointingly, in front of his home crowd at the German Grand Prix he was an early retirement, and at the season's end at Monza the BMW was sixth, behind four Gileras and an MV. But

19

that was really the end for, despite some good rides, 1957 was not a successful year for Zeller, and when the Italian factories withdrew at the season's end, BMW too announced an end to racing. It was a pity that they did not adhere to their decision. In 1958 they supported Geoff Duke and Dickie Dale, both of whom were at the TT. Duke lasted only two laps and Dale finished tenth.

In 1959 in the Senior TT run in stormy conditions, Dale fell at Glentraman on the second lap. Canadian private entry Ed La Belle battled on to finish 20th. In 1960 there were no BMW entries. Despite their original rarity, RS BMWs are still to be seen on the Continent in Classic events, and are well represented in the BMW factory museum.

BSA Gold Star

There was a Gold Star BSA before the war, the 82 × 94mm 496cc model M24, but the post-war Gold Star B32 and B34 models were not direct descendants. The 71mm × 88 348cc B32 Gold Star was introduced for the 1949 season, and from the start it was offered as a road machine, a trials model, a scrambler and a road racer. In all these different capacities, the B32 and its larger companion the 85 × 88mm 499cc, the B34 Gold Star were to prove eminently successful. Though, over the years, the demands of racing brought many detail improvements (which were incorporated in the road machines), the design of the engines remained essentially similar to the end. The cylinder was of light alloy with a pressed in austenitic iron liner, and the light alloy head had inserted iron valve seats. The steel flywheels had the mainshafts pressed in and secured by rivets. The valves, with coil springs, were operated by pushrods and rockers, and in every respect the engine was simple, workmanlike and robust – virtues that ensured its success. The cycle parts were conventional. The original machines of 1949 used a simple single-loop cradle frame with plunger-box rear springing, BSA hydraulically damped telescopic front forks and single leading shoe 7 in brakes fore and aft. A duplex twin-loop frame with pivoted rear fork and spring and damper units was introduced for 1953, as was the famous 200mm diameter front brake.

Converting from roadster to road racing specification involved the use of four close ratios in the separate gearbox, which was driven by a single-row racing chain, a cylinder head with larger valves, a larger racing carburettor, high-compression piston, special camshaft and straight-through exhaust, later using a megaphone. Testing the original B32 350cc model of 1949, *Motor Cycling* found that in full road trim it would attain a top speed of 78 mph in 29.8 seconds – a performance at that time equal to that of the average sporting machine of 500cc! With the racing options, the bike did 88 mph in third gear and well over 90 mph in top. The actual power output of the B32 was 25 hp at 6000 rpm, and the engine was safe to 6500 rpm, even 7000 rpm momentarily.

The B34 produced 28 hp at 5500 rpm and, equally, could be taken to 7000 rpm in the lower gears. Early Gold Star engines were built in a leisurely one-at-a-time fashion, but their immediate popularity called for more of a routine assembly line.

Every engine, however, was dynamometer-tested and had to reach a certain standard, which was detailed on a job card given to the customer. Engines which did not reach the target figure were sent back for rectification. Those which showed exceptionally good figures were carefully set aside for favoured riders! Over the years, developed by such legendary figures as Jack Ammott, Cyril Haliburn and Roland Pike, the power output of the 350cc engine was raised to 32.5 hp at 7500 rpm and that of the 500cc to 41 hp at 7000 rpm.

A 350cc BSA Gold Star at a test day at Oulton Park in May 1954. Geoff Duke lapped at over 67mph. On the bike is D. A. Wright and kneeling is Vic Willoughby.

W. C. Hancock in the 1955 Senior TT on a 350 Gold Star – he finished 45th at 77.34mph.

Kenny Brown with Hap Alzina (left) and Ted Hodgon after winning the 1957 Daytona 100 miler at 93.89mph.

There is no doubt that American tuners, as with several other British machines, obtained even better results, and there was considerable feedback of development both ways across the Atlantic. The Gold Star BSA was particularly associated with the Clubman's TT. Instituted in 1947, this series of races for standard production road machines was at first very popular. Though several riders had entered B32 and B34 BSAs, not, of course, Gold Star models, in 1947 and 1948, the only result of any note had been Fron Purslow's fifth place in the Junior race in 1948. The Gold Star altered all that. In the 1949 Junior, Harold Clark won easily at 75.18 mph. Gold Star BSA riders won *every* subsequent Junior race for the next seven years! Also in 1949 another four Gold Star riders finished inside a time which gained them a free entry for the Manx Grand Prix – not necessarily, of course, riding a Gold Star. One who did was Rod Hallett. He finished 28th at 74.10 mph – not too terribly impressive until one considers that he finished ahead of forty other riders! The best ever performance by a Gold Star BSA in the Manx Grand Prix was Jackie Woods' remarkable third place in the 1954 Senior race, when he averaged 85.81 mph against winner Geoff Tanner's speed on a Manx Norton of 88.46 mph.

Rather curiously the B34 500cc Gold Star had not been as successful in the Senior Clubman's race as the B32 had in the Junior. Not until 1954 did Alastair King win, followed in 1955 by Eddie Dow and finally, in 1956, Bernard Codd, who that year won both Junior and Senior races – finally, because after that the Clubman's races were dropped from the TT programme. It is often said that this was because the races were dominated by the Gold Star BSA, but this is surely an over-simplification. Nobody at the same time suggested dropping the Senior Manx Grand Prix because it was dominated by Nortons! Much more of a reason was the reintroduction of the sidecar race in 1954 (in which year the short Clypse course was first used) and the lack of time, exacerbated by the amateurish organization of the ACU. Be that as it may, the Gold Star had not only been raced in the Clubman's TT. Many an impecunious rider began his career using the famous 'Goldie' as a stepping stone, perhaps to a Manx Norton or 7R AJS. But many riders were to remain faithful to the 'Goldie', valuing its reliability, the cheapness of the spares and the way in which year by year it could be uprated.

America has been mentioned, and there the Gold Star had been an immediate hit with the discerning and ingenious rider-tuners who were such a feature of the American scene in the fifties. Not only did BSA riders earn a name at flat tracks, scrambles and 'TT' events, but they also did well at the celebrated Daytona Beach races. In 1949, Tom McDermott, an American who had spent some time in Europe and had actually worked at the BSA factory, finished sixth in the 200-mile race, and the following year did even better to finish third behind the ohc Nortons of Bill Matthews and Dick Klamfoth. In 1951, no fewer than 17 Gold Stars were entered in the 100-mile amateur race, and 15 in the 200-mile event. In the amateur race, Al Gunter finished third, but in the 200 miles, the best result on a Gold Star was Jim Garber's seventh place.

The Gold Star's weaknesses were being exposed by the severity of the race and the very success of American tuners in raising the power output, and this mechanical carnage was witnessed at first hand by BSA designer Bert Hopwood, then on a goodwill trip to the USA. Back in England, the engines were redesigned for 1952. In that year, the weather was unremittingly awful – so much so that the Amateur race was not run. By now the Star Twin – racing version of the A7 – was in use, and it was with one of these that Al Gunter finished fifth, having earlier made fastest lap, but later being slowed with a broken clutch lever.

But though the twins impressed, the big Gold Star single continued to surprise. In 1953, Nick Nicholson won what was really the previous year's Amateur race held over, a special 50-mile event. Tommy McDermott took third place in the 200 miles in 1954. In 1955 the Harleys were really flying, and few British bikes got a look in, yet, extraordinarily, the following year, four BSA Gold Stars ridden by Dick Klamfoth, George Evett, Tommy McDermott and Gene Thiessen finished

Works-prepared Gold Star for Daytona in 1954. Tommy McDermott finished third in the 200-mile race.

Yards from the water's edge, Chuck Jordan on a Goldie at Daytona, 1958.

in line astern behind winner John Gibson's Harley in the 200-mile race.

But 1957 was really the end, with BSAs finishing second, third and fifth. Thereafter nothing but a Harley would do.

Elsewhere Gold Stars continued to score wins and places in the late fifties – even into the sixties, though little factory development was done after 1955. In point of fact the 'Goldie', with its single cylinder and separate gearbox, had become something of a nuisance to a management that wanted to satisfy an apparently insatiable market for vertical twins, and production was deliberately slowed down after the demise of the Clubman's TT. Latterly the 350cc model was available only to special order, and not at all after 1962. The 500c model was withdrawn at the end of the following year.

By a curious quirk of fashion, many genuine racing BSA Gold Stars which survived into the 1980s have been converted back into road bikes, such is the demand for them and such are the prices paid!

Benelli
The 250cc Single

At Pesaro in 1911, the six Benelli brothers established their business of the same name, and for sixty years, until taken over by Alessandro de Tomaso, Benelli was very much a family business. Perhaps for that very reason, their racing policy, especially after the war, was curiously erratic and indecisive at times. In 1939, British rider Ted Mellors had won the Lightweight TT with a single-cylinder Benelli with gear drive to its two overhead camshafts, a covered-in outside flywheel and with a conventional brazed-up frame with girder front forks and plunger rear suspension. When racing began again after the war, Benelli used an almost identical machine in the Lightweight class. Works rider Dario Ambrosini rode in the 1949 TT, but fell at the end of the first lap at Governor's Bridge. The following year, he won the race and made a new record lap of 80.90 mph. Indeed, in 1950,

The 1947 single-cylinder Benelli differed little from that on which in 1939 Ted Mellors had won the rainsoaked Lightweight TT.

Ambrosini won every one of the Classic rounds except the Ulster Grand Prix, where he finished second, thus becoming Lightweight World Champion and bringing the Manufacturers' title to Benelli. In 1951 Ambrosini won the Swiss Grand Prix and was second in the Lightweight TT. But in practice for the French Grand Prix at Albi, part of the Championship series for the first time, he skidded on a patch of melted tar, hit a telegraph pole and was killed.

Following this, Benelli withdrew from racing, although in 1952 they appeared at the Swiss Grand Prix with a machine using the same 250cc single-cylinder engine

The Benelli of 1952 – note the huge front brake, telescopic forks and swinging-fork rear suspension and the contoured fuel tank.

but with a new welded duplex frame with telescopic front forks and swinging arm rear suspension. Ridden by Les Graham, it finished a creditable third, but no more was heard of it, and Benelli did not show any further interest in racing until early 1959. They then revealed another single-cylinder machine that in essentials was yet another updated version of their traditional design. Once again the 70 × 64.8mm engine had gear-driven overhead camshafts, but now it used a light alloy cylinder with a chrome bore. There was a twin-spark cylinder head with magneto ignition, and a six-speed gearbox was used. Benelli claimed 33 hp at 10,200 rpm, a very creditable figure for the time. But, typically, little was heard of the new bike outside Italy until in September, at Locarno, in one of his last rides, Geoff Duke used it to win the 250cc race. In 1960, it was used spasmodically in Italy by Silvio Grassetti and was offered to Dickie Dale for the TT, but though entered by Bob Foster, Dale in fact practised and raced on an MZ. NSU rider Jack Murgatroyd rode the Benelli at Imola and was loud in its praises thereafter, but nothing further came of this ride.

In June 1960, Benelli revealed their 250cc four, thus making the single obsolete, and at the end of 1961 two machines were sold to English sponsor Fron Purslow. Purslow entered John Hartle in several events, but an accident early in the year prevented Hartle from riding, and at Mallory in April 1962, Mike Hailwood had a runaway win in the 250cc race. At the same venue a month later, the machine was ridden by Percy Tait, and dropped a valve. Purslow entered Ron Langston and Allen Dugdale for the Lightweight TT, but at the last minute Mike Hailwood took over Langston's entry; Dugdale ran out of petrol on his second lap, but Hailwood rode a fine race and was lying fourth on the last lap when the engine blew up in spectacular fashion. That was virtually the end of the line – the expense and difficulty of maintaining such machinery far from its home, and the appearance in 1963 of ultra-competitive British machinery meant the overnight eclipse of such machines. Fortunately, several racing Benelli dohc singles have survived in museums and in private hands.

The Fours

It is often implied that the four-cylinder Benelli, first revealed in June 1960, was some sort of inferior copy of a Honda, but such a view begs two facts. Firstly that Benelli needed to copy nobody, having themselves designed and built a four-cylinder 250cc racer in 1939, and secondly that at the time that they laid down the design for the post-war four, Honda had achieved little or nothing. Not until a year later were the four-cylinder Hondas to come into their own.

Considering Benelli's size and profitability in relationship to Honda, their achievement over the next decade was astonishing, and yet had it not been characterized by typical Benelli vacillation, it might have been even greater.

Like Honda, designer Giovanni Benelli set his engine transversely and in unit with the six-speed gearbox. Bore and stroke were 44 × 40.6mm with two valves per cylinder, and drive to the two overhead camshafts was by a central train of gears. The oiling system was dry sump with a capacious oil tank, but this was soon replaced by a cast sump, and coil ignition was replaced by a Lucas magneto.

Forty horsepower at 13,000 rpm was claimed, reasonable enough in view of Benelli's vast experience of racing engines. Unfortunately, but typically, Benelli then allowed the project to lose its impetus, so that not until April 1962 did rider Silvio Grassetti take the four to the starting line at Imola.

Grassetti rode a fine race, but bent a valve, leaving victory to Tarquinio Provini on the ultra-rapid Morini single. One week later, at Casenatico, the comparatively inexperienced Grassetti was, amazingly, to win the 250cc race, beating Tom Phillis and Jim Redman on the by now 'invincible' Hondas! But one swallow does not make a summer, and the Japanese were rapidly consolidating their grip on international

Nobody could teach Benelli much about a 250cc 'four', after they had built this superb supercharged model in 1939.

road racing. At the end of 1963, Benelli sent for that extraordinary riding genius Tarquinio Provini to assess and develop the 250cc four. On his advice the frame was lightened and lowered and the machine took on quite a different appearance. A seven-speed gearbox was fitted and power raised to over 50 hp at 15,000 rpm. For 1964, Provini won the Italian National Championship, finishing first in every single round.

In 1965, there was an eight-speed gearbox, a disc front brake (though Benelli soon reverted to a drum), a little more power and another Italian Championship, though with Honda now fielding a six-cylinder machine with at least 60 hp (and ridden moreover by Mike Hailwood), Benelli despite their gallant efforts could hardly have expected to win Grand Prix races. Undaunted they produced a 50 × 40.6mm 350cc version of the four with four-valve heads, planned to make a 250cc Vee-eight and actually started to build a 500cc four. They might have done better to concentrate their resources. After a promising start to 1966, Provini crashed badly in practice for the TT, finishing his racing career. Benelli, in an inspired moment, engaged the young Renzo Pasolini for 1967, though in that season he was quite overshadowed by the Honda and Yamaha teams. At the end of 1967, Honda

The original Benelli four in 1960.

Silvio Grassetti on the Benelli four in 1962, winner at Casenatico.

withdrew from racing, and for 1968 Pasolini showed his, and the bike's, mettle by winning both 250cc and 350cc Italian Championships, and by finishing second in the 250cc TT to Bill Ivy's Yamaha and second in the 350cc to Agostini's MV. Pasolini began 1969 brilliantly by riding the 350cc to such effect in Italian meetings that he beat Agostini on six occasions out of seven!

At the first Grand Prix round at Hockenheim, he crashed badly enough to be out of action for the TT, and Benelli did not hesitate in engaging Phil Read and Kel Carruthers to ride for them in the Island. Read was an early retirement and did not ride again for Benelli, but Carruthers gave Benelli their first TT win since 1950 and went on to win for himself the Championship and for Benelli the Constructor's Championship in the 250cc class. Pasolini, despite another accident late in the season, finished second in the World Championship and won both 250cc and 350cc Italian titles. Very sadly that was the end, or the end to all intents and purposes. For most of 1970, Benelli, and much of Italy, were paralysed by orchestrated Communist strikes and early in 1971 the company sold out to Alessandro de Tomaso. He, alas, proved just as volatile and equivocal about the racing pro-gramme as ever the Benelli family had been! More as a publicity stunt than a serious policy, the 500cc four was dusted off, and entered at Pesaro late in 1971 for Finn Jarno Saarinen to ride. Previous outings for the big four in the hands of Mike Hailwood had been abortive – he had fallen off once and retired on the other occasion with front brake trouble.

Now, to everyone's considerable amazement, Saarinen won both the 350cc and 500cc races at Pesaro against the might of Agostini and MV! Much fantasizing followed, most of which ignored the fact that in the 350cc Agostini had retired and that he had twice visited the pits in the 500cc race. Actual statistics – lap times – told a more sober story. Saarinen's fastest lap in the 500cc race had been at 84.76mph, whereas in the 350cc race Agostini had lapped at 87.36 before breaking down. Nor had Saarinen the slightest intention of involving himself with an obsolescent and

Isle of Man 1964: work on the 250cc Benelli four.

grossly underdeveloped project when he was on the point of signing for Yamaha, in the knowledge that for the following season he would be riding their new 500cc four-cylinder two-stroke. Nevertheless, the episode, trivial as it really was, had provided de Tomaso with a good deal of inexpensive publicity!

So ended the Benelli saga. The 350cc fours made a few more spasmodic appearances, but were rapidly outclassed. The 250cc machines could not be used, that class since 1970 having been restricted to two cylinders and six gears.

Happily, examples of all three capacity fours have survived in unusually original condition, and are frequently to be seen in continental Classic events.

Bianchi

The very old-established Milanese firm of Bianchi had a long and honourable history of racing, including entries in the Lightweight TT in 1926, but they had long been inactive, when, in the 1950s, they re-entered Italian domestic competition with successively uprated versions of their 175cc push-rod ohv 'Tonale' sports model, culminating in a full 250cc version with chain-driven single ohc operation of the valves. It is often assumed (and one author has categorically stated) that it was with two such single-cylinder Bianchis that Derek Minter and Osvaldo Perfetti competed in the 1960 Lightweight TT. In fact, the Bianchis were vertical twins of 55 × 52.5mm designed by Lino Tonti. The visit to the Island was part of a publicity exercise aimed at launching Bianchi lightweight motorcycles in Britain and in Ireland, in which well-known dealer and sponsor Terry Hill of Hill of Belfast was involved. Terry Hill entered TT riders Jack Brett, Ray Fay and Peter Middleton, while the factory themselves entered Derek Minter and Italian riders Ernesto Brambilla, Gianfranco Muscio and Osvaldo Perfetti. Even in the easy-going sixties, riders of such calibre would have demanded quite substantial

A rare shot of Derek Minter testing the bulky 250cc Bianchi twin at Monza in March 1960.

retainers and expenses, and one way or another Bianchi must have faced up to quite a heavy bill for their services.

In the event, rarely can a major factory have engaged in such a fiasco, and as a publicity stunt it turned into a nightmare when, after a practice session full of trouble, Bianchi could only muster two machines by the time of weighing in! The choice of Minter as one of the riders was obvious, that of Perfetti was attributable to his previous employment by Bianchi as a development rider.

The story of their Lightweight TT is soon told. Minter screeched to a halt on the first lap at Sulby with a seized engine and Perfetti finished ninth at 77.56 mph, two places behind Mike O'Rourke's twin-cylinder two-stroke Ariel Arrow, alongside which he had started.

The 250cc Bianchi twins secured some surprisingly good results in 1961 ridden by Grassetti, Dickie Dale and Hugh Anderson, but there was no TT entry and by mid-season they had faded away. Tonti later admitted that they had been disastrously overweight and that the lubrication system left something to be desired. Bianchi next produced another vertical twin of 65 × 52.5mm, 350cc. Regarded objectively, it was one of the most remarkable racing engine designs of the Classic era, and it incorporated some very advanced thinking. Unfortunately, in practice it was an almost complete failure! The 360-degree crankshaft ran in four roller main bearings, the two separate pressed-up cranks being united by a centre coupling which incorporated a primary drive gear.

This drove not only the gearbox, but a train of spur gears to the inlet camshaft, the exhaust camshaft being driven by two idler gears. The gearbox could carry five or six speeds, according to the demands of different circuits, and there was a robust external dry clutch. The oil was carried in a capacious sump beneath the crankcases, and two oil pumps fed oil to the hollow crankshaft and to the hollow camshaft. Only in the matter of lubrication did Tonti's approach appear less than meticulous, but in an engine without a single plain bearing in sight, perhaps his reliance on splash was justified. The separate light alloy cylinders had pressed-in iron liners, but the cylinder heads were unusual in not having inserted valve seats. Instead, the valves ran directly on seats cut in the light alloy, which was of a

The 250cc Bianchi twin engine as raced at the 1960 Lightweight TT.

specification subject to obduration or work hardening by the impact of the valves. This, Tonti claimed, resulted in the valves running notably cooler. The cylinder heads themselves were of very advanced design, with superbly shaped inlet tracts, offset to promote swirl. The layout broke away from tradition by using a very narrow valve included angle of 78 degrees with the inlet valve set six degrees closer to the axis of the cylinder than the exhaust valve, the object being to minimize the loss of incoming charge to the exhaust port.

The Bianchi was successively uprated in capacity. It is seen here in 482cc form, as Italian Championship winner in 1964.

Both piston crowns and heads were machined to provide a very definite squish area, and a compression ratio of 9.8 to 1 was used. Carburation was by 32mm Dell'Orto racing instruments and ignition was at first by battery and coils, but later a generator replaced the battery. An eccentric feature of the design was the use of needle-roller bearings *within* needle-roller bearings – and also inside roller races – to reduce friction to an absolute minimum. But such attention to detail was counter-productive as far as weight, complication and opportunities for mechanical failure were concerned, and in any case begged the question of the main area of frictional losses – no less than 30 per cent being attributable to the pistons! Be that as it may, there seems no reason to question Tonti's claim of 48 hp at 10,500 rpm for the Bianchi twin. The conventional cycle parts were large and bulky and the machine weighed close to 300 lb, but even its detractors freely admitted its phenomenal speed – while it kept going! Alas, only too often it did not, and in its first season scored only three places, one second, one third and one fourth, the best being Bob McIntyre's second in the Dutch Grand Prix. At the TT McIntyre did no more than half a lap before the gearbox broke. Alastair King stopped at Kirkmichael with fuel-feed problems, restarted and worked his way back up the field, obviously as fast as anyone in the race, until he too was eliminated with gearbox trouble on his second lap.

At the East German Grand Prix, Bob Mac was joined by Ernesto Brambilla, but neither rider could keep up with Gary Hocking on the MV, or Franta Stastny on the Jawa. After a well-fought race, McIntyre finished in third place, and Brambilla in fifth, behind Gustav Havel on another Jawa. At the Ulster Grand Prix, Hocking shot into a commanding lead, but McIntyre lay second and Alastair King third. Then on the seventh lap, McIntyre came to a halt with, yet again, a broken gearbox. Alastair King then rode the race of his life to take second place, after 20 laps, only 38 seconds down on Hocking's four-cylinder MV, and over a minute ahead of Stastny's Jawa, not to speak of many highly considered AJS and Norton riders. It was a tantalising hint of what the Bianchi twin could have achieved had the brilliance of the design been matched by a commitment from the factory.

At the Italian Grand Prix no fewer than five machines were entered, to be ridden by Bob McIntyre, Alastair King, Alan Shepherd, Paddy Driver and Ernesto Brambilla, but only Alan Shepherd finished, in fourth place and a lap down on the leaders.

For 1962 McIntyre had no hesitation in signing a contract to ride for Honda. Bianchi decided to confine their efforts to racing in domestic Italian events, but they also wasted valuable time (that might have been better spent on developing the twin's reliability) on the design of a four-cylinder machine that was never completed. The Bianchi emerged from relative obscurity again at the end of 1962 at Monza where Silvio Grassetti was entered in the 350cc class, and also on a bored-out 385cc model, in the 500cc event. Even now, the twin dramatically demonstrated its continuing unreliability as, when Grassetti was about to go to the line in the 350cc event, his machine jammed in first gear! Bianchi were forced to call back second rider Renzo Rossi and have him hand over his machine to Grassetti! In a hard fought race Grassetti rode brilliantly to finish a good third to the Hondas of Jim Redman and Tommy Robb. The twin was successively bored and stroked to increase the capacity and in its final form in 1964, when Remo Venturi won the 500cc class of the Italian Championship, it was 482cc. To the end, the twin was unreliable though it always gave a display of speed that made its failure all the more heartbreaking. Its record did not do justice to the brilliance of its design. Bianchi stopped racing and went out of business in 1967, selling out to the giant Piaggio concern. Any connection with motorcycles ceased forthwith, and today the Bianchi name adorns a range of exquisite high technology racing and sporting bicycles. Unfortunately, the break with tradition was complete, and the contents of the race shop (such as they were at that time) were dispersed.

Bultaco

Bultaco, located near Barcelona and named after the company's founder, Francisco Bulto, came into being in late 1958 when Bulto left Montesa, the company that he and Pedro Permanyer had started a dozen years before. The reason for his departure was a strong disagreement over Montesa's withdrawal from racing, a policy from which Permanyer and the other Montesa directors would not be moved. Bulto had at first no intention of setting up in competition with his old company, but he was approached *en masse* by mechanics, technicians and riders, in all about a dozen men, who had made up the Montesa competition shop. Working in some very primitive premises, in less than a year the new company were in business with a smart little sporting machine of 125cc, the Bultaco Mettralla 101, which was an instant commercial success; nor were racing versions long in appearing. One early prototype was ridden to a lucky win at Zaragoza by Marcello Cama, when, on a wet track, an accident simultaneously eliminated his team-mate Johnny Grace and the favourite to win, Carlo Ubbiali on the MV. For 1960 Bulto entered a 125cc Bultaco in the Isle of Man TT to be ridden by Johnny Grace, but the bike failed to start because of what was said to be a broken wire to the ignition coil. The engine of this machine, and of later racing 125cc Bultacos, had the rather long stroke dimensions of 51.5 × 60mm. The design was entirely conventional with all the ports piston-controlled, but for a machine built in isolated Spain, it showed an up-to-the minute awareness of the most advanced thinking in regard to two-stroke racing engines. A 29mm Dell'Orto carburettor made under licence in Spain was set at a steep downdraught angle. A squish configuration between piston crown and head with a central plug was used; ignition was by flywheel low-tension magneto and external high-tension coil; and primary drive was by chain to a close-ratio constant mesh four-speed gearbox. During 1961 this engine, fitted into a sturdy duplex cradle frame, with telescopic front forks and swinging arm rear suspension, and with large

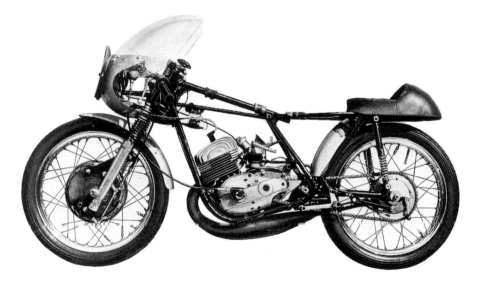

Bultaco's first TT entry of 1960 which failed to start. The engine altered little over the next few years.

ventilated brakes, was successfully raced by the factory in Spanish and other continental events. A power output of 20 hp at 10,300 rpm was claimed (for the factory machines), almost certainly a wild exaggeration. This model, the TSS 125, was offered for sale in Great Britain, but in fact availability was poor and the price was a fairly staggering £370 complete with fairing but without a rev counter.

Racing in the 125cc class was ill-served in Britain in 1961, and when Dan Shorey, a capable and experienced rider, was given a works-prepared TSS 125 for the season he had little difficulty in accumulating enough points to win the ACU 'Star' for the year. During the same season Ralph Rensen finished sixth in the 125cc TT at 83.26 mph (Hailwood on a works Honda twin won at 88.83 mph) and Shorey and Grace finished ninth and tenth. These results caused an upsurge of interest and orders from British riders for the 1962 season. It has to be said that these machines were, to put it politely, 'of variable build quality'. Such was the Spanish government of the day's economic policy that no motorcycle maker could import any materials or accessories – every component had to be of Spanish manufacture. Frames were made of heavy, poor-quality tubing, crudely welded. Chassis and tyres were also of poor quality, castings were porous and gears were badly heat-treated. Some items could be replaced with better-quality British components (at a cost that had not been bargained for), but not such components as gears and engine castings! The Bultaco soon earned a name for fragility, which was largely deserved.

Nevertheless, once again in 1962 Dan Shorey won not only the 125cc Star, but the 250cc Star as well, using for the latter a 196cc Go-Kart engine fitted to a TSS chassis, and for 1963 customers were offered a six-speed 125cc TSS and a four-speed 196cc TSS. Unfortunately for Bultaco, this coincided on the one hand with the availability of the double overhead camshaft 125cc twin-cylinder Honda CR93 and, on the other, the full 250cc Greeves Silverstone, a machine that ironically enough had been to some degree inspired by Shorey's 196cc Bultaco of 1962! In both classes the Bultaco was absolutely outclassed by the newcomers. The 125cc Honda was not cheap, but its specification, its speed and above all its astonishing reliability made the TSS 125 look like a joke in poor taste! Equally the Silverstone

The Bultaco 125cc TSS of 1962. Even the hideous fibre-glass tank was original equipment.

The water-cooled TSS 250 of 1965. By and large, it was Spanish rubbish.

was faster and more reliable than the TSS 200 and considerably cheaper. Quite coincidentally, Bultaco's heretofore modest, but not insignificant, works successes petered out during the 1963 season, and uprating the TSS 125 to a water-cooled version and introducing a water-cooled 72 × 60mm 250cc TSS 250 with a five-speed gearbox could not put Bultaco back in front. In fact the TSS 250 was horribly erratic and unreliable and a notorious breaker of primary chains.

Perhaps Bultaco did not really care about road racing any more, because certainly at this time 'off road' machines were beginning to become of considerably more importance to the company. The switching of imports into Britain to Rickman Brothers for 1965 and the signing at the end of that year of Sammy Miller to ride and develop the Bultaco trials machinery accelerated the change of emphasis. A brief interest in the 350cc class, and the production of the TSS 350 of late 1968, was a flash in the pan. Bultaco's successes had always been more apparent than real. After trying very hard they had been rolled over by the appearance upon the scene of the Japanese. Not as many Bultaco racers were sold as might be thought, and today, handicapped by poor quality and the rarity of spare parts, they are by no means common, but doubtless interest in them will be revived and more will be seen eventually.

DKW

DKW had a long and eminently successful racing history before the war. They had been Champions of Europe four times during the 1930s in the 250cc class, and at the 1938 Lightweight TT Ewald Kluge had achieved one of the most convincing wins of all times, lapping at over 80 mph and finishing no less than eleven minutes ahead of second-place man Ginger Wood on his Excelsior Manxman. But post-war, DKW had to start again from scratch. Germany was not allowed to compete in

International events until the 1951 season, and in domestic events, pre-war machines were frequently used. But of course they were dependent upon a form of forced induction, and supercharging had been banned by the FICM in 1946. Furthermore, though relations between East Germany (the 'Russian Zone') and West Germany were comparatively relaxed, the majority of DKW technicians opted for the West and a new factory was set up at Ingoldstat in the Western Zone, the old factory at Zschopau becoming first IFA and subsequently MZ. Not altogether surprisingly, both the old factory and the new chose a very successful pre-war design, the famous RT 125, as the starting point for experiment. In charge of development at Ingoldstat was Erich Wolf, who was to guide DKW fortunes, perhaps misfortunes would be a better word, for three seasons.

For the 1951 season the 125cc DKW was supplemented by a 250cc twin. Both were air-cooled, with dimensions of 54 × 54mm, with integral four-speed gearboxes. Forward-facing exhaust pipes terminated in typical DKW open megaphones. Induction was by way of a rotary sleeve valve, gear-driven, lying between the Amal racing carburettors and the inlet port. (This gave the opportunity for asymmetrical inlet timing, but with hindsight it is easy to see that compared with Walter Kaaden's disc valve it was complicated, restrictive, and took far more power to drive.) These early machines had a power output of approximately 80 hp/litre, the 125cc claimed 10 hp at 7,000 rpm, the 250cc 20–22 hp at the same speed. However, by the use of exotic materials and to some extent by ingenious design, they were extremely light, and were immediately successful in German national races. First appearance at an international meeting was at the West German Grand Prix at Solitude in August 1951, where the 125cc class was particularly well supported, although there were no Italian entries.

In a hard-fought race, H. P. Müller, on one of the three factory DKWs, made the fastest lap at nearly 69 mph and won comfortably from Otto Daiker on one of the new 125cc dohc NSUs. Ewald Kluge was third on a DKW, Krumpholz and Petrushke were fourth and fifth on IFAs and Dietrich on another factory NSU made up the leaderboard. In the 250cc race, the DKWs were not so impressive,

A win first time out! H. P. Müller speeds to a win at the German Grand Prix in 1950 at Solitude on the new 125cc DKW.

Müller again on the 1951 250cc twin – note the megaphone exhausts.

Wünsche finishing fourth behind two Guzzis and a Parilla. Roland Pike on his home-tuned two-valve pushrod ohv Rudge beat Karl Lottes on another DKW into sixth place.

However, DKW did not follow up this promising start, and in the 125cc and 250cc class thereafter were almost always overshadowed by NSU. They did not feature in any of the Grand Prix results in 1952, and in fact attended at least one meeting and abandoned their entries after practice. It was early in 1952 that the strikingly original three-cylinder 350cc racing model was first announced. With bore and stroke reduced to 53 × 52.8mm the three cylinders were arranged in line, but with the centre one inclined forward at 75 degrees to the outer pair. As the firing intervals were at 120 degrees this called for a crankshaft with unevenly spaced crankpins. Like the smaller models, the 'three' was almost unbelievably light-weight, but it was not, at this time, particularly powerful – 30 hp was spoke of – and the engine was not particularly reliable. The three-cylinder machine's first appearance was at the Swiss Grand Prix in May 1952. There was a single entry, ridden by Siegfried Wünsche, and for half of the race he held on to fifth place before the engine failed. Unfortunately, this was only too often to be the story of the DKW 3.

The 1953 version of the DKW twin with fully tapered exhausts of very advanced design.

1953 was also a disappointing season for DKW in International racing. Wünsche crashed in practice for the Belgian Grand Prix, and again much of the story was one of cancelled entries and non-appearances.

However, strangely, 1953 saw DKW supporting the TT with entries for Wünsche and Ewald Kluge in the Lightweight 250cc and Junior 350cc classes. However, at the Nürburgring, shortly before DKW were due in the Island, poor Kluge fell, breaking his leg. The factory hastily substituted Rudi Felgenheimer who practised, and to everyone's dismay, crashed and broke *his* leg! Wünsche, therefore, was DKW's only starter. The 3 did only one lap before it expired, but in the Lightweight race Wünsche finished in third place behind Fergus Anderson's Guzzi and Werner Haas' NSU twin. It was the best result ever obtained with the 250cc model.

The German Grand Prix in July 1953 was described by *The Motorcycle* as 'a farce' – the circuit at Schotten being judged so dangerous that the factory entries from Norton, Gilera, AJS and Moto Guzzi were withdrawn. DKW decided to race, and August Hobl finished third in the 250cc race, Karl Hofmann second in the 350cc.

In the Swiss Grand Prix at Berne in August 1953, the 250cc DKWs were completely outclassed, Len Parry and August Hobl finishing in 11th and 12th places. In the 350cc race, despite Wünsche making the running for the first few laps, the only 3 to finish was that of Hoffman in sixth place. And again at Monza in September it was a similar story and DKW's only finisher was Hobl in the 350cc race, fourth behind three works Moto Guzzis, a lap adrift.

For the 1954 Junior TT, DKW entered Wünsche, Hobl and Parry, but neither men nor machines arrived in the Island. In an astonishingly frank letter to the ACU, DKW admitted that their machines were neither fast enough nor reliable enough to take part with any chance of success. In fact, during 1954 DKW did very little indeed.

In his obsession with weight saving, designer Wolf reduced the gauge of frame tubing to a dangerous level of fragility, and on several occasions riders experienced terrifying moments with frames that actually broke!

Siegfried Wünsche rides the 250cc twin to a third place in the 1953 Lightweight TT.

Wolf's failure to develop the obvious potential of the 3-cylinder engine can be laid squarely at the door of his own prejudices. Despite his background with DKW, pioneers and leaders in loop scavenge and the distortion-free flat-top piston, the pistons in the 3-cylinder racer had exaggerated deflectors to separate the gas streams during the exhaust and transfer phases! Such a fundamental error explains both the unreliability and the inadequate engine development that characterized the factory DKWs between 1951 and 1954. At the end of the 1954 season, recently appointed technical director Eberan von Eberhorst gave Erich Wolf his marching orders and turned development over to long-time technician Helmut Georg. Von Eberhorst himself completely redesigned the frame, using a combination of tubes and sheet metal pressings, provided large, twin, hydraulically operated brakes, and leading link front forks that owed quite a bit to those used on Giulio Carcano's Guzzis.

The resulting machine was considerably heavier than before, but the riders were spared the fears that had come to haunt them in 1954 with Wolf's desperate attempts to gain an advantage by reckless weight reduction. The rise in weight, too, was much more than offset by the improved power and reliability of the new engine, subject of a complete redesign by Helmut Georg. Most obvious of Georg's improvements was the use of pistons with lightly domed symmetrical crowns and cylinder heads with a matching 'half-moon' squish band. Georg continued the use of American-made spring steel piston rings, but had the thickness raised from .030 in to .040 in. The crankcase was completely redesigned in the interests of stiffness. Three Dell'Orto carburettors were fitted, with conical wire gauzes over the ends of the bellmouths. Despite assertions that these gauzes 'stabilized the air flow', the likelihood is that they were, sensibly enough, designed to stop stones thrown up by the wheels from entering the engine.

In one respect, Georg's design took a backward step. Wolf's exhaust systems had been of absolutely exemplary layout. Now Georg substituted exhausts that must have cost him as much as 10 per cent in power output. But the other alterations to the engine raised its power from around 30 hp to a claimed 38 hp–42 hp over the next two seasons.

DKW did not contest the 1955 TT, but they showed much improved speed and reliability at the few Grands Prix they did contest. In Belgium, Hobl, Hoffman and Bartl finished fourth, fifth and sixth. At the German Grand Prix Hobl finished a

The original 3-cylinder racer of 1953.

remarkable second to Lomas on the four-cylinder MV, ahead of the Norton of John Surtees and the Guzzis of Cecil Sandford and Ken Kavanagh. Karl Hoffman and Siegfried Wünsche took their DKWs to sixth and seventh places. At the Belgian Grand Prix, Hobl was second to Lomas on the Guzzi, and Bortl was sixth. At the Grand Prix des Nations at Monza in September Hobl did far better than the bare result indicates to finish fifth behind a do-or-die effort by the Moto Guzzi team.

In 1956, DKW did not, directly, support the TT, but allowed British dealer Arthur Taylor to enter Cecil Sandford in the Junior race, in which he finished a very creditable fourth.

At the Dutch Grand Prix, Hobl finished third in the 350cc race, and Sandford was fourth. Riding in the 125cc class with redesigned DKWs, Hobl was again third and Hoffman fifth. At the German Grand Prix in July, Hobl was second to Bill Lomas on the Guzzi, with Sandford and Bartl fourth and fifth. Truly, DKW now had both speed and reliability, but, it was too late: despite third, fourth and sixth places in the Belgian Grand Prix and fourth, fifth and sixth at the Grand Prix des Nations, the DKW management had had enough! One could scarcely blame them. In October 1956 they announced that there would be no more racing DKWs. The expenditure on racing and development had been enormous, the returns in comparison mediocre. At the end of its life, Georg claimed 42 hp at 9700 rpm for the three-cylinder engine, but though this power, in conjunction with intrinsically light weight and effective streamlining, was enough to beat private Manx Nortons and 7R AJSs it was not enough to hold off the single-cylinder Moto Guzzis. Georg asserted that fuel injection would have raised the power to something like 48 hp and he may well have been right, but the experiment was never tried. The race department was closed and the bikes were dismantled. All the parts were scrapped or sold, and according to Erwin Tragatsch, only one 125cc and one 350cc were restored to as new condition, only to be stolen from the factory!

Be that as it may, at least one 350cc 3-cylinder DKW has survived and been restored.

DOT

When the ACU announced that for the 1951 TT, in line with continental Grand Prix meetings, there would be a 125cc class run over two laps of the Mountain circuit, there was considerable scepticism in Britain, where many of the riders and commentators were, as usual, obsessed with the 500cc class. In fact, the race was won by Cromie McCandless on a Mondial at a staggering 74.85 mph, which only seven racing seasons before would have won the 250cc event! The tiny British firm of DOT, with no hope of success in terms of speed, entered a team of three machines with Villiers 9D engines canted forward so that the cylinder was near horizontal in a neat duplex frame of square-section steel tube, with proprietary front forks, hubs and swinging arm suspension controlled by Armstrong units. The little DOTs were not fast – the engines, apart from slightly larger carburettor and short open exhausts, were virtually standard – but they were reliable. Ted Hardy finished seventh at 57.86 mph, C. Horn 11th and G. Newman 12th. The following year, Hardy finished tenth and Newman retired on the first lap. The DOTs did not race again.

Throwing caution to the winds indeed! DOT rider, G. Newman, at the start of the first 125cc TT

Derbi

Old-established bicycle makers and later manufacturers of 250cc and 350cc two-strokes, the Spanish Derbi factory decided to concentrate upon 50cc machines for 1961 and to race for the sake of advertisement. In 1961 they contested domestic events with a simple air-cooled machine with a five-speed gearbox. In 1962, designer Francesco Tombas produced a 38 × 42mm disc-valve induction model for recently engaged rider José Busquets to use in the Spanish round of the newly instituted Coupe d'Europe at Montjuich Park. To everyone's surprise Busquets finished a close second to Hans George Anscheidt on a factory Kreidler, ahead of various other Kreidlers, Hondas, Ducsons and Itoms. Though very successful in 50cc racing in Spain, Derbi did not join in the ensuing World Championship series, so fiercely contested by Kreidler, Suzuki and Honda. But they did not neglect development, and at the 1964 Spanish Grand Prix, José Busquets amazed everyone by leading until, four laps from the end, a rear suspension unit broke.

For 1965, Derbi offered a 50cc racing machine to private owners and with one of these English rider Ian Plumridge finished fifth in the 1965 TT. Quite a few of these 'over the counter' racers were sold, but they were not really successful; though fast whilst they were going, reliability was notoriously marginal. Furthermore spares were not readily available. Though Derbi confined most of their efforts to racing in Spain, they loaned one or two racing machines to private owners in other countries. One such was Australian Barry Smith, who, with an ex-works machine, won the non-classic Austrian Grand Prix in 1966.

It was Barry Smith who, after Japanese withdrawal from the 50cc World Championship, won the last 50cc TT with a genuine factory racing Derbi in 1968.

Andres Magaz leads team mates José Busquets and Franco Farne, all on Derbis in the 1963 Spanish Grand Prix.

After team-mate Angel Neito threw his machine down the road, Smith deliberately slowed down, 'to give the others a chance of a replica', and won at 72.90 mph. Derbi went on to greater things, but during the Classic era, their participation in international racing was limited by Spain's peculiar political situation. Today Derbis *do* survive, but they are a rare sight at Classic events.

Ducati

Only for one full season, 1958, did the Ducati company of Bologna take part in the World Championship road racing series, and neither they nor any of their riders won the title. Nevertheless, their astonishingly fast and reliable 125cc racers, featuring 'desmodromic' valve gear, made an impact upon the class that is remembered to this day. Strangely, no other maker followed the way that they had pointed out, and only Ducati were ever to offer production road-going motorcycles with desmodromic valve gear, yet their best-known production racers, sold to the customers, employed orthodox valve gear!

Ducati were well established before the war as makers of electrical and radio equipment, and their first entry into mechanical engineering was by government directive after the war, when they were chosen to manufacture a tiny 'clip-on' four-stroke engine unit for attachment to ordinary pedal cycles. This, the truly excellent 'Cucciolo' (little pup), soon led to the manufacture of a proper miniature motorcycle, still of only 60cc. Not until 1954 did Ducati raise their sights to the 125cc class, when the chief executive of Ducati Meccanica, Dr Giuseppe Montano, recruited the young Ing. Fabio Taglioni from Mondial.

Taglioni (still with the company on a consulting basis in the 1980s) used Ducati's existing 49.4 × 52mm, 98cc first as the basis for the 98 Sport model and then in 1956 the 55.25 × 52 mm, 125cc 125 TV. Both these models were used with considerable success in the long-distance races on open roads unique to Italy and were at the height of their popularity in the 1950s. However, the first pure racing Ducati was the 100cc single overhead camshaft *Gran Sport* model, which in turn led to an experimental double overhead camshaft engine of 125cc. This engine gave 16 hp at 11,500 rpm – good, but as Taglioni well knew, not good enough. It was at

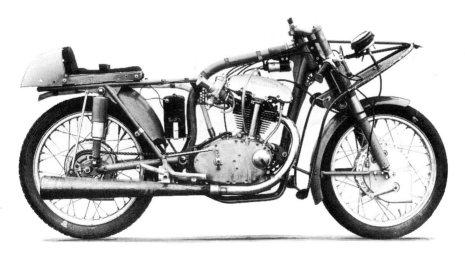

The 125cc Ducati Grand Prix dohc production racer.

The real thing. The 125cc desmodromic Ducati that made such an impression, but was never followed up.

this point that he decided to experiment with desmodromic valve gear, a system that had been brought sharply into focus by its successful use on Mercedes-Benz Grand Prix and sports-racing cars in the 1954 and 1955 seasons. Mercedes-Benz had indeed won the Grand Prix World Championship in both those years, and largely dominated sports car racing in 1955. 'Desmodromic', derived from the Greek, means 'Running in a bond' and alludes to the fact that the sequence of valve events is at all times positively controlled – the valves are closed as well as opened by cams. As long ago as 1924 James L. Norton had taken out a patent on 'desmodro-mique' valve gear, listing as one of the advantages the fact that heavy double and even triple valve springs would not be needed to prevent valves floating off their seats at high revs. Norton also perceived that quite a lot of power would be saved through not having to overcome the resistance to compression of such springs.

Fabio Taglioni did not copy Mercedes-Benz' system, which it hardly needs to be said was comprehensively protected by patents, but used a simple system of three camshafts and four cams with pivoted followers and forked rockers to close the valves. The illustration opposite shows how this was achieved better than pages of explanation. To allow for expansion, a certain amount of play is necessary in desmodromic valve gear. Like Mercedes-Benz before him, Taglioni relied upon gas pressure in the cylinder to seat the valves for starting rather than (as has sometimes been used in the past) light springs.

In almost every respect other than its valve gear, the 125cc Desmodromic engine was entirely orthodox, and was in fact based upon 98cc ohc Gran Sport components. The pressed-up crank with caged needle roller big end ran in ball and roller bearings and end float was controlled by a peculiar spring steel 'star washer' interposed between the drive-side flywheel and main bearing. The four-speed (soon converted to five and later to six) gearbox was in unit with gear primary drive. Lubrication was comparatively simple, a gear pump raising oil from a sump formed in the crankcase casting and feeding it via a fine strainer to the big end through crankshaft drillings and by outside pipes to the hollow camshafts, where again by drillings and centrifugal force it lubricated the rubbing surfaces of the valve gear. From the top end, surplus oil drained back down into the 'semi-wet' sump. This oil was shared by the gearbox, hence the careful filtration.

The light alloy cylinder employed a shrunk-in austenitic liner, and the two valves, set at quite a wide included angle, seated directly on the light alloy head. The 'closing' cams were driven by vertical shaft and bevels and in turn drove the 'opening' cams by spur gears. Ignition was by battery and coil, either a 27mm or a 29mm Dell'Orto racing carburettor was used according to the demands of the

various circuits, and this engine/gearbox unit was fitted into a simple loop frame with entirely conventional front and rear suspension. Dynamometer tests had been extremely encouraging, showing a steady 18 hp at 12,500 rpm with apparent reliability up to a hair-raising 15,000 rpm! Nor did extended bench and road testing show up any weaknesses.

Thus encouraged, Ducati entered two machines at far-away Hedemora in Sweden, venue of the non-Championship 1956 Swedish Grand Prix. Riders were their own Giani Antoni on the desmodromic model and local star Olle Nygren on a 'twin cam'. Antoni went through the opposition 'like a cannonball' as *The Motorcycle* said, winning with ease, at record speed and with a new record lap at 87.5 mph, having lapped every other finisher! Ducati immediately made an entry for the Grand Prix at Monza, but, alas, practising at that circuit, poor Antoni crashed and was fatally injured. Ducati drew back from Grand Prix racing, although by now the 125cc Grand Prix twin-cam customer racers were doing well in continental events. At the 1957 Swedish Grand Prix they filled the first six places!

However, for 1958 the Ducati management had regained their equanimity, and a

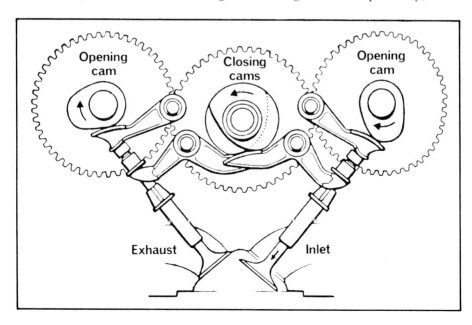

team of three full-time riders was retained by the factory: Romolo Ferri, Alberto Gandossi and the Swiss riders Luigi Taveri. In addition, Irishman Sammy Miller and Englishmen Dave Chadwick and Fron Purslow were promised machinery and appropriate support at certain meetings. Unfortunately, just before the TT Gandossi was injured in a road accident. His place, although not at the TT, was taken by Bruno Spaggiari, who was to become one of Ducati's most successful riders at a later date.

In 1958 both 125cc and 250cc Lightweight TT races were run over 10 laps of the 10.79-mile Clypse course, nothing like so demanding and testing as the famous 37¾-mile Mountain circuit, but still a genuine road-racing event. Five 125cc Ducatis were entered, Fron Purslow's being one of the twin ohc models with the valves controlled by springs. The MV factory had entered Tarquinio Provini, Carlo Ubbiali and Franco Libanori, and there were no fewer than ten other MVs privately entered. The East German MZ factory had riders Horst Fugner and Ernst Degner, and there were three Montesas entered by Englishman Jim Bound, one of them ridden by himself. A trio of ingenious British 'specials', the LCH, the LEF and the Fruin, together with a solitary EMC, completed the field. One MV entry, the young and up-and-coming Mike Hailwood, substituted a 125cc Paton at the last moment. At an early stage in the race, Luigi Taveri led on his 'Desmo' Ducati, but was soon passed by both Ubbiali and Provini, but Provini crashed on the third lap and Taveri retired with engine trouble on the fifth, leaving Ubbiali well and truly in the lead. Romolo Ferri, who had made a slow start, passed team-mate Dave Chadwick and set off in pursuit of Ubbiali – but he had left it too late.

The MV rider won the race, with Ferri, Chadwick and Sammy Miller behind him. The two MZs completed the leaderboard, and Fron Purslow on his 'conventional' Ducati was a gallant eighth, just behind Mike Hailwood's Paton.

At Assen, Ubbiali on the MV was the winner, but Taveri took his Ducati to second place ahead of Provini's MV. Gandossi, Chadwick and Miller were fourth, fifth and seventh. Then in Belgium, sensation, as Ducati riders Gandossi and Ferri finished first and second, relegating Ubbiali and Provini to third and fourth places, whilst Chadwick and Taveri were fourth and sixth.

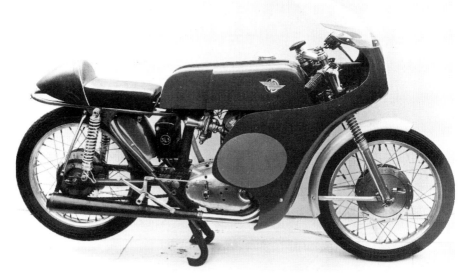

Imitation racer – the Mach I faked up by Vic Camp from a standard model.

A fairly disastrous German Grand Prix outing saw Ferri crash and sustain a broken leg, whilst Taveri and Gandossi both retired, and at the Swedish Grand Prix, now a Championship round, Gandossi and Taveri were first and second. At the Ulster, Taveri, Chadwick and Gandossi finished in line astern behind Ubbiali's MV – and with that the MV factory and Carlo Ubbiali secured the Constructor's and the individual championship. It was a considerable shock to the MV factory therefore when, at the final Grand Prix at Monza, their riders were soundly beaten by the Ducatis, with Bruno Spaggiari, Alberto Gandossi, Dave Chadwick, Luigi Taveri and Francesco Villa finishing in line astern, neither of the MV riders having ever been in the lead, and both machines having expired by half-distance!

But, having so convincingly shown their speed and reliability to their 'home crowd', Ducati then effectively withdrew from the Grand Prix scene. Bruno Spaggiari and Francesco Villa were at the 1959 TT, Villa on one of the 42.5 × 44mm twins, but neither finished, Villa falling whilst chasing Dave Chadwick's MV and Spaggiari retiring with engine trouble on the third lap. Mike Hailwood practised on a twin which had been sold to his father by the factory, but rode a single to third in the race, claiming that the twin had too narrow a powerband. Mike preferred the single. He was later to acquire 250cc and 350cc desmodromic twins which promised and promised – in his hands and those of others – but never delivered! A well-known authority on Ducatis, Mick Walker, remarked to me that these machines should never have left the factory, for they were completely undeveloped. Ducati's parlous financial plight at this time of Europe's wide depression in the motorcycle trade may have been responsible for this action, as it most probably was for the cessation of sales of the 125GP 'production' racer. A few years later, according to the British expert quoted above, Ducati threw away a 'golden opportunity' to break into the 250cc class with a racer which, known in America as the Ducati 'Manxman', was simply not sold in England.

In the Island, Ing Taglioni watches, as the mechanics work on the desmodromic heads and camboxes.

This machine was fast and – in strong contrast to the abysmal 250cc Aermacchi of the time – ruggedly reliable. But Ducati did not exploit these virtues for the benefit of the European private owners. Instead, it was left to Vic Camp, the British importer, to produce a 'pseudo' racer in the early 1960s by simply stripping off the road-going equipment from the 250cc Mach 1 of late 1964 and fitting a rev counter, megaphone exhaust and glass-fibre fairing. The resulting machine, though reliable, was embarrassingly slow by the side of the British two-strokes of the time. That indicator of what might be called British National level racing, the Manx Grand Prix, gives some idea of the 250cc Ducati's capabilities. In the first of the revived 250cc Manx Grand Prix races in 1964, no Ducatis finished in replica time, and in 1965 the best result was ninth at 83.61 mph. The following year, when the race was won by Bob Farmer on an Aermacchi at a speed 2.17 mph slower than the previous year, Ken Watson finished second, over a mile an hour slower than Farmer. Never again was a Ducati to so much as win a replica, never mind a place on the leaderboard!

In contrast, with the introduction of Classic racing by the CRMC, the 250cc Ducati became enormously popular, and – due to intelligent tuning and the knowledge that had been amassed in the interval between 1972 and 1979 – extremely competitive. The owners of Greeves and Cotton two-strokes with no such tradition to fall back upon, were riding machines that in the majority of cases were slower than they had been ten years earlier!

The Ducati company, with undoubtedly brilliant machines (and riders) at their disposal in 1958, were frustrated by financial difficulties. Within a couple of years they had been eclipsed by Japanese machinery. Today the sight of a 'Desmo' Ducati is rare, but several have been preserved for all that, and the cheap and cheerful 'production' 250cc models make up something like 60 per cent of CRMC racing in their class.

EMC

Joseph Ehrlich, an expatriate Austrian who had lived in England since 1938, started his EMC (Ehrlich Motorcycle Company) activities at Park Royal in London in 1946. Here were produced EMC road-going motorcycles of generally orthodox design, but powered by a 350cc 'split single' two-stroke engine. The first most people heard of Joe Ehrlich was his extraordinary claim at the 1946 Manx Grand Prix that the handful of split single DKW two-strokes that were entered infringed his pre-war patents, and must race as EMCs. As a publicity stunt it was a washout, the DKWs putting on a most undistinguished show!

In 1951, sales of the EMC roadster having fallen away to nearly nothing, Ehrlich marketed the 125cc EMC Puch racer, which owed far more to Puch than it did to EMC. It, too, was a split single, of which layout Puch were pioneers in motorcycle racing, with two carburettors and a megaphone exhaust. The cycle parts were conventional with telescopic front forks, a double-sided twin front brake and pressed steel pivoted fork and spring damper units at the rear. A large and shapely light alloy tank gave the little bike a very racy appearance.

Facing negligible opposition in British racing, the EMC Puch sold quite well and performed respectably. In the 1952 lightweight TT works-entered F. H. Burman finished sixth at 63.14 mph – as against MV's Cecil Sandford's winning speed of 75.54 mph, which puts the EMC's capabilities into perspective. Two other EMCs finished ninth and twelfth, but another retired on the first lap. Later that season at a very wet Silverstone meeting, Burman rode his EMC to win the 125cc class of the

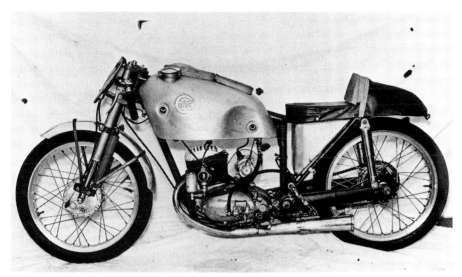

The Puch engined EMC of 1951 – more noise than go!

Hutchinson 100 race, thereby beating both Albert Fern on a Mondial and R. L. Graham on a works MV! It was a high spot that the EMC Puchs never reached again. In 1953 Joe Ehrlich left to work for Austin cars in Birmingham, but there were EMCs at the TT that year and in 1954, though with miserable results.

In 1958, somehow having come by an old DKW 350cc three-cylinder racing engine, Ehrlich cobbled up a 117cc single-cylinder racer with this engine in an old EMC Puch frame. In a notably naïve article, *Motor Cycling* revealed the engine's origins without saying so in as many words. The outer crankcases of the three-cylinder engine were blanked off, the connecting rods removed and the crankcases half-filled with oil!

This crude beginning might have led to something better, but in 1960 Ehrlich

The de Havilland EMC of the 1960s. Ridden by Rex Avery, Mike Hailwood and others, it was surprisingly fast.

was to join the de Havilland aero engineering company and in July was made head of small engine development. Now there appeared the first of a new line of EMC racing motorcycles, unashamedly based upon the East German MZ. It was paddock gossip at the time that Joe Ehrlich had been made a present of a clapped-out MZ engine in a 'swap' with Walter Kaaden, Joe's side of the bargain being fulfilled with a new pair of Norton racing front forks! Be that as it may, the new EMC's 54 × 54mm water-cooled engine and six-speed gearbox was certainly made in the the de Havilland workshops, and was fitted into a neat frame with a large-diameter spine, and at first EMC Puch front forks and hubs, although these were quickly replaced with Ceriani forks and Oldani hubs and brakes. When the bike reappeared in 1961 it had become a serious contender in the 125cc class, as was shown at the Brands Hatch meeting early in April, when rider Rex Avery, a de Havilland employee, walked away with the 125cc race, and in so doing raised the lap record by no less than 5 mph! At the end of April he won again at Brands Hatch and in the TT Tony Godfrey finished eighth.

1961 and 1962 certainly saw the EMC produce some exciting performances, notably at the 1962 TT, when Mike Hailwood, no less, rode one in the 125cc race and chased Luigi Taveri's leading Honda for two laps before a main bearing broke up. Rex Avery took his EMC to sixth place. Unfortunately, things began to go wrong later in 1962 and 1963 and development seemed to be going backwards. There were no EMCs at the 1963 TT and de Havilland seemed to have lost interest, which was confirmed when the small engines section was closed.

Today the de Havilland EMCs seem to have gone underground, but quite a few of the cheap and cheerful (and noisy!) EMC Puchs survive to race and parade at CRMC events.

FB Mondial

Like the Aermacchi company, Fratelli Boselli (FB) were makers of small industrial vehicles and delivery trucks before they manufactured motorcycles. Before and during the war these were manufactured at Bologna, but in 1948 Count Giuseppe Boselli, who in the 1930s had himself been a successful motorcycle competitor, opened a new factory in Milan. The intention was still to manufacture industrial equipment, but Boselli reasoned that to build and race a successful motorcycle would be excellent advertising for the company's engineering abilities.

At that time, the 125cc class was something of a novelty and was to be included in the newly instituted World Championship series in 1949. Almost all the machines involved, including the Italian Morini and MV and the Dutch Eysink, were two-strokes, but Count Boselli was farsighted enough to perceive that a scaled-down double overhead camshaft single-cylinder four-stroke engine would have the legs of all of them. Determined to have the best, he was lucky enough to be able to recruit the brilliant veteran designer Alfonso Drusiani. Drusiani's engine had bore and stroke of 53 × 56mm and used an outside flywheel to enable the crankshaft and crankcases to be kept as compact and stiff as possible. The four-speed gearbox was built in unit. Drive to the two overhead cams was by vertical shaft and bevels, and though the valve gear was enclosed, the valves were controlled by exposed hairpin springs. Ignition was by magneto, carburation by a Dell'Orto instrument. On test, the engine produced 12 hp at 9000 rpm and could safely be taken to 11,000 rpm. This unit was fitted into a frame and cycle parts that have sometimes been criticized as 'old fashioned', but were in fact soundly based on the state of the art. Front forks were fabricated girders made of welded pressings, with parallel ruler action and a

1952: Cromie McCandless and the 125cc FB Mondial in the Isle of Man. He pushed in from Governor's Bridge to finish fourth.

single central spring. The front brake was very large and powerful for the time. The double cradle frame was entirely conventional with plunger-box springing at the rear. The weight was well under 200 lb with fuel and oil.

The machine was known as the FB Mondial and made its first surprise appearance in 1948 at the Italian Grand Prix at Firenze. Ridden by Franco Lama, the Mondial simply walked away from the two-stroke competition and into a commanding lead, but had to be retired with a split petrol tank. A record-breaking session followed and revealed the little bike's speed as being over 80 mph, a good 10 mph faster than the two-strokes. A final outing at Monza at the Grand Prix des Nations saw Nello Pagani easily winning the 125cc race.

FB might well have saved the Mondial as a surprise until the 1949 season and thus have doubly assured themselves of winning the new World Championship, but through showing their hand had forewarned rivals MV and Morini, who immediately set about designing four-strokes of their own. Count Boselli and Drusiani were confident enough of the Mondial's superiority to take that risk and they were not mistaken. There was no Ultra-Lightweight TT until 1951 (when Mondials ridden by Cromie McCandless, Carlo Ubbialli, Gianni Leone and Bruno Ruffo finished first, second, third and fourth), but in 1949, 1950 and 1951, FB Mondial riders won *every* round of the 125cc World Championship, despite their 'anachronistic' cycle parts, and despite the best that any of their rivals could do. Nello Pagani took the title in 1949, Bruno Ruffo in 1950 and Carlo Ubbialli in 1951. That they fell back in 1952 was almost entirely because in 1950 they had begun production of road-going machinery and during 1953 had launched single overhead camshaft bikes of 125cc and 175cc which were quickly developed into 'production racers' to be sold to customers.

After the 1953 season, at the end of which Ubbialli finished second in the World

51

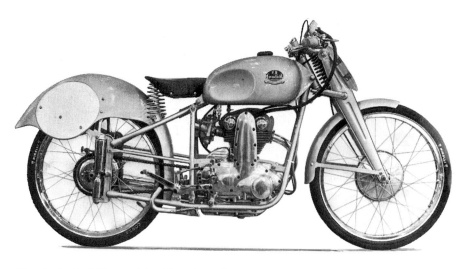

The single ohc 125cc model, sold to the cash customers.

Championship to MV's Cecil Sandford, FB Mondial withdrew, but not permanently. Drusiani redesigned the 125cc engine and cycle parts and the company
engaged that remarkable rider Tarquinio Provini to ride it in 1955. Although he
won the 125cc Italian national championship in that year, Provini was fighting a
losing battle in the 250cc class which he contested on a mercilessly overbored 70 ×
56mm, 216cc model. Thereafter Drusiani lost his way with a grotesquely bulky and
overweight 53 × 56mm twin, which proved quite hopeless. Late in 1956 he
returned to the idea of a scaled-up version of the still viable 125cc single and drew
up new single cylinder 125cc and 250cc designs. The only significant difference
with the smaller machine was the use of a seven-speed gearbox, but the 250cc at 75
× 56.4mm was heavily 'oversquare' and used a train of spur gears to drive its two
overhead camshafts. Alternative five- and seven-speed gearboxes were available

*The full 250cc dohc Mondial raced in 1957 by Cecil Sandford to win the World
Championship. 'The perfect moment'.*

and the cycle parts were as up to date as the engine unit. There was no hint of 'anachronism' about the beautifully streamlined all-enclosed 'dustbin' fairings, the twin leading shoe brakes and the suspension fore and aft. Power outputs were later quoted as 18 hp at 12,000 rpm for the 125cc, 29 hp at 11,000 rpm for the 250cc.

Mondial were very confident for 1957, as well they might be. The factory team of riders was led by Tarquinio Provini, and he was joined by Englishman Cecil Sandford and Dublin's Sammy Miller. To make the story brief, Provini won the 125cc Championship, Sandford the 250cc, a reflection in fact of the TT results, where Provini had won the 125cc race at 73.69 mph, Sandford the 250cc at 78.00 mph – both races being run at that time over the 10.79-mile Clypse course. Count Boselli later recalled, 'It was the perfect moment that could never be repeated.' And so, when at the end of the 1957 season he was approached by Guzzi and Gilera management, anxious to cut down on ruinous expense of Grand Prix racing, he took little persuading to join them in withdrawing for 1958.

In later years, FB Mondial occasionally lent their assistance and even their name to motorcycle racing escapades, but never with any great conviction. Quite a few of the works racers were sold to private owners, who were still racing them into the 1960s.

In Britain, Mike Hailwood, Norman Surtees and Brian Ball all used them with success. But the Mondial racing department, which continued for some time to service such machines, still retained a dozen or more earlier models. With a wonderfully intelligent gesture, Count Boselli helped Torinese engineer Oreste Daddario to set up the so-called Mondial Owners' Club International to restore and preserve these racing motorcycles. This enterprise, and the efforts of several private owners, ensures that the sight and sound of the wonderful FB Mondials is not lost forever.

Gilera
The early days

The Gilera company, long established by Giuseppe Gilera at Arcore near Milan, though enjoying an excellent sporting reputation, did not give any consistent support to road racing until the late 1930s. How they came to do so, achieving World Championship domination before retiring from racing whilst apparently insuperable, is an involved story.

It goes back as far as 1923, when two newly graduated engineers, Piero Remor and Carlo Gianini, drew up a design for a four-cylinder motorcycle engine and gearbox unit. It was air-cooled, had a single overhead camshaft and was to be mounted in the frame transversely. In 1924, this design attracted the attention of a wealthy enthusiast with interests in aero engineering. He was Count Luigi Bonmartini, and he set up a company GRB (from the initials of the three principals), to pursue the design to reality. Even for a small research company, progress seems to have been slow. No doubt consulting work for other concerns had to take priority and pay the bills, but even so it seems to have taken nearly five years to build a complete motorcycle.

Not a lot of that time had been spent on the frame, which, even for 1928, was a crude affair, and in the meantime the original engine design had been altered considerably. It was now of 51 × 60mm bore and stroke, with air-cooled cylinders and, according to some accounts (the engine has not survived), with water-cooled cylinder heads. A rare surviving photograph appears to confirm this contention and although too battered to reproduce, it has been copied by artist Greg Velichenko, whose minute examination of the photograph reveals that water pipes and hoses disappear into the underside of the petrol tank area, although no radiator is visible. Twin overhead camshafts were driven by a central train of gears.

An up-and-coming young rider who was making his name in Italian racing on a Norton, Piero Taruffi, was engaged as development rider. However, to Taruffi's chagrin, when Count Bonmartini entered the machine, now known as the OPRA from the initials of another of his companies, for the Rome Grand Prix, he was passed over in favour of the veteran rider Umberto Faraglia. After leading briefly the OPRA blew up and the race was in fact won by Taruffi on his Norton! If progress had been slow to date it was very little better thereafter, and not until 1934 was the project revived by Bonmartini as the Rondine. Now Taruffi was re-engaged, given much more authority, and produced a completely new frame with carefully thought-out geometry, a composite affair of steel pressings and essentially straight lines, with no rear springing.

The front forks were girder-type fabricated from steel pressings. Single leading-shoe brakes of ample size by the standards of the time were fitted front and rear. The engine was now completely redesigned by Carlo Gianini alone. Bore and stroke were 52×58mm, and the fully water-cooled cylinders and integral heads were cast in pairs. Twin overhead camshafts were driven by a train of gears, and there was gear drive too for the gearbox and a Roots-type supercharger mounted above it behind the steeply inclined cylinders. There was magneto ignition, a single carburettor and four long, plain exhaust pipes. Incredibly, six machines were built! Bonmartini entered Taruffi and Amilcare Rossetti for the prestigious Tripoli Grand Prix against formidable opposition, which included works teams from Benelli and Guzzi. The outcome must have been a heartening one for Count Bonmartini, for in a dramatic struggle with Omobono Tenni's Vee-twin Guzzi, Taruffi and Rossetti finished in first and second places. At Pescara, Taruffi again won easily, but in front of a home crowd at Monza the result was disappointing, only Carlo Fumigalli finishing out of three entries, and even his machine had a sick engine, so that although he had made fastest lap, he dropped back to fifth place at the finish. And that, surprisingly, was that!

Apart from a record-breaking session by Taruffi when the Rondine, fitted with an astonishingly modern-looking Dolphin fairing, achieved 152 mph over the

The OPRA of 1928 with water-cooled cylinder heads. The drawing is by Greg Volichenko.

flying kilometre, the Rondines never raced again. Bonmartini sold his business interests, including the Rondine, to the Milanese aero engineering concern of Caproni and was heard of no more in connection with the project that he had fostered for a dozen years!

Caproni had no interest in nor desire to enter motorcycle racing. Taruffi, however, was vitally concerned that the project should not die, and with the willing co-operation of Caproni, he approached Giuseppe Gilera. Gilera, whose thoughts had lately turned to road racing for advertising's sake, was only too happy to oblige, and straightaway purchased all rights and patents, six machines and spares, and retained Taruffi's services as rider, team leader and development engineer. But there was no question of actually racing the Rondine as it stood. Gilera was too shrewd an engineer not to have seen the machine's weaknesses as well as its strengths, and so set up a development department. Most of the engine parts were used in building the new Gilera engines, but in particular the crankshaft was entirely redesigned with caged roller bearings.

The supercharger too was modified in the interests of both reliability and efficiency and a new Weber carburettor was tested. New frames were constructed, retaining the Rondine steering geometry, but made of steel tube, and incorporating Gilera triangulated swinging arm rear suspension controlled by horizontal coil springs and friction dampers. Front forks from the Rondine were retained. A rather handsome wedge-shaped fuel tank holding five gallons sat on top of the sloping frame tubes, and oil was circulated through two slab-sided tanks carried on each side of the frame below the saddle. (Most photographs of the Gilera show the heavily ribbed tanks that were adopted for 1939, and which, despite their intended function as oil coolers, were left bright, thereby reducing their efficiency!)

The Gileras, with blood red fuel tanks and black cycle parts, were very impressive-looking machines and claims of 80 hp at 9000 rpm were no less impressive, even if they were probably exaggerated by 20 per cent! Unfortunately, despite all the time and trouble taken, the machines had a disappointing season throughout most of 1937, occasionally showing a wonderful turn of speed but plagued by infuriating troubles until the season's end. Then, at the non-championship, but still prestigious, Italian Grand Prix at Monza, Gilera rider Giordano Aldrighetti led almost from start to finish. Despite a bad start, a slow pit stop to refuel and another to change a sparking plug, he soundly beat Omobono Tenni's Guzzi, having raised the lap record to 111 mph! Even so, 1938 was another year of disappointment,

Serafini's Gilera in the Paddock at the 1939 Ulster Grand Prix. Champions of Europe.

though notable for the excellent riding of Dorino Serafini, whom Taruffi had chosen as his own replacement, intending to concentrate on managing the team. Unfortunately, during 1938 Aldrighetti crashed at the Swiss Grand Prix so severely as to virtually retire from motorcycle racing thereafter. 1939 was the season which paid for all the hard work and disappointment; the machinery was reliable for the most part, and Serafini had found top form. For the first half of the season the Championship was virtually a duel between Serafini on the Gilera and Georg Meier on the supercharged BMW, with Meier in the lead, having won the Senior TT, which Gilera did not contest, and at Assen and Spa. Then, in a furious duel at the Swedish Grand Prix at Saxtorp, Meier crashed heavily and was out of racing for the rest of the season.

Serafini won the race, and his subsequent wins at Sachensring and at the Ulster Grand Prix, plus his second place at Spa, gave him, and Gilera, the European Championship for 1939. It was a triumphant moment, the culmination of a vision and historic in the sense that it signalled the inherent superiority of the multi-cylinder motorcycle, and especially the four-cylinder engine, over the single. But history and what might have been were soon to be swept aside by the war. In many ways, the Ulster Grand Prix of 1939 was the end of an era.

The Saturno

The ancestry of the Gilera Saturno, sometimes known as 'the Italian Manx Norton', can be traced back to a 1933 design by Mario Mellone that was developed into the pre-war VT 'four-bolt' and 'eight-bolt' sports machines. The bolts referred to were those which secured the cylinder and head to the crankcase. Though not sold as a racer, many were used in Italian long-distance races on (unclosed) public roads, and in 1939 Ettore Vella won the Milan-Tarranto race on an eight-bolt. Immediately thereafter the machine was redesigned by Giuseppe Salmagi as the 84 × 90mm 499cc Saturno, a single-cylinder sports motorcycle of orthodox but very

The 500cc Saturno racer of 1946 ready for the 1947 season.

The 1954 Gilera Saturno.

advanced specification. Riding a prototype racing model, Massimo Masserini won first time out in the Targa Florio, held on the Favorita Park circuit in Palermo, Sicily, and again at Modena before Italy's entry into the war. Post-war, Gilera built 13 Saturnos to full racing specification over the winter for the 1947 season.

These machines had girder front forks of tubular construction, a tubular frame that used the engine as a stressed member, and at the rear a swinging arm controlled by two horizontal coil springs contained within the frame tubes and damped with adjustable friction dampers. The single leading-shoe brakes, though larger than standard, look very inadequate to modern eyes. The push-rod ohv engine had a massive appearance, with a very large integral oil sump and four-speed gearbox in unit, with gear primary drive. The light alloy cylinder carried an iron liner and the light alloy head had bronze valve seats inserted, a large 35mm Dell'Orto carburettor was fitted and ignition was by a racing magneto carried high on the front of the crankcase. Confined like everyone else to using fuel of low octane rating, Gilera did well to attain a power output of 36 hp at 6000 rpm. For all its massive appearance, the racing Saturno weighed less than 270 lb, so that its performance was not to be ignored. The Saturno's post-war racing debut was at Massimo Masserini's home town of Bergamo, on the tortuous circuit of the Walls. His machine had some last-minute alterations, including a sheet-metal section in the rear part of the frame and fork girders also fabricated from sheet steel.

The other factory bikes soon incorporated these modifications. Unfortunately, Masserini did not finish the race (some reports say he fell, others that he was taken ill), but at San Remo three weeks later Carlo Bandirola, supported by team-mates Alfredo Pagani and Jader Ruggeri, won handsomely. The racing Saturno was thereafter known as the San Remo model. Unfortunately, after winning at Lugo, poor Ruggeri was killed in practice for the Swiss Grand Prix and the team was withdrawn. At the Dutch TT and the Belgian Grand Prix, Oscar Clamencigh took second and sixth places respectively. In 1947 the Italian Grand Prix was held not at Monza, but over the Fiera Campionaria street circuit in Milan itself. Hero of the hour was Arcisco Artesiani, who took the lead when Guzzi riders Belzarotti and Lorenzetti collided. Undoubtedly lucky for Artesiani, but he had stayed in a consistent third place for many laps. Even after the four-cylinder model had been completely redesigned, (and, not without problems brought to viability), development of the Saturno still took place, though rather by fits and starts than as part of a steady policy. Remor-designed torsion bar suspension for the rear end was tried in 1948, and cooling was improved and telescopic front forks fitted for 1951.

A year later there was a new all-tubular frame and conventional spring and damper units at the rear. The final version, or nearly so, had a larger 38mm carburettor and gave 42 hp at 6500 rpm. Production of the racing model ceased when Gilera withdrew from international road racing at the end of 1957.

One hundred and seventy of the genuine racing Saturnos had been made, and in Italy in particular had earned a wonderful reputation. They rarely appeared in Great Britain in the Classic years, and those that are seen today are often not genuine racing machines at all, but road-going bikes stripped and cosmetically altered to look like racers. Consequently, few British followers of Classic racing have any appreciation of how extremley competitive the Saturno was in its day. As with the Manx Norton, to which it has been compared, the Saturno was not sold to any Tom, Dick or Harry with the necessary cash, but only to up-and-coming riders of proven above-average ability, and again, like the Manx Norton (which was made in considerably large numbers), the Saturno was one of the mainstays of the 500cc class of the Continental Circus.

The experimental dohc Saturno of 1953.

Fortunately, a large number of Saturnos survive, even though a few of them may not have started life as genuine racing models. Curiously, one of the rarest Saturnos of all ran in the Senior Manx Grand Prix of 1953 ridden by an Englishman, Harry Voice. This was one of only two entirely redesigned double overhead camshaft models drawn up by Franco Passoni for 1952. It was not raced until 1953 and gave disappointing results, its only win being in the hands of French veteran Georges Monneret in the non-championship Bordeaux Grand Prix. Voice had asked his friend Geoff Duke if he could get him a Saturno for the Manx and to everyone's astonishment, Gilera sent over not only two DOHC racers but an attendant works mechanic as well. It was to no avail, as the bike sprang an oil leak early in the race and Voice had to retire. Despite instructions from the Gilera management that both machines be destroyed after the 1957 withdrawal from racing, one, according to Italian authority and collector Brizio Pignacca, survived complete and is currently in a Swiss collection.

Guzzi, who were not above exaggerating wildly in their claims for power outputs of the four-cylinder machinery, never made any such inflated statements about the Saturno. In fact they may deliberately have understated its power output as a form of gamesmanship! Riders, even those who raced against them, recall the machine with great affection as having tremendous torque, forgiving handling, excellent brakes and gears and a turn of speed that belied the simple specification. To fall back on a piece of modern jargon, the Saturno was 'user-friendly' and for that reason many have survived.

The four-cylinder 500cc

Italian industry, by and large, emerged from the Second World War in better shape than that of most of the European combatants, and the Gilera factory at Accore was no exception, having neither been bombed by the Allies nor vandalised by the retreating Germans, as some factories were. Domestic competition was again soon in full swing and Gilera raced the pre-war water-cooled fours on a number of occasions, rider Nello Pagani scoring several wins despite the engine being shorn of its supercharger. During 1946, Giuseppe Gilera had Ing. Remor working on an entirely new design. Though the FICM were not officially to ban superchargers until the Autumn Congress, Gilera anticipated the decision and indeed so did the Italian governing body, and in Italian racing supercharging was not allowed during 1946. Putting the Gilera business back to peacetime production in an ordered fashion took time, and not until well into 1947 did the new normally aspirated air-cooled racer start to take shape. The engine had its four 52 × 58mm cylinders inclined forward at 30 degrees and the one-piece crankcase casting set on top of a huge and liberally finned oil sump. Though there were four separate plain exhaust pipes, only two 28mm Weber carburettors were used at first.

As before, the two overhead camshafts were driven by a central train of spur gears. Drive to the gearbox – some accounts say that it had four speeds, some five – was by spur gears between the first and second cylinders, and the clutch ran wet. The frame was a peculiar affair of combined steel tubes and pressings with, at first, Gilera's patent rear suspension and pressed-steel parallel ruler front forks and the brakes were very similar to those fitted to the pre-war supercharged fours. There was not a trace of streamlining, perhaps indicative of the fact that at this time Piero Taruffi had left Gilera to pursue his car-racing ambitions. Testing of the new four took place in the spring of 1948 on the Milan to Bergamo autostrada and was carried

Straight from the hand of the designer, the 1948 4-cylinder Gilera.

out by riders Carlo Bandirola and Massimo Masserini. Unfortunately, the machine was straightaway in trouble with lubrication problems, which took an unduly long time to resolve, but when the problem was cured, there was no doubt that the bike, with 48 hp at the rear wheel and weighing a mere 270 lb, had the speed and acceleration to live with any racing motorcycle of its time. Its handling was another question. At the machine's very first outing at Cesena in May 1948, Nello Pagani retired the Gilera as 'unrideable', to the extreme annoyance of designer Piero Remor.

Nevertheless, the problem seems to have been very real, and 1948 was not a good season for Gilera. Even the Italian National title eluded them, being won by Bertacchini on a Guzzi Bicilindrica. Some consolation came at the season's end when Norton and AJS chose not to race at the Italian Grand Prix in September and Masserini gave the four its first International win at Farenza. With this victory Masserini retired from racing. Most unfortunately the best rider at Gilera's disposal, the experienced Nello Pagani, was locked into a counter-productive feud with Remor over the handling of the four. Such was Remor's temperament that rather than admit to the machine's shortcomings (which were plainly visible to everyone else) he forbade Pagani to ride, condemning him to race the single-cylinder Saturno!

A measure of the Gilera's handling can be gleaned from the fact that during 1949, the year in which the FIM instituted the World Championship both for riders and constructors, the honours went to Les Graham and the AJS Porcupine, a machine which weighed around 310 lb and produced approximately 45 hp, whereas the figures for the Gilera were 275 lb and 50 hp respectively! So annoyed were the Gilera management at the way the season was going, that Remor was overruled and Pagani rode a four at Assen. He won comfortably, having shadowed Les Graham until the last lap and then used the four's superior power to win. That, and the Italian Grand Prix at Monza, another victory for Pagani, were Gilera's only outright wins in 1949.

At the season's end, matters came to a head with Piero Remor, whom most of the riders not only detested but regarded as, in the words of one of them, 'a charlatan'. He had certainly caused considerable problems by his early failure to sort out the lubrication, and by his refusal to acknowledge and cure the evil handling.

It is hard to understand why Remor occupied the position that he did post-war as much of the credit for pre-war success was attributable to the work of Taruffi and Giuseppe Gilera himself. Remor was not the only man in Italy with the capability to design what was after all a fairly simple four-cylinder engine. Be that as it may, he departed, along with rider Arcisco Artesiani and technician Arturo Magni for the MV factory at Gallarate. It is interesting to note that with the return of the much more sympathetic Piero Taruffi, and the promotion of designer Franco Passoni, some fundamental changes were made to both engines and frames. (It is also interesting to note that the MV four was by no means an instant success.)

For 1950, with four 30mm carburettors and revised cylinder heads, power output was 52 hp at 9000 rpm. There was a full-width front brake and the rear suspension was altered back to Gilera's distinctive design rather than the system favoured by Remor. For 1950 the Gilera riders were Carlo Bandirola, Umberto Masetti and Nello Pagani. In a season of mixed fortunes, it was, astonishingly, the virtual novice, Masetti, who was to win the Individual World Championship, though the Constructor's Championship went to Norton. Masetti achieved his triumph with wins at the Belgian Grand Prix and the Dutch TT, second places at the Swiss and Italian Grands Prix, and sixth in the Ulster Grand Prix.

For 1951, Gilera tackled the problems that still persisted with the handling, built fully tubular frames, employed conventional coil spring and damper units to control the swinging arm rear suspension, and used oil-damped telescopic front forks. The riders were Masetti, Pagani and Alfredo Milani. Despite the undoubted improvements to the handling, and a little more power from the engines, in 1951 Gilera were overshadowed by Norton, whose featherbed frame had given them a new lease of life since 1950 and whose number one rider, Geoff Duke, stood head and shoulders above any other European rider of the time. Norton and Geoff Duke became Champion Constructor and Champion Rider in the 500cc class for 1951.

Masserini on the Gilera in the Dutch Grand Prix 1948. He led, but fell back and crashed in heavy rain.

Along the way Masetti had won for Gilera at the Spanish Grand Prix and Milani had won in France and Italy.

1952 was again an indeterminate year for Gilera. Not until the Dutch TT at Assen did Masetti score for Gilera, beating Geoff Duke fairly and squarely and then repeating his win at the Belgian Grand Prix. These two victories, plus his placings in the other rounds, once again brought Masetti the individual World Championship for 1952, but the Constructor's Championship went to Norton for the third year in succession. Giuseppe Gilera was reluctant to engage foreign riders – which at the time effectively meant Englishmen. Taruffi had no such scruples, and indeed for the Ulster Grand Prix had had the satisfaction of seeing Ulsterman Cromie McCandless win for Gilera. He now persuaded Gilera that he should swallow his chauvinistic pride and persuade Geoff Duke to leave Norton, which was not a difficult thing to achieve. Duke's position with Norton was by no means what it might have seemed to an outsider – he was employed at Bracebridge Street as a mechanic and tester, and paid £10 per week. His considerable starting money was paid to Norton Motors Ltd, and apart from his basic wage, all he earned from his racing career was his prize money and some none-too-generous bonus payments. He was, in fact, early in 1953, disillusioned about his career, and was hoping to join the David Brown Aston Martin sports car racing team. However, he was in a strong bargaining position *vis-à-vis* Gilera, and stuck out for a good contract. In the event, neither he nor Gilera were to regret it. To complete the team, Piero Taruffi signed up Reg Armstrong and Dickie Dale, thus apparently

With Remor's departure, Piero Taruffi assumed control of racing. Here, hands in pockets, he watches Nello Pagani warming up a four with telescopic forks and rear suspension dampers.

dealing the Norton factory team a mortal blow, but Norton were not as bothered as they might have been, for they were finding that racing successes were bringing rapidly diminishing returns, and only a year later were to withdraw from contesting the World Championships.

Without a doubt, one reason for Gilera's decision to secure the services of ex-Norton teamsters was Taruffi's conviction that the time was ripe to challenge for victory in what was still the world's premier motorcycling event, the Senior TT. In 1953, for the first time in the company's 40-odd-year history, entries were made and accepted. Guided by the ex-Norton riders and especially by Geoff Duke, Franco Passoni completely revised the cycle parts in the light of their experience, though the engines remained substantially the same.

Showing their serious approach to the TT, Gilera took no fewer than eight complete machines to the Island (plus a large consignment of spares) for riders Duke, Dale, Armstrong and Alfredo Milani, but after an incident-free practice Gilera had a disappointing Island debut. The race was a tragic one in any case, overshadowed by Les Graham's fatal accident on Bray Hill on the second lap. Duke broke the lap record from a standing start at 96.38 mph and continued to draw out a lead over Ray Amm on the Norton – at the end of the second lap it was over a minute – even though Amm had lapped at 97.41 mph! But on lap three, at Quarter Bridge, Duke, perhaps trying a little too hard, 'lost it' at Quarter Bridge and split his petrol tank. Reg Armstrong was down on power all through the race, and did extremely well to finish third to Amm and Jack Brett on the Nortons after having to refit his rear chain to the sprockets on the last lap. Milani was never on the leaderboard and Dickie Dale fell at Hillberry.

The TT apart, 1953 was a good year for Gilera, and Geoff Duke was to win the individual 500cc World Championship (and Gilera the Constructor's Championship) with outright wins at the Dutch TT and the French, Swiss and Italian Grands Prix.

By the end of 1953, Gilera might have been excused for feeling complacent, but Taruffi and Passoni were both realists, and allowed themselves no such luxury! The works Nortons were still incredibly fast, perhaps not as fast in a straight line as the Gilera, but just as fast around a demanding circuit! MV were beginning to make progress, especially now that Piero Remor had departed, and development had been made the responsibility of Arturo Magni, and Guzzi could never be ignored! Consequently, for 1954, Passoni undertook a major redesign of the 500cc four. The engine was lowered in the frame no less than three inches by an alteration to the sump. The included angle of the valves was increased and detail alterations made to the cylinder heads. Power was now measured as 64 hp at 10,500 rpm, and transmitted through a five-speed gearbox. A new lower and narrower frame gave the bike a far neater appearance. Braking was not neglected, and a full-width ventilated two leading-shoe unit was used at the front. Geoff Duke appeared with this new machine at the April meeting at Silverstone, fresh from testing at Montl-héry. In the so-called BMCRC Championship race, Ray Amm challenged Duke strongly, but over-revved his engine and could only finish second, with Derek Farrant third on an AJS Porcupine.

It was a magnificent introduction of the Gilera to the British enthusiasts, and the fact that Amm on the Norton had made fastest lap suggested that some exciting racing lay ahead. Duke and Armstrong also rode at the famous 'North West 200' in Ulster. In fact, it was Reg Armstrong's race all the way, for though Duke took the lead when the Irishman refuelled, he was soon out of the race with broken valve gear, and Armstrong went on to win. After a few minor setbacks, 1954 proved another good season. The TT was, literally, a washout, being stopped at the end of the fourth lap after two postponements of the start. Duke, having refuelled at the end of the third lap, was a minute and six seconds down on Amm, and Armstrong, fourth to Jack Brett's Norton, was fully three minutes behind. Suggestions that the

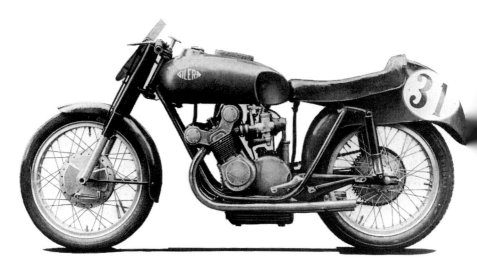

The 1951 Gilera, although much improved, still looked high off the ground and carried its oil below the engine.

ACU stopped the race to 'allow' Ray Amm (and Norton) to win were ludicrous. Amm needed no help! Duke's fastest lap was his first, in 25 mins 41 secs. That apart, each of Amm's successive laps was faster than Duke's – lap two by 12 seconds, lap three by 30 seconds and the last lap by an astonishing 38 seconds. Admittedly Duke's third and fourth lap times were affected by his pit stop, but by nothing like a minute and eight seconds! But thereafter Gilera had a good year, winning six of the Grands Prix; Frenchman Pierre Monneret won the Belgian, and Geoff Duke the Dutch, German, Swiss and Italian rounds. At Monza, surprisingly clumsy-looking streamlining of the full-enclosure 'dustbin' type was used, though Duke expressed his belief that it did little to enhance the bike's performance. These results were enough for Duke and Gilera to retain their World Championships, though officially the FIM awarded no Constructors Championship for 1954.

In 1955 the machines were virtually unaltered except for a larger and better-cooled front brake, but there were team changes: footloose Umberto Masetti left to join MV, as did Norton's Ray Amm. Poor Amm was to lose his life at Imola in his very first race for the Italian factory – a sad end to a brilliant career. The basic Gilera team of Duke and Armstrong was joined by the up-and-coming Libero Liberati, who indeed won at Imola when Duke fell and Armstrong had engine trouble. Once again Geoff Duke gave British fans a treat at the April Silverstone meeting, winning the Championship race, though hotly pursued by another promising rider, John Surtees on the Norton. In Spain, Duke retired after only six laps, but the race was safe with Reg Armstrong, who won, ahead of the MVs of Carlo Bandirola and Umberto Masetti. At the French Grand Prix, Taruffi once again experimented with full streamlining, but the riders appeared to prefer to ride with the bikes unfaired in later events.

Alas for British prestige, there was no Norton team at the TT for 1955, almost the only time since the races began in 1907. The Senior race was run in beautiful weather, and conditions were ideal for breaking records. It was a total triumph for the Gileras of Geoff Duke and Reg Armstrong, who finished ahead of Ken Kavanagh (Moto Guzzi), Jack Brett (Norton), Bob McIntyre (Norton) and Derek

Geoff Duke, Giuseppe Gilera and Alfredo Milani at Monza in 1953.

Ennett (Matchless G 45). Duke won at 97.93 mph, and lapped at 99.97 mph on lap three, which was mistakenly announced as 100 mph exactly! When, nearly forty minutes later this was corrected, there was an audible storm of protest from the infuriated and disappointed crowd! Controversy raged for months about the 100 mph lap, even to the extent of the course being unofficially re-measured, and found rather surprisingly, in view of alterations over the years, to be, if anything, slightly *short* of its stated $37^{3}/_{4}$ miles.

At the Nürburgring Duke won again. At Spa he retired, but fortunately Giu-

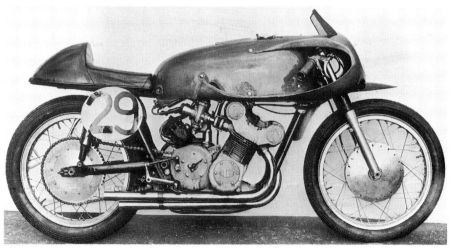

Geoff Duke 'Nortonised' the four – note how much lower it appears in this 1954 photograph.

*Views of the Gilera
4-cylinder engine,
showing the centrally
disposed sparking plugs,
the liberal finning, large
oil sump between the
inner pair of exhausts
and central drive to the
camshafts.*

seppe Colnago, Pierre Monneret and René Martin were all Gilera-mounted that day and finished first, second and third. The Dutch TT at Assen was on the face of it another triumph, with Duke and Armstrong first and second, but the 'Dutch' had been the scene of a mass protest by private owners over the poor conditions and starting money that they claimed prevailed. In the 350cc race, 23 of them pulled into the pits at the end of the first lap, leaving only the works bikes and a few Dutch riders running. In the face of angry demonstrations by the huge crowd the organizers hastily caved in to riders' demands before the 500cc race, which was run as normal. But the KNMV (Dutch equivalent to the British ACU) pursued the matter in a sickeningly vengeful manner. Incredibly, at the end of November, the FIM suspended 14 riders, including Duke and Armstrong, from riding in International events in the first half of 1956! Three other riders, all Italian, were suspended for four months. More than thirty years after the event, the mind still boggles at the unethical way in which the inquiry was rigged and the petty spitefulness of the Dutch governing body. Neither Duke nor Armstrong had taken part in the demonstration, and their only crime, if crime it was, was to have argued the case of the private entrants with the organizers in a reasonable fashion. Never before or since has the history of motorcycle racing recorded any injustice comparable to this infamous and disgraceful decision by the FIM. Nor was there the slightest indication beforehand that such Draconian measures would be taken, so that when Piero Taruffi finally parted company with Gilera (on the best of terms) at the end of the 1955 season, the team had no reason to suspect that 1956 would be other than a good year. This was especially likely because, in Taruffi's place, Ferrucio Gilera, only son of founder Giuseppe Gilera, became manager of the racing organization with which he had worked since 1954. Twenty-five years of age, enthusiastic and unquestionably able, Ferrucio Gilera was universally liked and respected. He had been responsible for both the 125cc twin that appeared in practice at Monza in 1955 and for the 350cc four that was raced in 1957.

Now came the bombshell that was tantamount to the FIM robbing Gilera of the 1956 500cc World Championship and presenting it on a plate to MV Agusta, who had for five years shown little chance of earning it by their own efforts! MV shrewdly took advantage of the situation by signing up the brilliant young John Surtees, whom, under other circumstances, Gilera would almost certainly have employed in 1956.

Over the winter, Passoni stiffened the frame still further, and by now it was no longer possible to claim that the Gileras did not steer and handle. The exhaust pipes now terminated in megaphones, which, improved the power output at the lower end of the scale as well as producing a peak output of 70 hp at 11,000 rpm! The most striking and memorable improvement to the machines was the superb full fairing, to call it a 'dustbin' would be to insult a beautiful example of genuinely aerodynamic styling that was also the creation of Franco Passoni. Because Giuseppe Colnago and Alfredo Milani were amongst the riders suspended for the first four months of 1956, Gilera did not contest any event before the TT. Duke, who was allowed to ride in non-Championship events, rode the new model at Aintree in May and won against negligible local opposition. As was only to be expected, Surtees and MV won in Holland and in the Isle of Man, accruing valuable Championship points. They won too at Spa in Belgium, but not before Geoff Duke had convincingly demonstrated the Gilera's utter superiority over the MV. Alas, with a mere two laps to go, he was forced to retire when a piston completely disintegrated. By the time of the German Grand Prix, Gilera's hopes of the Championship looked thin, and though John Surtees crashed in the 350cc race, breaking his arm, Duke's chances of the individual title vanished with another retirement as Reg Armstrong went on to win.

The Ulster Grand Prix was another disaster, with Duke falling heavily at half-distance and Armstrong retiring only moments later with a burned-out clutch.

Any chance of a title had vanished. Nevertheless, Gilera fielded four machines at Monza, giving one of them, which was quite obviously faster than the others, to Libero Liberati at the last minute! This perhaps understandable chauvinism stung Geoff Duke into an exhibition of how sheer riding skill could overcome an advantage in the hands of a lesser rival, and he won easily, with Liberati, Pierre Monneret and Reg Armstrong in line astern behind him. It had not been a good season for Gilera, with only two classic wins, and it ended in downright tragedy when Feruccio Gilera, only 26 years of age, died of a heart attack on a business visit to Gilera's factory in Buenos Aires. The effect upon his father was devastating, and from that time onward, he progressively lost interest even in the day-to-day affairs of the factory. To the outside world this was not apparent, but Geoff Duke claimed that early in 1957 he noticed a slackening of effort. Nevertheless, with Duke, Liberati and the brilliant Bob McIntyre (signed up to replace Reg Armstrong, who had now retired), the team seemed a strong one. Most unfortunately, at the non-championship meeting at Imola which began Gilera's season, Duke fell not once, but twice, first from the 350cc machine. Though shaken he was not badly hurt, but the bike was comprehensively wrecked. In the 500cc event, he fell heavily once more and not only hurt his left eye, but exacerbated the shoulder injury that he had received at the Ulster Grand Prix in 1956. McIntyre was forced to retire with ignition trouble.

Although it was said at the time that Geoff would be fit and well for the TT, this was not to be the case, and as this became apparent, Gilera hastily signed Australian Bob Brown at McIntyre's suggestion. It was the 50th anniversary of the TT and the Senior race was to be run over eight laps. There was tremendous excitement at the prospect once again of an MV–Gilera duel and anticipation that, given good weather, the long-awaited 100 mph lap would materialize. And so it did. The weather was described as 'perfect', and from a standing start McIntyre lapped at 99.99 mph! Already he was an astonishing 39 seconds ahead of the MV, some indication of the Gilera's superiority. Furthermore, McIntyre's fastest lap at 101.12 mph was no less than 29 seconds faster than Surtees' fastest at 99 mph. In a truly thrilling race, although he visibly eased the pace in the last two laps, McIntyre came home first at 98.99 mph with John Surtees in second place and Bob Brown (whose fastest lap, his sixth, had been at 98.4 mph) third.

The man, the style, the machine – Geoff Duke at La Source hairpin in the 1956 Belgian Grand Prix.

Moment of triumph! The Golden Jubilee TT, of 1957: Bob McIntyre laps at 97.42mph in the Junior and Bob Brown finishes third. With his arm around Bob is chief mechanic Giovanni Fumigalli.

They all finished ahead of the Vee-eight Guzzi of Dickie Dale, the single-cylinder Guzzi of Keith Campbell and the works-supported Norton of Allan Trow. It had been perhaps both McIntyre's and Gilera's finest hour, and a victory by which both man and machine are still remembered by those lucky enough to have been in the Isle of Man that last year of what many people remember as a golden era of road racing.

At Assen, Bob McIntyre fell whilst chasing John Surtees. That he was behind, not in front of the MV, was because of a pit stop to change a sparking plug. Liberati finished second. At Spa, a stupid and chauvinistic decision by new team manager Roberto Persi cost Gilera any points that they might have accrued. Because Liberati's machine would not start, Persi sent him out on Bob Brown's bike without having the wit to register the change with the officials. The result was that Brown did not ride (nor did McIntyre, still suffering from a neck injury from his fall at Assen), and though Liberati won, he was disqualified! Liberati, whose self-esteem sometimes outran his actual capabilities, showed real form at the Ulster Grand Prix and won with ease from McIntyre and Duke after Surtees retired. In the final race at Monza, Liberati again won from Duke and Milani (McIntyre, being ill, did not ride). Thus, with wins at four Classics, Gilera became Constructor's Champion, and Liberati, who had scored three of them, became individual World Champion. Development for 1958 began immediately, and Passoni set to work on the design and development of a new cylinder head. Then, sensation! Gilera, Moto Guzzi, Mondial and MV Agusta jointly announced that they were withdrawing from international road racing! For all its tremendous entertainment value, and the technical advancement that it undoubtedly stimulated, racing had become ruinously expensive, which was bad enough. Worse was that in the economic climate of the day it was no longer selling motorcycles, and the Italian industry was in no position to continue its extravaganza. That MV almost immediately broke the agreement to withdraw from racing is understandable, for they were not serious motorcycle manufacturers but depended upon aeronautical engineering for their profits – racing was quite literally a hobby activity for the wealthy Count Domenico

Agusta. But Gilera were nearing the very brink of financial disaster. Though they drew back, the company never prospered again, struggling through the next decade, handicapped by lack of capital, an ageing management, horrendous strikes and a depressed market for motorcycles. By 1968 a receiver was appointed and Gilera was sold to Piaggio late in 1969. Giuseppe Gilera died two years later.

That in 1963 Gilera were mistaken enough to be tempted back into racing indicates a fatal weakness of purpose, and though in theory they only provided the machinery and the mechanics, they doubtless incurred far more expense than they bargained for. It was Geoff Duke's belief that the 1957 Gilera was in every way superior to the 1960 MV, and at that time he tried to persuade Giuseppe Gilera to release a machine for Bob McIntyre, but nothing came of this. Duke must have been persuasive and persistent, because in late 1962, a bike was sent over to England for tests and assessment by Derek Minter and John Hartle. Both men were immensely experienced and successful – Minter, indeed, being at that time arguably a better rider even than Mike Hailwood.

Tests in Britain showed great promise, and Duke secured financial support from Avon Tyres and Castrol Oil. But in retrospect mistakes were made from the very beginning. It was over-ambitious to race the 350cc models as well as the 500cc – extra expense and extra work for the mechanics, and the 350cc Gilera (only raced in 1957) had not had the development of the big bikes.

After tests at Monza in the spring of 1963, Derek Minter claimed that the change from full fairings to the now obligatory 'Dolphin' resulted in a lack of aerodynamic downforce, and that the suspension was too hard. He made various other suggestions in the light of the six years that had elapsed since the Gileras had been raced and later claimed that he was ignored.

However, the 1963 season apparently opened on a promising note with Minter winning at Silverstone, Brands Hatch and Oulton Park. Even more heartening was to have Minter and Hartle finish first and second at Imola, ahead of MV's new star Mike Hailwood. In May, Derek Minter on his Norton crashed at Brands Hatch during the course of a lurid and downright terrifying battle with Dave Downer on Paul Dunstall's 650cc Domiracer. As anyone who saw the race will testify, it could only end one way and the resulting accident killed Downer and put Minter into hospital with serious back and wrist injuries. Up-and-coming Phil Read was recruited to take Minter's place. His first race was in the 350cc event at Hockenheim, and led to instant disillusionment about the smaller Gilera! Nor did the Junior TT give any comfort.

In the Junior race Jim Redman on the Honda led from start to finish, closely followed for three laps by Mike Hailwood on the MV. On the second lap, Read's Gilera blew up, and John Hartle was in third place. On the fourth lap, Mike Hailwood's MV lost all its power, and Hartle moved up to second. But he was lucky to finish at all, even luckier to finish in second place, for his engine was dreadfully 'off song' and his last lap was at a derisory 77.49 mph on three cylinders! Redman's race average on the Honda was 94.91 mph – Hartle's was 90.58 mph, and he finished less than a minute and a half ahead of Franta Stastny on the Jawa! The Senior race was nothing like so humiliating, and Hartle finished second to Hailwood on the MV, at 103.67 mph compared with Mike's 104.64 mph. Read, by no means as experienced, was third at 100.10 mph. To give some perspective, Mike Duff on a G50 Matchless finished fourth at 99.29 mph.

At this point reason prevailed, and the 350cc machines were sent back to Italy. At the Dutch TT Hailwood's MV broke down and Hartle and Read were first and second in the 500cc class. It was their last moment of Classic glory. Read finished second to Hailwood at Spa. Derek Minter, though still suffering from his injured back, returned and won (breaking the lap record) at Oulton Park. In the Ulster Grand Prix, Hailwood demonstrated the MV's now superior speed not only by an easy win over Hartle and Minter, but by going through the speed trap at 143.5

mph, fully five and half miles an hour faster than the fastest Gilera.

Read had crashed, demolishing a second bike (for Minter had written one off in tests at Monza when the front forks failed at over 100 mph). At the East German Grand Prix, Minter was second to Hailwood, but yet another bike was written off when Hartle fell! Now only one machine remained raceworthy and was sent to Finland for Hartle to ride, but trouble with the gearbox frustrated his effort. Everything now concentrated on putting on a show for the Italian crowd at the last European Classic of the season at Monza. Alas it proved a dismal fiasco. Hartle crashed heavily in practice, writing off yet another machine that had only just been rebuilt. In the race, hasty preparation and poor machining slowed the bikes and caused them to retire with oil leaks and faulty gearboxes. An infuriated and humiliated Gilera management over-ruled any suggestion of continuing racing in 1964, and so ended Geoff Duke's attempt to revive Gilera's greatness. It is all too easy, with hindsight, to be wise. Both Derek Minter and Phil Read have said some harsh things about Duke's approach which, summed up, amount to the fact that not having raced himself since 1959, he did not and *would* not acknowledge that there had been subtle changes in road racing, and that the bikes did not handle as well, compared with the opposition, as they had done six years before. Probably quite true. That the team was financed at all was a minor miracle, but it was almost certainly under-financed with all the irritations and decisions made with crossed fingers that such a condition entails. The factory, too, were almost certainly over-optimistic about the expense and effort that the exercise would demand of them. The wonder is, not that 'Scuderia Duke' did badly, but that with so many handicaps, they did so well.

Incredibly, the fiasco at Monza was *not* the end. Machines – and factory mechanics – were loaned out to various riders in 1964 and again in 1966, even though the factory was now a shambles and production virtually at a standstill.

Benedicto Caldarella, Silvio Grassetti, Remo Venturi, and even Derek Minter all had occasional outings with the by now largely uncompetitive fours, with just enough success that Giuseppe Gilera could not bear to cry 'enough'. That he did so for 1967 was probably forced upon him by sheer circumstances.

The four-cylinder 500cc Gilera's last appearance in the Isle of Man was in practice for the 1966 TT. The bike, and mechanic Luigi Columbo, were taken to the Island at Minter's own expense. Fitted with a seven-speed gearbox, the outcome of a brief association between Gilera and Lino Tonti, the bike was in trouble throughout practice with poor handling, only cured for the final practice session. Minter later claimed that with new rear dampers the machine was all that it should have been and entirely competitive. But he was not to be able to prove it, for at Brandish he fell heavily, breaking his wrist. When the circumstances are considered, that *any* of the Gileras have survived is something at which to marvel. In fact, none of the early ones have: they were broken up, crashed and not repaired, and constantly cannibalized. Two of the machines apparently of 1954–57 are in museums, one in Milan, one in Turin, but they are probably both built up from whatever parts came to hand and possess no real integrity. The same applies to three that are in Gilera's own museum, and three more that are in private collections in Italy. Only the machine retained after 1964 by Benedicto Caldarella in the Argentine is 'original' and even that was totally rebuilt by Gilera's Argentine factory. That the few survivors were not stolen or smashed up in spite by agitators in the anarchic mid- and late 60s is remarkable.

Most fortunately, although Piaggio hard-headedly disapprove of racing, they do allow the bikes in the Gilera Museum to appear in public, and to take part in demonstration runs. Long may they continue to do so!

The 350cc four-cylinder Gileras

That Dean of motorcycling journalists, himself a one-time International competitor, and for several years Technical Editor of *The Motorcycle*, Vic Willoughby has, on more than one occasion, asserted that the way to a successful 350cc racing machine is to scale up a two-fifty rather than to scale down a five hundred. Gilera, of course, not having a 250cc racer had not much choice, but their 350cc four-cylinder bike of 1957 certainly bore out Willoughby's contention that a scaled-down 500cc made for a 350cc that was heavy and bulky.

John Hartle, Geoff Duke and Phil Read contemplate the 350cc Gilera at the 1963 TT.

Derek Minter tests the 350 Gilera four early in 1963.

Once again, the stimulus for the 350cc model came from Ferrucio Gilera and the design from Franco Passoni. In most respects, except the internal dimensions of the engines, the 350cc and 500cc Gileras were identical. Bore and stroke of the 350cc was 46 × 52.6mm, carburettors were 25mm Dell'Ortos and the engine produced about 45 hp at 11,000 rpm. The bike first appeared at Monza right at the end of 1956. Why Gilera (like so many other Italian manufacturers) chose to show their hand to the opposition in this way is one of life's mysteries. The fact that in this instance, although Geoff Duke retired, Libero Liberati won with ease only served to stimulate Moto Guzzi's Giulio Carcano to undertake a concentrated development programme over the winter.

At the first Classic round in 1957, the German Grand Prix at Hockenheim, run in a rainstorm, most of the top runners fell (including Bob McIntyre) and Liberati won. At the TT Bob McIntyre rode a new, lighter development machine to victory in the Junior race over Keith Campbell on the Guzzi, and on a second, ordinary machine, Bob Brown finished third. Thereafter, Keith Campbell won at Assen and at Spa, with McIntyre taking second place at the one and Liberati at the other. At the Ulster Grand Prix, Campbell secured the individual championship by winning. At the final round at Monza, McIntyre, though still suffering from the after-effects of a fall at Assen in the 500cc race, soundly beat Liberati, whom the Gilera factory had hoped would win in front of a 'home' crowd and to whom they had therefore given a faster machine. That should have been the end of the 350cc Gilera, for though it won its makers the Constructor's title in the 350cc class for 1957, it was a flawed concept, and when in 1963 Geoff Duke chose to have his team ride it alongside the larger bikes, its performance, in contrast to the developed MV and Honda opposition, was abysmal. At the 1963 TT John Hartle profited from numerous retirements to finish second to Jim Redman's Honda, but a succession of disasters soon meant that the team hastily abondoned their assault on the 350cc class.

The rapid destruction of three 500cc machines in a row towards the end of 1963 led to the cannibalization of the 350cc machines for their cycle parts. Whether, during the anarchy that prevailed at Arcore between 1964 and 1969, the engines were stolen is not known, but today not a single 350cc Gilera four is known to survive.

The 125cc Gilera Twin

Although its career was brief and it never saw the Isle of Man, the very promising 125cc twin that Romolo Ferri rode for Gilera in 1956 deserves a mention. The concept was Ferrucio Gilera's, the design was entirely Franco Passoni's, and had not events overtaken Gilera, the bike would almost certainly have done far better in 1957 than it did in the one season, 1956, in which it contested the Classic meetings. It was designed during 1955 and, with bore and stroke of 40 × 49.6mm and twin overhead camshafts driven by a train of gears between the two cylinders, it resembled a scaled-down 500cc four without its two outer cylinders. A six-speed gearbox was also centrally driven. With coil ignition and a pair of 22mm Dell'Orto carburettors, the engine gave about 20 hp at 12,000 rpm, which was well within its safe limit. The cycle parts were conventional (and none the worse for that) and the engine sat low in a duplex cradle frame with leading-link front forks (later altered for 1956 to telescopics), and at the rear, swinging arm and spring/damper units and large twin leading-shoe brakes were used. A beautiful full fairing with tail streamlining was designed by Passoni and doubtless contributed to the bike's top speed of around 120 mph – fast at that time for 125cc.

An entry for Pierre Monneret at Monza at the end of 1955 was withdrawn, and Gilera engaged Romolo Ferri to test the machine and to ride it in the 1956 season; it was at Ferri's urging that the telescopic forks were fitted. At Monza in May 1956

The beautifully streamlined 125cc twin, here ridden by Romolo Ferri to a convincing win in the 1956 German Grand Prix.

Ferri led from start to finish in the bike's first race and averaged a staggering 96 mph. At Spa, he lapped at 100.85 mph, but the engine overheated and he was forced to retire. Pierre Monneret, not quite as fast as Ferri, survived to finish third. With small ducts for extra cooling cut in the fairing, Ferri won the German Grand Prix at Solitude, breaking the lap and race records.

At the Ulster Grand Prix, the bike was off-song, and Ferri finished a poor second to Ubbialli, at Monza he retired with a burned piston and in Sweden, a non-Championship race, he won again. Ferri finished second to Ubbiali in the Championship and, in the normal way, Gilera would have enthusiastically pursued development of this remarkable little machine. But Ferrucio Gilera's untimely death at the end of 1956 cast a blight on everything, and with a sole Classic win at Solitude to its credit, the 125cc twin was virtually retired. A few none-too-impressive appearances in 1957 by factory riders (and by private riders in domestic events) were anti-climactic. The twins never raced again. Today one survives in the private Gilera Museum, the fate of the other is not known.

Greeves Silverstone

By the early 1960s the Essex firm of Invacar Ltd, makers of Greeves motorcycles, were tremendously respected for their Motocross and trials machinery with Villiers-based engines and gearboxes. Greeves motorcycles had been in contention for a number of years when first Brian Stonebridge and then Dave Bickers showed that they were well able to beat the best that the Continentals could field in the Motocross Coupe d'Europe. Nevertheless, the appearance at the 1962 Motorcycle show of a road-racing model was not taken altogether seriously by many people.

Before the show designer Bert Greeves had already announced the machine, the RAS model 'Silverstone', as a learner's introduction to road racing. But developments over the winter of 1962–3 were to turn the bike into a serious contender at national road-racing levels. The Silverstone's original inspiration had been a modified 24MDX scrambler ridden with some success in club and national road races by Reg Everett. Contributions to engine development made in late 1962 by an acquaintance of Everett's, Brian Woolley, raised the power at the rear wheel from 24.5 hp at 7500 rpm to 30.5 hp at 7800 rpm, a figure which, allied to the bike's amazingly light weight and excellent handling, meant that on its appearance for the 1963 season it was outstandingly competitive at all but works-supported international events.

The engine was based upon the single-cylinder Villiers 36A unit of 66 × 72mm (246cc) and used a light alloy cylinder (with cast-in iron liner) and cylinder head of Greeves' own manufacture. Ignition was by Villiers flywheel magneto, carburation by a $1^3/_8$ in Amal GP 2 carburettor with 'matchbox' float chamber. Close ratios were specified for the Villiers four-speed gearbox. The frame closely resembled that of the 24MDX, with leading front-link forks using large-diameter rubber bushes in torsion as springs, with twin telescopic dampers concealed in the fork stanchions. The frame itself resembled the scrambler in using the Greeves cast light alloy 'beam' instead of a front tube, and the swinging arm was square-section tube, controlled by orthodox Girling spring and damper units. Proprietary hubs and brakes were fitted, and tank, saddle and head fairing were of glass-fibre. The bike was extremely well made and finished, and at £275 (when a very second-hand NSU Sportmax would change hands for three times that sum) was remarkable value for money. If that had not been immediately apparent, it certainly became so after the bike's first appearance at Oulton Park, where private owner Tom Phillips' shattering wins in both the 250cc events called forth headlines in the motorcycle press.

Similar results by other owners meant a surge of demand for the Silverstone that the factory (who had expected to sell at most 25 machines) were hard put to meet: in all, 144 model RAS Silverstones were sold during 1963, a quite remarkable number. It was as a short-circuit machine that the Greeves shone brightest, but a little-noticed eighth place in the 1963 Lightweight TT by Rhodesian rider Alan Harris on a Silverstone entered by London dealer Reg Orpin was of some significance. The 1963 ACU 'Star' for the 250cc class was won by Tom Phillips. Normally, the factory would have built upon such a brilliantly successful start and

Simple, cheap, and reliable and so quick in its day! The original Greeves RAS Silverstone took British 250cc racing by the scruff of the neck in 1963.

The later Greeves with their own engine were not slow either. Here, Trevor Burgess fends off Phil Read and Bill Ivy on works Yamahas at Mallory Park in 1965. And yes, he was in the lead – not being lapped!

merely undertaken detail development for the following year, but Bert Greeves was tired of the expensive waste involved in using Villiers engines in which the crank had to be replaced with Alpha full-circle flywheels, the piston with one by Hepolite, the cylinder and cylinder head with parts made by Greeves themselves and the carburettor with a racing instrument. He therefore designed and made the Greeves 'Challenger' engine, which thereafter was to power both scramblers and road racers. Unfortunately, for the RBS road-racing version he chose to use the lightweight five-speed Albion gearbox (as fitted to the road-going Royal Enfield Continental GT model), which proved horribly fragile in use. The radical redesign of the engine, which had a new Alpha crankshaft considerably more robust than that used in the RAS, as well as a new cylinder barrel and head, led to initial troubles on the dynamometer which were not easily overcome.

Few RBS Silverstones were delivered during 1964, and those soon had their five-speed gearboxes replaced with a heavy four-speed gearbox that was robust enough but detracted from the performance. Though the RAS models continued their successful ways, had it not been for a win in the newly reintroduced Lightweight class of the Manx Grand Prix, 1964 would have indeed been a wasted year for Greeves. Shrewd strategy by entrant Reg Orpin, meticulous preparation by factory mechanic Bob Mills and a cool level-headed ride by Gordon Keith resulted in a win for the Silverstone at 86.19 mph, well ahead of assorted Yamahas, Aermacchis, Cottons and Ducattis. A year later, Dennis Craine, backed by the same team, won again at the even higher speed of 88.37 mph. With detail improvements and uprating, the Greeves Silverstone ran through from the RBS of 1964 to the RES of 1967, still very successful and wonderful value for money. But with Greeves' commitment to Motocross, for all the publicity and free advertising that its results brought to the Company, the Silverstone had, by 1967, become almost an embarrassment, and production came to an end. Its demise coincided with the arrival upon the scene of the remarkable Yamaha TDIC and soon the Greeves Silverstone was totally outclassed. Many British riders made their names – or significantly advanced them – on the Greeves Silverstone. Though they never directly employed factory riders, Greeves gave support to several – briefly John Cooper and later Peter Williams through dealer Reg Orpin. Famous tuner Francis Beart entered Joe Dunphy with considerable success. Perhaps the most successful

– certainly the best known Silverstone rider – was Northerner Trevor Burgess who, on Brian Woolley's works assisted development bike, was very rarely ever beaten in 1966 and 1967. A 350cc model, the Oulton, which had been promising in prototype form, was launched for 1968, but due to lack of development at the crucial moment, it was not successful and was dropped after only about twenty-five had been sold. Although a respectable number of Silverstones survive and are raced and paraded today, their performance hardly matches up to their hold on the 250cc class between 1963 and 1966, probably because of the continuing tuning of Ducati and Aermacchi machinery in the late 60s and early 70s, in contrast to the abandonment of the Silverstone in the face of the apparently overwhelming dominance of Yamaha.

Honda

Late in 1945, in the traumatic aftermath of Japan's defeat in World War II, 39-year-old Soichiro Honda put behind him the evidence of a successful (if sometimes erratic) business career when he sold his Tokai Seika piston ring company to his largest customer, Toyota Motors. Despite his avowed intention of taking a rest from business affairs, seemingly he could not stay idle for long, and he soon drifted into making and selling motorized bicycles of the crudest and most primitive sort. Having set out on this more as a hobby than anything else, in late 1948 he reorganized the rather ramshackle little business and designed and began to manufacture proper 98cc two-stroke-engined motorcycles which were, for the first time, sold as Hondas. Production was tiny, improvements easy to incorporate as and when necessary, and the process culminated in the Honda 'Dream' of 1949. With 3 hp propelling a sturdy pressed-steel frame, this model sold well enough to allow a modest mass production to begin. But in 1949 Honda were only one very small and virtually unknown Japanese manufacturer amongst scores of similar concerns. That Honda survived, which almost none of their rivals of 1949 did, that they grew and prospered beyond belief, and that within Soichiro Honda's active lifetime the company became by far the largest and most successful motorcycle maker that the world has ever known, is a matter of history.

That this happened is attributable to the remarkable abilities of three men; Soichiro Honda himself, an intuitive and volatile genius, who sometimes played as hard as he worked, sales administrator Takeo Fujisawa, whose contribution to Honda's growth would take a book to expound, and young graduate engineer Kiyoshi Kawashima, who interpreted Honda's ideas and contributed many valuable ones of his own.

Fujisawa's brilliant grasp of markets was accompanied by a financial acumen that over and over saved Honda from the mistakes that ruined other manufacturers despite the excellence of their products. Kawashima's earliest contribution was the design of the ohv four-stroke-engined 150cc type E Dream, which, launched in 1951, soon became of overwhelming importance to the company. By 1954, Honda was the largest manufacturer of lightweight motorcycles in the world. But Soichiro Honda and Takeo Fujisawa were in complete agreement that to rely upon the Japanese market alone could have disastrous consequences, and that exporting would, at no very distant date, become of life and death importance. Motorcycle competition in Japan in 1954 was scarcely even in its infancy, but Honda recognized that racing successes conferred great prestige.

The factory's successes in domestic racing in the next few years were to become monotonous, but in 1954 that was part of an uncertain future, and in any case, of

The very first photograph seen in Europe of a racing Honda. The 125cc twin of 1959.

what interest was Japanese racing to customers in Europe and America? The most prestigious and most highly exposed motorcycle racing in the world was the TT series in the Isle of Man, and Honda decided that if the company were to race at all it must be with the firm and fixed intention of winning the TT!

One wonders that Honda and Fujisawa expected to find on their trip to Europe in June 1954. What they *did* find in the Isle of Man was the cruelly demanding 37³/₄-mile mountain circuit, which even after 40 odd years of improvement was still the most difficult and unforgiving in the world. They found, too, British and European racing motorcycles, refined by years of competition to a peculiar perfection (as far as that is ever possible) and suitability for the job in hand. It was brought home to both men with the force of a blow that here was no ordinary event, and that to compete with the slightest chance of success would entail some *years* of hard work and rigorous planning.

Naturally enough, the 125cc and 250cc events were of particular interest to the two Japanese visitors. The 125cc race was, for the first of six occasions, run over ten laps of the short but still demanding Clypse course, but in 1954 the 250cc race was still run on the Mountain circuit, through its duration had been more than halved to a mere three laps compared to the seven that had prevailed until 1951.

Both races were won by riders of German NSU machines. Rupert Hollaus won the 125cc event after his fellow team rider Werner Haas had tried too hard and crashed. Haas had made no such mistake in the 250cc race, leading from start to finish. He and Hollaus between them broke the lap record on each successive lap, Haas leaving it at a staggering 91.22 mph – over five mph faster than the previous record. He was also the first man to win the 250cc race at over 90 mph, at 90.88 mph. NSU twins filled four of the next five places and the only other make to feature on the leader board was Fergus Anderson's Moto Guzzi in fifth place. It was not only this remarkable result that impressed itself so deeply on Soichiro Honda's mind. He carried away, too, a vivid memory of the efficiency and confidence of the NSU organization. He said later, 'I decided there and then that when Honda went racing that was how we too would do it, and that those were the sort of results that we too would obtain.'

Even in 1959, Honda did not do things by halves! The mechanics are working on the 125cc twins, before practice in the Isle of Man.

Back in Japan and reunited with Kiyoshi Kawashima, the two men started to plan for the future. But though the name of Honda quickly sprang to the fore in Japanese racing, not until 1959 was an entry made for the TT and even then it materialized because of a misunderstanding. By 1958 the company was ready to launch the revolutionary new C72 125cc parallel twin and its sporting version the CB72. The CB72 was to be sold with a race kit available. What better publicity could there possibly be than a good result, maybe even a win, in a 'Formula' TT for 125cc machines? But Honda had misunderstood the scope of the 'Formula' regulations (Formula 1 races were run in the TT in 1959 only for the benefit of owners of 350cc and 500cc machines of series manufacture – in effect AJS and Norton) and when Ichiro Nitsuma, head of Honda research, and American adviser Bill Hunt called at the ACU offices in London at the end of January 1959 they were quickly

Rider-manager William C. Hunt rides in the 125cc Lightweight TT race in 1959, before falling and retiring.

disabused. The decision was then taken to enter what were described at the time as 'three factory specials', in fact, experimental double overhead camshaft twins of 125cc which had been built and tested half-way through 1958.

It may be that from this incident and subsequent discussions that there later arose the folklore (still repeated today) that Honda were so ignorant of conditions in the Isle of Man that they arrived with machines shod with knobbly scrambler tyres! They did no such thing, but the story was perhaps reinforced by one or two curious (but quite incidental) resemblances between those early 125cc racers and the British Greeves scrambler, in particular in the use of a curved 'spine' frame and the use of bottom link forks with a swinging fork that passed around the rear of the front wheel, and had its damper units concealed within the front fork stanchions. In fact these elements of design were just as relatable to the 250cc NSU twin of 1952, and it is more than likely that the Honda company had acquired one of these to study, although in no significant way was the Honda a copy.

The neat 44 × 41mm 125cc twin-cylinder engine had its cylinders set vertically, was built in unit with a six-speed gearbox with gear primary drive and a dry exposed clutch, and was cantilevered from the sturdy main spine tube of the frame. However it was also braced to the frame from the cylinder head so forming a stressed number. Oil was carried in a heavily finned sump beneath the light alloy crankcases. The light alloy cylinders had pressed in austenitic iron liners, and these were cast in iron valve seats, four of them in each light alloy cylinder head. The valves were closed by conventional coil springs. The advantage of using paired valves (no new thing in itself) was the reduction in reciprocating weight of each valve (those in the Honda were of very low weight) and subsequent better control at high rpm – and the 125cc Hondas allegedly ran up to 13,500 rpm! There were two overhead camshafts driven by spur gears from a vertical shaft and bevels of the left. Ignition was by magneto and carburation by flat-slide Keihin instruments which in reality were not entirely satisfactory. Honda claimed for their four-valve layout that cylinder filling was improved, but it was not a claim that was made with much conviction, for there is evidence that over the next year or two they experimented over and over again with two-valve layouts, including desmodromic valve gear, and even with two carburettors per cylinder before firmly coming down on the side of their original layout.

As soon as practice began it was plain to see that reliability was good, and that the bikes ran consistently, but they were not fast, and so it proved in the race. American rider-manager Bill Hunt retired after a fall on the first lap and Japanese riders N. Taniguchi, G. Suzuki, T. Tanaka and J. Suzuki finished in that order, sixth, seventh, eighth and eleventh, Taniguchi winning a silver replica, G. Suzuki and Tanaka bronze replicas. Honda also won the team prize. Taniguchi's average was 68.29 mph against winner Tarquinio Provini's speed of 74.06 mph on his MV. Honda had nothing to be ashamed of, and although lacking speed, the machines had been remarkably reliable.

Later in 1959 there were rumours of a four-cylinder 250cc Honda, and in early 1960 pictures of this appeared in the British motorcycle press. Very much a 'doubled up twin', this had a five-speed unit gearbox, exposed clutch and shaft and bevel drive to the camshafts. Photographs showed similar bottom link forks to those seen on the 1959 125cc machines, and curiously a proprietary make of twin-leading-shoe brake. But when Honda appeared in the Isle of Man in 1960 both the twin cylinder 125cc and the 250cc four-cylinder were entirely new designs.

The engine dimensions remained the same in both cases at 44 × 41mm, but the shaft and bevel drive to the camshafts had gone on the four-cylinder machine and was replaced by a central train of spur gears. The cylinders were inclined forward, the frame was lowered and the whole appearance of the machines was longer and slimmer. The brakes were two-leading-shoe units of Honda's own manufacture, and the bottom link forks had gone forever, replaced by telescopic forks of Honda's

A rare picture of the 1959, vertical-engined 250cc four. Note the cooling ducts around the cylinders. It was never raced outside Japan.

The 125cc twin of 1960.

design and make. Honda now claimed 18 hp for the 125cc and 35 hp for the four-cylinder 250cc, modest enough claims one would have thought, but many people thought them exaggerated at the time and frankly did not believe the quoted peak engine speeds of 14,000 rpm.

In 1960, the 125cc and 250cc races returned to the Mountain circuit, the 125cc race being of three laps, the 250cc of five. Since their visit a year earlier, Honda had decided to take one or two European riders into the team, but for the chauvinistic Japanese this was not an easy decision and they would far rather have employed only riders of their own nationality. But they had ambitions to do much more than race in the Isle of Man, and Japanese riders were badly lacking in experience of racing on tarmacadam roads, as well as disliking spending long periods away from home in unfamiliar Europe. The language question too, was an ever present difficulty, and it was thought that having English-speaking riders in the team would help matters. But the Honda company quite deliberately refrained from signing 'stars'. Had such riders started to win races, then the credit would have gone to them and not to Honda. So they deliberately picked upon two dependable 'good runners' from the Continental Circus, both of them Australians, Tom Phillis and Bob Brown. Throughout practice, the riders complained that the machines were inconsistent, being occasionally as much as 1000 rpm down on speed for no apparent reason. Later this was attributed to the unorthodox flat-slide carburettors.

The race results were something of a disappointment. In the 125cc event, Taniguchi finished sixth behind three MV Agusta four-strokes and two MZ two-strokes, and Honda riders seventh, eighth, ninth, tenth and 19th, winning between them five silver replicas. But this time they did not win the team prize, which went to MV, and, again, Taniguchi was over five and a half mph slower than winner Carlo Ubbiali.

In the 250cc race, once again the four-cylinder Hondas were no match for the MV Agusta twins. Gary Hocking, MV's number one rider, broke the lap record time after time, although in fact Carlo Ubbiali made fastest lap at 95.51 mph, and led the race from start to finish to win. Ubbiali was second, Tarquino Provini on the Morini was third and in fourth, fifth and sixth places were the Hondas of Bob Brown, Kitano and Taniguchi. Tom Phillis, after being well up, retired on lap four. Bob Brown's speed was 89.21 mph compared to Gary Hocking's 93.64 mph.

Instead of returning to Japan as they had done the previous year, Honda now

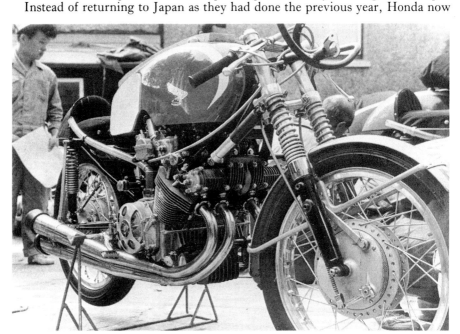

The 250cc four of 1960.

journeyed to Europe for the Dutch Grand Prix. Unfortunately the meeting was a catalogue of disasters, for, in practice, Tom Phillis and Taniguchi both fell, Phillis breaking his collar bone and Taniguchi his wrist. Hastily, the Honda team recruited Dutch rider Jan Huberts, and on Tom Phillis' recommendation, Southern Rhodesian Jim Redman. Unfamiliar with the 250cc fours, they could do no better than for Huberts to finish seventh, and Redman, a lap down on the leaders, eighth. In the 125cc race, Redman finished in a very good fourth place, only 1 mph behind winner Ubbiali on the MV. G. Suzuki finished sixth in the 125cc event.

At the Belgian Grand Prix the following weekend, the 250cc fours did not race. Apparently in the aftermath of Assen the team found that they simply could not put together even *one* machine with a decent chance of finishing! Spares were requested to be sent from Japan by air, but were not available in time. In the 125cc race Kitano, Shimazaki and Brown finished in seventh, eighth and tenth places. G. Suzuki finished in 12th place. Jim Redman, still not a permanent member of the Honda team, rode a Grand Prix Ducati into ninth place. If Francorchamps had been disappointing, the German Grand Prix at Solitude was a tragedy, for Bob Brown crashed fatally early in the 250cc race. There was no 125cc race at this meeting. Tanaka finished third in the 250cc event, Takahashi sixth and Sato seventh.

Then, after a pause, it was on to the Ulster Grand Prix. In the 250cc race, after an early charge, Gary Hocking retired his MV with clutch trouble, leaving teammate Carlo Ubbiali in the lead, but strongly pressed by Jim Redman and Tom Phillis on the obviously faster Hondas. But Ubbiali was a hard man to beat, and he finished first, but only two seconds ahead of Phillis, with Redman third, and with Takahashi and Sato finishing seventh and eighth. Writing in *The Motorcycle* a week later John Surtees said, 'The improvement in the Honda fours was maintained, though high-speed misfiring remains a problem. According to the riders the chief need now is improved handling, but their rapid development in such a brief time is fantastic.'

The 125cc race was anti-climactic, with only Fukada and Sato finishing, in seventh and eighth places. At Monza the 125cc Hondas were similarly poorly placed in fourth, sixth and seventh places, but in the 250cc race Redman once again finished second to Ubbiali's MV twin, and Takahashi finished fourth behind Ernst Degner's MZ. Gilberto Milani rode a Honda at this event and finished fifth ahead of Sato. The Hondas were definitely beginning to rattle the Italian establishment!

Then it was back to Japan and winter development. That this was effective was in no doubt whatever when the 1961 season dawned, furthermore Honda had effectively moved into Europe, with headquarters in Germany (later in Holland), so easing the spares situation, although in emergencies, spares and modifications were often air-freighted direct from the racing department back in Japan.

Over the winter, two notable British riders had been promised the use of Honda machinery. One was Mike Hailwood, whose father, Stan, head of the nationwide retail chain Kings of Oxford, had used his considerable influence to guarantee Mike a ride. The other was Bob McIntyre, who was to be sponsored by Irishman and ex-Norton and Gilera teamster Reg Armstrong. It may seem strange that Honda should allow an Irishman to have charge of one of their four-cylinder 250cc machines, but in the 1960s Eire was a prime market for the sort of road-going motorcycles that Honda intended to export into Europe.

The season opened in Spain at Montjuich Park at Barcelona, and the winter development programme had obviously succeeded, for Tom Phillis handsomely won the 125cc race and finished a close second to Gary Hocking on the MV in the 250cc event.

At Hockenheim in early May, Honda had their first Classic win. 'East scores on speed', said the headline in *The Motorcycle*, but the biggest surprise was a heart-stopping battle for the lead in the 250cc race between Gary Hocking's MV,

In the Isle of Man again in 1960, mechanics working in the sunshine on the 250cc fours. Tom Phillis looks on.

Tarquinio Provini's Morini and the Hondas of Takahashi and Redman. It was Takahashi who won fairly and squarely and made a new record lap at 117.79 mph as well! In contrast the 125cc twins were no match for the amazing single-cylinder two stroke MZs, which occupied the first four places in the 72-mile 125cc event.

The 1961 Hondas were again entirely new, with duplex frames replacing the previous 'spine' type, and a dry sump and external oil tank system allowing the engines to be lowered even further on the 250cc four. The 125cc twin retained the sump, but strangely went to a long-stroke configuration of 42 × 45mm.

In the 125cc TT there were three CB72 race-kitted Hondas entered as well as seven twins entered by the factory. Mike Hailwood, originally entered on a Ducati,

Early days – Tom Phillis in action on the 250cc four in the 1960 Ulster Grand Prix.

switched to a Honda during practice. Besides Phillis and Redman, Honda's European riders now included the Swiss Luigi Taveri. In the 250cc class, seven of the fours were entered. An entry had been made by Bill Smith for John Hartle on a factory machine, but contractual difficulties meant that Hartle did not start. Practice showed the Hondas consistently high on the leaderboard, very different from the two previous years. And the 125cc race was the triumph that Soichiro Honda had waited for, over seven long years, since his first visit to the Island.

Mike Hailwood won the race at 86.23 mph, narrowly beating Luigi Taveri, who, on his last lap, set a new record at 88.45 mph, and was second, and then it was Phillis, Redman, Shimazaki, filling the first five places, and Naomi Taniguchi in eighth place. As in 1959, Honda also won the team award.

The 250cc event was if anything even more of a sensation! Bob McIntyre fairly tore into a lead on the first lap, breaking the lap record from a standing start. This lead he held and increased, his second lap being made at an incredible 99.58 mph! But his fantastic progress was not to last. The change from semi-wet to dry-sump lubrication proved to have been of borderline reliability, and his oil tank had begun to empty itself on to the rear tyre. On the last lap he slowed dramatically and seized at Quarry Bends. Twice in a day, young Mike Hailwood took the chequered flag in first place, having averaged 96.36 mph. He was followed by Phillis, Redman, Takahashi and Taniguchi and, again, Honda won the team prize. It was the culmination of seven years' work by Honda, and it was only the start of a success story unprecedented in the history of motorcycle racing.

Between Hockenheim and the TT Honda had obviously found more speed from the 125cc machines, and for much of the rest of the season they had the measure of the MZ two-strokes, most of the time!

At the Dutch Grand Prix at the end of June, Hailwood, Bob McIntyre and Jim Redman finished one-two-three in the 250cc race. In the 125cc class Phillis and Redman were first and second. At Spa Francorchamps in Belgium the 125cc race was a Honda benefit with Degner on the MZ no higher than fourth behind Luigi Taveri, Phillis and Redman. Similarly the 250cc race saw Redman, Phillis, Hailwood and Shimazaki in the first four places. In East Germany Ernst Degner won the 125cc race ahead of Phillis and Takahashi, but the 250cc was no contest with Hondas led by Mike Hailwood in the first four places. By now, especially in the

Phillis again, in 1961, at the French Grand Prix 250cc race.

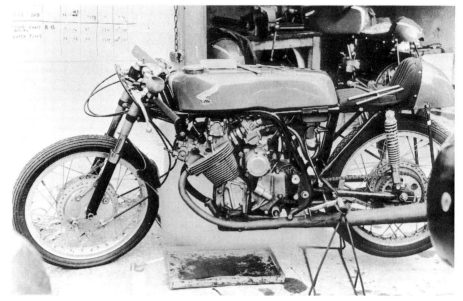

The much improved 125cc twin of 1962.

250cc class, Honda had a stranglehold. Bob McIntyre beat Hailwood at the Ulster, and Redman beat him at Monza. Then, at the Swedish Grand Prix, Mike made no mistakes and won the 250cc race and secured the World Championship for himself and Honda. At this point MZ's Ernst Degner, who was well in line to win the 125cc title, made his dramatic defection to Suzuki (although at the time this was not apparent). Because of the East German Motorcycle Federation's intervention, he was not allowed to ride in the Argentine Grand Prix on one of Joseph Ehrlich's EMC two-strokes (a close copy of the MZ), as he had hoped. Thus, Tom Phillis, winning the 125cc race, became Champion with a two-point lead over Degner. It was a wonderful end to the season, and the Honda personnel returned to Japan in triumph.

They now took stock. They had tried, tested and proved their theory that small-capacity cylinders, four valves, and very high crankshaft speeds was a winning combination. They had won two TT races, had beaten the European factories on their own terms, and won two World Championships. As the season progressed they had improved the power output of both capacity machines to close on 160 hp/litre and they were confident that this could be considerably increased as and when necessary with very little difficulty. By and large 1962 only confirmed their confidence.

Honda simply dominated the 125cc and 250cc classes in Spain that year. Their principal riders for the start of the season were Redman, Phillis, McIntyre, Luigi Taveri and Irishman Tommy Robb. In the TT Honda had mixed fortunes. To be sure, in the 125cc race they filled the first four places, and in the 250cc race the first three. Bob McIntyre made fastest lap in the 250cc event, but with his usual wretched luck, retired on lap two in a punishing race that saw only seven finishers! The surprise winner had been Derek Minter, not even a member of the works team, but riding a well-worn 1961 model loaned to British importers Hondis Ltd. Derek, probably the best racing motorcyclist in the world in 1962, inherited the lead from MacIntyre, and seeing no reason to slow, went on to win ahead of official team riders Redman and Phillis at 96.68 mph. Poor Derek probably thought that this would lead to an invitation to a works ride. Little did he understand the convoluted mental processes of the Japanese, who were in fact furious that he had

The full 350cc 4-cylinder engine of 1963.

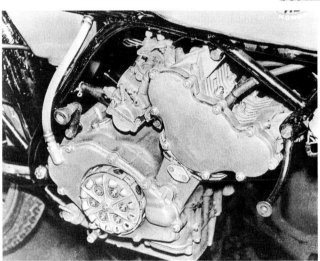

Back into the 50cc class with a vengeance! The incredible 50cc twin used in the 1964 season.

And why on earth not? Caliper brake on the front rim of the 50cc twin.

shown a touch of brilliance! They were still trying to project the image of *Honda* the winner, irrespective of the rider, and Minter's acknowledged 'star' status detracted from this.

The 350cc Junior race was sheer disaster for Honda. Tom Phillis and Bob McIntyre were riding 285cc fours. Chasing Gary Hocking and Mike Hailwood on their four-cylinder MVs, poor Phillis crashed fatally at Laurel Bank on the second lap. MacIntyre, who unknowingly inherited third place, retired on the next lap with engine trouble. Another sour note was the 50cc class. Honda had started the season with a single-cylinder, double overhead camshaft engine with a unit eight-speed gearbox, housed in a very neat, quite conventional frame with spine main tube that in fact handled as well and better than any of the other factory offerings from Suzuki, Kreider and Derbi. But with 9 hp at 14,000 rpm it just was not fast enough, and in practice for the TT the Honda team cabled home for ten-speed gearboxes. These were designed, made and flown over before the end of practice, some indication of Honda's awesome power and flexibility. But even this was not enough to win the 50cc race, though Taveri and Robb were second and third behind Ernst Degner on the disc-valve Suzuki two-stroke. Derek Minter and the Japanese rider Shimazaki trailed home in ninth and tenth places.

Jim Redman won the 350cc Championship for Honda, as well as the 250cc class, a considerable blow to the pretensions of the Italian MV! Luigi Taveri did the same in the 125cc class, and only in the 50cc class – where, ironically, Honda had their largest-selling market worldwide, were they soundly trounced by the Suzuki two-strokes and rider Ernst Degner.

Rather than suffer another season's public humiliation, Honda decided not to race in the 50cc class in 1963. Instead, in what turned out to be a masterly piece of timing, they launched the superb 50cc CR110 and 125cc CR93 machines for sale to paying customers. Both these machines, with gear-driven double overhead camshafts and four-valve cylinder heads, had in fact been conceived (and sold, in Japan) as super sporting street machines, but with racing carburettors, cams and exhausts, with eight gears for the 50cc model and six for the 42 × 43mm 125cc; both machines were immediately and overwhelmingly to dominate their classes. Not only did they epitomize the virtues of a racing motorcycle, being small, light, fast and simple, but they handled wonderfully well, and if properly (and rather expensively) maintained they were remarkably reliable. They were to remain a mainstay of British racing for the next seven years, a living advertisement for the factory that made them.

As an indication of how successful they were, in the first year in which they were available generally in time for the TT, 1964, no fewer than 18 CR93s finished in the

Ralph Bryans on the 50cc twin on his way to victory in the 1966 50cc TT.

The well-worn engine of Jim Redman's 250cc 6-cylinder after a season's racing.

Jim Redman on the six in 1966.

125cc race, 12 of the riders winning replicas. In the 50cc event, five CR110s finished and two riders won replicas.

For 1963, Honda 'stretched' the 285cc fours to 340cc (49 × 45mm). Jim Redman was to win a fairly easy World title for himself and Honda with this machine, but his 250cc title came only after a season-long battle against Tarquinio Provini and his amazing single-cylinder Morini. Honda were so concerned about the title position – with only the Japanese round to go, Provini actually led Redman with equal points scored and with four outright wins to Redman's three – that Jim Redman was provided with a brand-new specially tuned machine for the final Japanese Grand Prix. He won, and Provini could do no better than to finish fourth. There was no such last-minute rescue in the 125cc class, the ageing twins being soundly trounced by the Suzuki two-strokes, whose rider Hugh Anderson gave Suzuki the Constructors' Championship and himself the individual title.

It had been a rather lacklustre season for Honda, and although it was plain to see that Morini had overstretched themselves in contesting the 250cc championship – and having failed to win it, would not be back in 1964, there was another threat in the 250cc class from Yamaha, who since the TT, where Fumio Ito had finished a close second to Redman, had been snapping hard at Honda's heels. Furthermore for 1964, Yamaha were to be joined by English rider Phil Read, making them an even stronger challenger.

Honda chose to treat their defeat in the 125cc class and their default in the 50cc class more seriously than the threat from Yamaha. It was to cost them the 1964 title in the 250cc class. In line with their design philosophy, for the 1964 season Honda produced a 50cc *twin* of 33 × 29.2mm (with its crankpins at 180 degrees to one another) with, as usual, gear-driven overhead camshafts and four valves per cylinder. It was as well for Honda that they had two riders of small slim build in the persons of Luigi Taveri and new signing Irishman Ralph Bryans, for the twin was incredibly small and neat. In pursuit of low weight, it had a cable-operated caliper brake working on the front wheel rim, and to aid penetration through the air the spokes of the front wheel were almost completely covered by aluminium discs. It was logical to produce also a 125cc four, and this machine broke no new ground except for its size, being an almost exact scaled-down replica of the successful 250. Successful to date that is, for in 1964 Honda were to lose the 250cc Championship that they had won for three consecutive years. At the Spanish Grand Prix Redman was beaten in the 250cc class by his rival of the season before, Tarquinio Provini, now riding Benelli's 250cc four, but for most of the season Benelli confined themselves to Italian racing. Phil Read on the Yamaha was close behind Redman, and at Clermont Ferrand in France Read won on the two-stroke, so that Redman again finished second. At neither of these early meetings did the 50cc twins finish, but the new 125cc fours won at both events.

At the TT Ralph Bryans did well with the 50cc twin, finishing a close second to Hugh Anderson's Suzuki. The 125cc fours did even better; Taveri, Redman and Ralph Bryans finishing first, second and third. Redman won the 250cc and 350cc races, but Phil Read on the Yamaha had led him in the 250cc event before retiring and also made the fastest lap. Holland was a good meeting for Honda, winners in all four classes.

In Belgium, where there were no 125cc and 350cc classes, Bryans won the 50cc race, but Mike Duff on a Yamaha beat Redman in the 250cc class. Over the next four Championship rounds Read was the victor on each occasion. Bryans, who had won the 50cc races in Holland, Belgium and Germany, retired in Finland and thus lost the title to Anderson and Suzuki. Only in the 125cc class with Luigi Taveri and in the 350cc with Jim Redman were Honda to win Championships. Phil Read and Yamaha duly won the 250cc titles. But the season ended on a dramatic note and showed that it was never wise to write off Honda's reputation! With the title all but lost, Honda might have been better advised to have kept a low profile in the 250cc class at what was virtually the season's end, but at Monza (strangely echoing what the Italian factories had so frequently done) they chose to unveil their 'secret weapon', the remarkable 39 × 34.5mm Honda six. It was a mistake, for it warned Yamaha for 1965, and in fact the machine was not ready to race, being plagued by a high-speed misfire and suspect handling. Predictably Redman finished third to Read and Mike Duff. At Suzuka, Honda again wheeled out the six, and this time Redman howled round to victory, but the title had gone to Yamaha.

If 1964 had been a disappointing year, 1965 was one that Honda might have wished that they could forget. At the time the factory had become involved in Grand Prix motor racing, an enterprise that was to bring them nothing but frustration and humiliation and only one rather second-rate win in Mexico at the

Mike Hailwood on the six in 1967.

end of the season. That the motorcycle racing suffered is undeniable, and only in the 50cc and 350cc classes did Honda win the manufacturer's titles, the riders being Ralph Bryans and Jim Redman. At the TT their score was impressive enough, with Taveri winning in the 50cc class and coming second to Phil Read in the 125cc race. In the 250cc race Redman won and made fastest lap at 100.09 mph, but Phil Read, who had already lapped at 100.01 mph from a standing start, had led him by 15 seconds before an early retirement. Redman also won the 350cc race at 100.72 mph ahead of Phil Read on an overbored Yamaha and Giacomo Agostini (riding in the Island for the first time) on an MV. Once again, Redman could be said (perhaps unfairly) to have won only by default, for from a standing start Mike Hailwood had broken the lap record at 102.85 mph and led Jim by twenty seconds – increased to twenty-eight after three laps. But after a pit stop of some length Hailwood had lost all his advantage, and retired soon after rejoining the race.

Thereafter it was Phil Read and Yamaha all the way in the 250cc class, with the six cylinder Honda, still handling atrociously, only able to score a couple of wins in Czechoslovakia and Belgium. Suzuki won the 125cc title and Yamaha the 250cc.

As at Monza the year before, so at Suzuka at the end of 1965, Honda sprang a surprise. This consisted of, in effect, five of the 32 × 29.2mm 25cc cylinders from the 50cc twin on a crankshaft with crank pins at 72 degree intervals! Though the 125cc 'five' did not win first time out, it was clearly a future winner.

By the end of 1965, Jim Redman, veteran of six hard seasons with Honda, was beginning to feel that he was pushing his luck, and that perhaps now was the time to retire, before it ran out. Needless to say, after his long and loyal service, and five World Championships, Honda were reluctant to lose him. Apart from anything else, he was popular with the Honda management for keeping a low profile and being discreet with the Press. (By the same token, the Press, whilst acknowledging his mastery, were relatively unenthusiastic about a man whom they could not 'build up' into a 'personality'.)

Nevertheless, Honda could see Redman's point, and with his approval they approached Mike Hailwood at exactly the right time. Since Count Agusta had first 'spotted' Giacomo Agostini at Monza, when in 1964 he had been riding for Morini, he had been convinced that here was the Italian rider to win the World Championship on an Italian motorcycle. To this end, Agostini's interests had been promoted perhaps, as Mike Hailwood began to believe, at the expense of his. During 1965 it was no secret that Mike was becoming increasingly irritated by this chauvinistic approach, and yet, with four 500cc World Championships behind him on the MV, he was reluctant to, as he saw it, settle for less.

'No problem,' said Honda. 'We will build a 500cc motorcycle that will blow the MV into the weeds.' With the 250cc six, and the promise of an overbored version for the 350cc class, Honda offered a tempting prospect. Mike rode the 250cc six at Suzuka at the very end of the 1965 season. He later confessed that he had been shaken to discover just how appallingly bad was the bike's handling, and not being of Jim Redman's phlegmatic temperament he did not hesitate to make his opinions known to the Honda racing department at the earliest possible moment and in the strongest possible terms! Although no engineer, Mike knew enough about racing motorcycles to make some very strong recommendations. Handling had never been Honda's strong point and even the very early 250cc fours, with probably no more than 40 hp, had weaved and wobbled alarmingly on fast corners. Unsophisticated suspension dampers, insufficiently stiff swinging arms and wheel spindles of too small a diameter all contributed to this unsteadiness. However, the six was something else, and Hailwood made it plain that the handling had to be improved or he was not interested. Mike's blunt approach paid dividends, and thereafter the six in both 250cc and 297cc (41 × 37.5mm) forms was probably one of the best-handling Hondas of all time.

Not so the new 500cc four! As early as the end of January 1966, Mike was making worried noises about this machine. Although he was extremely confident about the engine, he expressed doubts about the wisdom of, in his words, 'sticking it into the

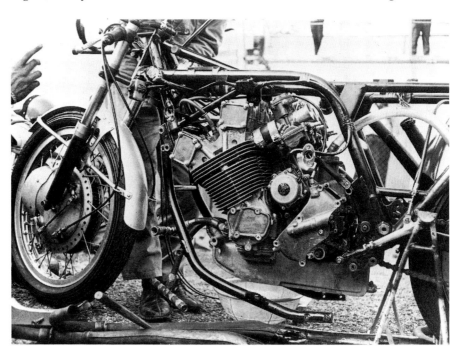

The engine of the awe-inspiring 500cc 4-cylinder. Note the detachable frame rails.

old three-fifty frame', thus indicating that the bike had been tested that early.

There was no 500cc race at the Spanish Grand Prix. Taveri won the 50cc class with Ralph Bryans third. Bill Ivy on the Yamaha beat Taveri and Bryans in the 125cc race. Hailwood won the 250cc event after Jim Redman had fallen and had the bike catch fire.

It was at Hockenheim that the big four first showed its potential. Honda had only the one machine present, and, bewilderingly, having built the machine with Hailwood in mind, they asked him to stand down and allow Redman to ride it!

The engine appeared to be an entirely typical four-cylinder on familiar Honda lines. There were six gears which were hardly needed, for the engine's spread of torque was phenomenal. The frame was, unusually for Honda, a full twin-loop with the bottom tubes detachable so as to facilitate work on the engine and with a massive-looking square section swinging arm at the rear and heavy-duty telescopic forks of a new design.

At Hockenheim, Jim Redman simply walked away from Agostini on the MV to record an easy win. Afterwards he remarked that the big machine had power 'from 100 rpm to 12,000 rpm' and that winning had been 'too easy'. That was the sort of attitude that endeared Redman to Honda, and it may well have been the reason for their response to Mike Hailwood's continual complaints about the handling – which was, from time to time, to appear to favour Redman at Mike's expense. At Hockenheim, Taveri could do no better than fourth in the 50cc race, though on the five-cylinder 125cc he won easily and Ralph Bryans was runner-up. Mike Hailwood won both 250cc and 350cc races.

At Clermont Ferrand there were only 250cc and 350cc solo classes, both of which were won with ease by Mike and then at Assen came his first real experience of the 500 cc four. It was not a particularly happy one! Having won the 250cc and 350cc races he made a poor start with the big machine, lying third behind Redman and

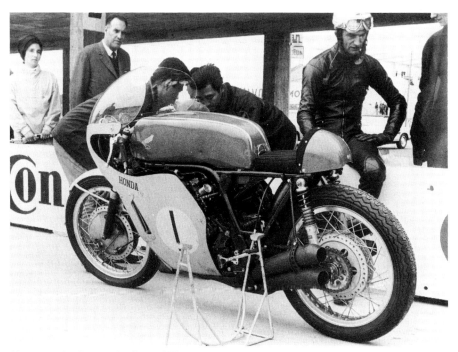

Never much of a one for drama! Jim Redman lets the mechanics argue over the big 4-cylinder 500. He just got on with riding it!

Agostini before taking the lead with a lap which broke his own record on the MV by more than two mph. On the next lap his gearbox broke and he slid (literally) to earth with little or no damage to himself or the bike, but it was obviously not an experience calculated to improve his opinion of either the machine or its preparation. Stolid, unglamorous old Jim Redman reeled in Ago's MV and won the race without fuss or drama. Taveri won the 50cc race, and was second to Bill Ivy on the Yamaha in the 125cc class. East Germany was something of a disaster. Although Mike won the 250cc race, he blew up both his 350cc six and his 500cc four. Jim Redman was not there to pick up the pieces. In the Belgian Grand Prix he had fallen and injured his shoulder, and with that surrendered all his ambitions. He never raced again in Europe. Jim Redman never attracted the glamour and publicity that accrued to a good many riders, who could scarcely hold a candle to him, but his record is secure. One day he will be reassessed for the remarkably professional rider that he was.

By August, Mike Hailwood already had the 250cc Championship and at the Ulster Grand Prix he secured the 350cc Championship as well. The 500cc title was another matter entirely. In 1966 the TT was delayed until September by a seamen's strike. The 50cc race was won by Ralph Bryans, with Luigi Taveri second, ahead of the Suzukis. However, Honda did not shine in the 125cc race. The Yamaha two-strokes of Phil Read and Bill Ivy were very much on form (Ivy lapped at 98.55 mph) and the best that Mike Hailwood could do was to finish sixth. Mike won the 250cc race and Stuart Graham (who had been recruited after Redman's final retirement) was second on another six. One wonders at Honda's logic in taking on another rider at all at the time. They already had some of the best and most experienced lightweight riders, and good as Stuart Graham was, he was not the man to ride the 500cc four! In any event, he was dropped at the season's end.

The 1966 Senior TT was the race that everybody had been waiting for, and they were not disappointed, as the battle between Mike on the Honda and Ago on the MV was joined. Giacomo Agostini's inexperience of the Island – it was only his second visit – was to some degree offset by the visibly evil handling of Hailwood's 500cc Honda, and by intermittent rain showers which made roads treacherous in the area around Ramsey. Nevertheless, it was Hailwood and Honda all the way. He led Agostini by nine seconds at the end of the first lap, and with a second lap at 107.07 mph, the fastest of the race, this was extended. Each of Hailwood's laps was

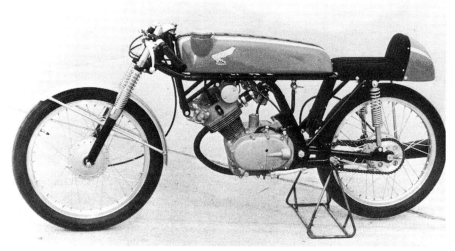

The superb CR110 dohc 8-speed 50cc single that transformed 50cc club racing.

faster than Agostini's and at the end he led by 2 mins 38 secs, having averaged 103.11 mph to Agostini's 101.09 mph. With that result, Hailwood retained a slim chance of winning the 500cc World Championship, but he was to lose it at Monza the following weekend. There Luigi Taveri clinched the 125cc title, but Ralph Bryans, who was in with a good chance of the 50cc title, was beaten in the 50cc race by Hans Georg Anscheidt on the Suzuki. Mike Hailwood won the 250cc race against negligible opposition. Now came the 500cc race, which, to retain the 500cc Championship that had been his for four consecutive years, Mike had to win. He led on the first lap, and then allowed Agostini to pass, adopting the familiar cat and mouse tactics of someone who knows that he can regain the lead as he chooses. So they circulated until the sixth lap, when fate – or poor maintenance – struck and the big Honda's engine comprehensively expired with a broken exhaust valve! Agostini thus became Individual Champion, though the Constructor's title went to Honda. To say that Hailwood was furious is to put it mildly. Normally the most philosophical of men, he felt with some justification that Honda had become slack and indecisive during 1966, and he had no hesitation in saying so. He had also become obsessive about the 500cc machine's handling, which, especially at the TT, had, he confessed, really frightened him. Whether at this stage he perhaps knew what the other riders most certainly did not, that Honda were about to reduce their commitment to racing drastically in 1967, is open to question. Whether he did – and risked dismissal – or did not, the certainty is that he told the Honda racing organization some very unwelcome home truths. It was even rumoured at the season's end that Honda were so annoyed that they had approached Agostini to ride for them in 1967! Be that as it may, Hailwood and Honda were to settle their differences and he was to sign for them again in the spring, with the promise of new and improved machinery.

Another of Honda's decisions at this rather unhappy time was to rob Irishman Ralph Bryans of an excellent chance of the 50cc title. The Japanese Grand Prix had been moved from Suzuka, Honda's 'home circuit', to Fisco. Whether Honda really objected as they said to the 'Wall of death' banking at this new circuit or whether their decision was taken in pique, they adamantly refused to support the event, and the 50cc title thus went to Hans Georg Anscheidt. So, although for the first and last time Honda had won every single solo title from 50cc to 500cc as Constructors, only Taveri in the 125cc class and Hailwood in the 250cc and 350cc classes won individual titles.

Sensational news early in 1967 was that after eight years' involvement, Honda were not contesting the 125cc class or, for that matter, the 50cc class. This in effect meant that the factory team in the 250cc, 350cc and 500cc events was Mike Hailwood backed in the 250cc class by Ralph Bryans. Nor was Mike a happy man in 1967. To his dismay and disgust he discovered that instead of working on the handling, Honda had simply got more power from an engine that was already too fast for its chassis! In desperation, Mike had Colin Lyster build a complete new frame with disc front brakes. This was tested, even raced a couple of times in unimportant events before the Grand Prix season began, but Honda firmly forbade its use in the Championship rounds. Whether it would have cured Honda's problems is doubtful, because with the benefit of hindsight, they were probably as much attributable to the tyres of the time as to the actual frame.

There was no 500cc race in Spain. In the 250cc event a punctured rear tyre caused Mike's retirement. He retired again in the 250cc class at Hockenheim a week later, won the 350cc race, beating Agostini, and after leaving Ago trailing in the 500cc race retired once again – with a broken crankshaft!

Again, in France there was no 500cc race, nor was there a 350cc event, so Mike rode only the 250cc six. After convincingly demonstrating that he could leave Phil Read and Bill Ivy on the Yamahas, raising the lap record and gaining a commanding lead, Mike found to his dismay that he had lost first and second gears and that

The equally brilliant CR93 125cc twin that made the 125cc class into one of the most popular in the later 1960s.

the other ratios were hard to select. After an unavailing pit stop he slowed to finish third and win his first championship points of the year. Ralph Bryans had no problems, but could do no better than fourth place. The TT was a happier affair altogether. The Diamond Jubilee of the races, the weather was wonderful throughout the whole week. With his win in the 250cc race at 103.07 mph and a fastest record lap at 104.5 mph, Mike set the pattern. He won the 350cc race at 104.68 mph, beating Agostini on the MV, and made a new record fastest lap of 107.73 mph that was faster than his own Senior 500cc lap record of the year before! And this with a machine of only 297cc!

The Senior race was as exciting as any ever run. Agostini, incidentally celebrating his 25th birthday, looked well placed to win. From a standing start he raised the lap record to 108.3 mph and led Mike by 12 seconds. A lap by Mike at 108.77 mph cut Agostini's lead to eight seconds, but Hailwood was being hampered by of all things, a loose twist grip! At the end of the third lap both riders came to the pits to refuel at the same time. Hailwood took the chance to bash the twist grip with a hammer, hoping to make it grip. After four laps, Agostini was back to leading by twelve seconds. Then on the penultimate lap poor Agostini suffered a broken rear chain and was out of the race. Mike went on to win at 105.62 mph, a lucky man indeed.

For the first time since 1959 there were no factory Hondas in the 125cc race. In their place there were no less than thirteen Honda CR93s amongst the finishers, highest placed being Kel Carruthers in fifth place with Jim Curry close behind him in sixth.

Mike was to win the 250cc race in Holland, and to retire in East Germany. He won on the 500 in Holland and was beaten by Agostini in Belgium. In East Germany he retired in both 250cc and 500cc races, winning only the 350cc event.

Having secured the 350cc title for himself and Honda, Hailwood attempted to do the same in the 250cc class at the Japanese Grand Prix, which Honda supported in 1968 following an alteration to the circuit which excluded the steep banking. Both he and Phil Read had 50 points. In the race, both retired, and on the basis of second best performance, Hailwood and Honda won. There was no 500cc race. Agostini and MV were 500cc World Champions.

Despite rumour and speculation in the press over the winter, it came as no very great surprise when, early in 1968, Honda ended their nine years of Grand Prix

The 125cc 'five' based on the 50cc twin. Note the routing of exhaust!

racing, during which they had come to dominate the world as no other manufacturer had ever dreamed of. The last unhappy season of 1967 could not tarnish what had gone before. It is often forgotten or ignored (or perhaps not even realized) in what doldrums racing had been after the Italian factories withdrew at the end of 1957. It was to Honda more than any other factor that we owed the huge resurgence of interest that made the 1960s such a golden era for everyone concerned. It should not be forgotten that they did not support only the Classic Grands Prix, but allowed their riders to compete in domestic, international and even national races, so that many people in England thrilled to their screaming exhausts who might otherwise only have read about them.

Honda never pursued the policy of sawing up and/or burying their old racers, but maintained their own comprehensive museum. At one time or another they gave away machines to various riders – (at the time of writing, Mike Hailwood's estate owns several, including the 1968 500cc four) – and even to other museums. But such machines rarely possessed any integrity, being cobbled together (nicely enough to be sure) from whatever parts came to hand. Several machines have been built up by private owners, who have gone to the lengths of re-manufacturing such items as castings, pistons, crankshafts and gears, thus outraging a few purists. So long as they do not then fabricate a spurious 'history' to go with their machines, does this matter? Any Honda twin, or four, or six is worth a king's ransom!

Itom

The tiny Itom Competizione 50cc racer is of vital interest, because its success in British road racing from 1959 onwards really led to the acceptance of 50cc racing in Europe and the eventual decision of the FIM to institute an International 50cc class in 1962. From that arose the 50cc TT in the Isle of Man and some quite remarkable races. The Itom's introduction to Britain (and much of its success) was due to an independent dealer, Dick Chalaye, who persuaded the Milanese company to supply their already respectably rapid sports models in stripped form and he fitted locally made rev counters, tanks, saddles and fairings. His firm also offered a whole range of racing parts, including larger racing carburettors, tuned cylinders, etc. The iron-barrelled engine was in any case very responsive to intelligent tuning and spares were ridiculously inexpensive. Early models had a three-speed gearbox,

This beautifully restored Mark 8 Itom is typical of those raced in Britain in the 1960s.

with gear primary drive and a twist grip operated gearchange. With the Mark VII there were four gears, and with the Mark VIII four gears with a positive-stop foot change. Early bikes had a tiny 'cow horn' megaphone attached direct to the exhaust port with ear-splitting results from a tiny engine turning at between 9000 rpm and 12,000 rpm!

The first of the British Racing 50 Club's 250-mile road race 'Enduros' held at the Snetterton circuit in 1960 was won by two riders on an Itom at 47.82 mph. A year later another Itom-mounted pair averaged 51.44 mph to win. As much as anything the success of this event led to the FIM's Coupe d'Europe the following year. In that series, an Itom ridden by Piero Verisoegen won the Belgian round, but it was a private entry, the Itom factory never giving the least support whatever to racing, a short-sighted attitude that cost them dearly. Itoms and Itom-based specials made up the bulk of private entries in the first 50cc TT of 1962, but their owners were bitterly disappointed to discover how badly they were outclassed by the factory Hondas, Suzukis and Kreidlers with their multi-speed gearboxes. Nor did Itom respond by offering a six- or eight-speed engine, for which many Itom enthusiasts would cheerfully have paid a high price. Though perforce British 50cc racing depended upon the Itom for several years after 1962, the end was inevitable, and whereas events had been oversubscribed they were soon poorly supported, resulting in lack of interest.

Today the virtues of the Itom and its significance in racing history are well appreciated. Many have survived, and quite a few appear in CRMC parades and even in races.

Kreidler

The Kreidler Company, originally specialist suppliers of alloy steels, started manufacture of 50cc mopeds and later light motorcycles at Kornwestheim near Stuttgart in 1951. When news of 50cc racing reached Germany in 1959, a group of enthusiasts at the factory sought permission from their autocratic chief, Alfred Kreidler, to build a racer. Kreidler agreed, stipulating however that only modified parts·from the standard 'Florett' model should be used. Thus the very early Kreidler racers used even the pressed-steel frame of the road bikes, and though the Earles-type front forks were tubular, they too incorporated standard parts. Internal parts from different models of gearbox were swapped about to give a set of four close ratios with the first gear far higher than usual. The engines were virtually standard but for raised compression ratio, alteration of the ports in the light alloy chrome bore cylinders and use of a 20mm Dell'Orto carburettor on a short straight inlet pipe. Even the fan cooling of the Florett engine was retained, as was a shortened exhaust pipe and *silencer*, which gave an eerie effect as these models whistled past their noisy rivals in almost complete silence!

Kreidler's already considerable experience with 50cc engines assured that from the start they were very competitive in German events, winning the 50cc Championship in 1960. By 1961, 50cc racing had become popular enough throughout Europe for the FIM to institute the Coupe d'Europe, eight rounds in Belgium, Germany, Spain, Holland and Yugoslavia. Kreidler, with machines now incorporating a rotary inlet valve and with purpose-built steel tube frames, won the series hands down, riders Hans Georg Anscheidt scoring four victories and Wolfgang Gedlitch one. The success of the Coupe d'Europe led to an International 50cc class for 1962 with a World Championship of ten Grand Prix rounds. For this, Kreidler were prepared to set up a full-scale racing department to design and build machines of what, at the time, seemed astonishing sophistication. In charge was Johannes Hilber, who had joined Kreidler from the aircraft industry. As before, the single-cylinder engine of 40 × 39.7mm was slung horizontally below a frame of narrow-diameter steel tubes. Earles-type front forks were used, with a large range of different springs and damper settings for different conditions. Similar spring-damper units controlled the rear suspension. The engine was normally air cooled

A shoestring works racer! Only the fork stanchions were specially made. Even the standard silencer was retained!

Jan Huberts descends the Mountain on his 12-speed Kreidler in the 1962 50cc TT.

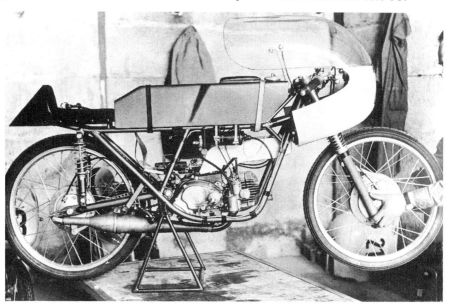

The 1963 50cc Kreidler, still not fast enough to catch the Japanese bikes.

and heavily finned and induction was now by *two* rotary disc inlet valves and Bing racing carburettors, one each side of the crankcase. Ignition was by battery and coil. The most unorthodox feature was the way in which an external three-speed gearbox was combined with the normal four-speed gearbox to provide, in theory, twelve ratios! In fact, this arrangement was used to prevent the engine speed from falling below the very narrow power band at the top of the range. It had the advantage over a true multi-speed gearbox that the riders could change *down* through the foot-controlled four speeds without having to manipulate the hand-controlled auxiliary box. With 10 hp at 14,000 rpm and with highly developed streamlining (tested in a wind tunnel), Kreidler had every right to feel confident of winning the first 50cc World Championship. Riders were Anscheidt and Gedlich, joined by Dutchman Jan Huberts – Holland was always a vital market for Kreidler.

But to sum up the story of the next half-dozen seasons briefly, Kreidler, despite gallant efforts and organization second to none, were always overshadowed by the

Japanese Honda and Suzuki teams. In 1962 they won only three Championship rounds, and at the TT, where they had such hopes, could do no better than for Anscheidt to finish fourth, with Huberts seventh, Englishman Dan Shorey 11th and Gedlich 12th! Though Anscheidt finished third in the 1963 TT on a model with larger brakes, telescopic forks and a stiffer frame, Kreidler's only outright Grand Prix win that year was in Spain. Over the years, the racing Kreidlers, though incorporating detail improvements, remained substantially the same.

In 1964 the same trend continued. Kreidler engaged the immensely experienced Luigi Taveri and Tarquinio Provini, but at the TT all they could achieve behind Anscheidt in fourth place was seventh and eighth respectively! 1965 was disastrous – the best that Anscheidt could do at Montjuich Park in early May was to finish fifth – beaten even by José Busquet's Derbi! At the French round at Rouen, he retired. Following this, Kreidler announced their withdrawal from Grand Prix racing and did not appear at the TT, and for 1966, Anscheidt departed to ride for Suzuki. During 1966 Kreidler worked out with their Dutch importer Van Veen a policy whereby for 1967 Van Veen took over all racing activities.

In 1967 Kreidler marketed a race kit for the standard Florett giving 9.5 hp at 11,000 rpm, which sold freely for use in club racing; many bikes so equipped have survived, as have a few race-kitted engines fitted into old works chassis.

When the CRMC was first formed, old 50cc racers were little regarded, but with the formation in 1986 of a Classic 50cc racing register, interest was rekindled and a reasonable number of 50cc machines, including Kreidlers, began to appear again.

MV

Ask almost anyone interested in the history of motorcycle racing to name the most successful factory of all time and, depending upon age and prejudices, you will probably hear the names of Norton, Honda or Yamaha. Surprisingly few people realize that the answer, amply supported by hard statistics, is MV Agusta.

Between 1952 and 1977 Meccanica Verghera, founded in 1945 by Count Domenico Agusta as an offshoot of his aero-engineering business, won no less than *thirty-seven* world titles – more than twice Honda's 17 and making the 11 won by Yamaha appear derisory. To further point to MV's statistical superiority to any other make, consider these figures: the 125cc World title won seven times between 1952 and 1960; the 250cc title four times between 1955 and 1959; in the 350cc class no less than nine titles between 1958 and 1972; and in the Senior class – most glamorous of all – quite staggeringly, 17 World Championships in the years between 1956 and 1974! All this from a company that had no long history of excellence stretching back into the past and which even in its heyday never matched its racing image to the generally dull, uninspired and horribly badly styled machines offered to the public. For all MV's racing successes, the firm never sold more than a handful of machines in England. Truly a case of the right hand, the commercial division, not knowing what the left hand, in this case the competition department, was doing.

MV first raced a 125cc two-stroke in 1948 and won the 125cc class at the Italian Grand Prix that year. In 1949, however, the two-stroke, a simple piston-ported affair with plain pipe and megaphone exhaust, was completely outclassed by Alfonso Drusiani's wonderful little double overhead camshaft FB Mondial. Count Agusta was quick to see that this was the path to travel, and before the season's end he had poached from Gilera not only their up and coming chief mechanic Arturo Magni but racing designer Ing Piero Remor, designer of the pre- and post-war

The very 'clean' exterior of the Remor-designed 500cc MV 'four' of 1950.

Rear suspension that might have made sense with chain-drive, but not with a shaft!

Gilera four-cylinder racers. Remor's brief was to lay out a 125cc single and logically enough a 500cc four. Quite incredibly quickly, Remor and Magni had 125cc single-cylinder and 500cc four-cylinder prototypes built and running. In late April, pictures of the 125cc machine appeared with the announcement that replicas would be on sale later that year at £425 (for today's prices multiply 1950 prices by at least 20!) and though no pictures were published, the four-cylinder 500cc model was described in some detail.

Confidently, the factory spoke of 'replicas' for sale at £750 and 'sports' versions at £600. This was, of course, sheer fantasy, and the primitive MV set-up – scarcely at this stage a 'factory' – was in no position to fulfil such wild promises. Nevertheless, there *was* a four at the Belgian Grand Prix, in itself something of a minor miracle, and even more remarkable, rider Arcisco Artesiani finished an excellent fifth behind Umberto Masetti and Nello Pagani on the Gileras, Ted Frend on an AJS 'Porcupine' and Carlo Bandirola on another Gilera. Admittedly, the factory Nortons were eliminated with tyre trouble, but it was an encouraging result for MV. Their next outing was at the Dutch, where not only was Artesiani present, but another machine was provided for Irishman Reg Armstrong!

Unfortunately, the promise shown in Belgium was not sustained. Artesiani, after a scintillating start, retired early with gearchange problems and Reg Armstrong, after lying in fifth place, had to change a plug and finished well back in ninth place. MV did not race again until the Grand Prix des Nations at Monza at the season's end. The French Grand Prix was cancelled, and though machines were entered in both the 125cc and 500cc classes at the Ulster, they did not arrive, which convinced Reg Armstrong that he was wasting his time.

Monza was, again, encouraging and Artesiani rode a fine race to finish third to Geoff Duke's Norton and Umberto Masetti's Gilera. For a first season, with a brand new design, not at all bad. But, paradoxically, the complicated four had

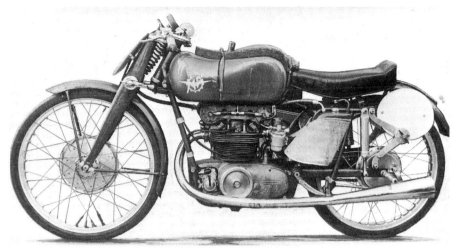

The 125cc MV that suddenly came on song in 1952.

made far more of a show than had the simple single-cylinder 125.

What were these brand new designs like from a technical point of view? The answer is that as far as the engines were concerned, very much the Piero Remor formula as before! The 125cc engine could be regarded as one-quarter sliced off the four, sharing the same bore and stroke of 52 × 58mm and gear drive (central on the four) to the twin overhead camshafts. The 125cc machine was typical of the Italian racers of the time (did Remor copy Drusiani's Mondial or did he independently arrive at the same solutions?), with twin-loop cradle frame, blade-type parallel-ruler front forks and simple pivoted fork rear suspension. As with the larger machines, primary drive to the five-speed gearbox was by spur gears.

The 500cc four was in many respects no more than a rehash of the Gilera, with a number of what Remor doubtless considered to be 'improvements'. Unfortu-

As early as Monza at the end of 1951, the 'four' had telescopic forks and spring damper units at the rear. Note the extraordinary 'streamlining'.

nately, that is just what they were *not*. In defiance of common sense, the engine had only two carburettors, which fed adjacent cylinders through two Y-shaped inlet pipes. For whatever reason, upward gear changes were effected by a pedal on one side of the bike, downward changes by another pedal on the other side. The blade-type parallel ruler front forks were perhaps something of an anachronism, but at the time, and especially in Italy, telescopic front forks were by no means universally accepted as the ultimate answer.

The rear suspension and final transmission amply illustrated Remor's unhappy tendency to use several untried elements of design at the same time. The twin loop cradle frame itself was, like that of the Gilera, partly in steel tube, part sheet steel pressings. There were two pivoted rear forks, one above the other, Watts linkage fashion, united at the rear on each side by a forging which carried the rear wheel

Les Graham, seen here in 1952, insisted on chain-drive for the four. Less happily, he also advocated the highly suspect Earles forks.

spindle. Such a design might have its merits if it were designed to maintain a constant chain tension, but used as it was on the MV with shaft drive, it simply looks like unnecessary complication. The possibilities of rapid wear and flexing of the joints is also readily apparent. Nor was this double swinging arm controlled, as one might have expected from an aircraft manufacturer, by sophisticated oil-damped spring units, but by torsion bars and crude friction 'snubbers' of the sort to be seen on a typical Vintage sports car.

Using shaft drive was no doubt motivated by the desirability of keeping oil off the rear tyre, but with its use, Remor exchanged one evil for several others. The torque reaction of the shaft could not fail to exert itself on the multiplicity of small joints in the rear suspension with consequent unpleasant handling on acceleration and deceleration. The drive-shaft on a motorcycle is necessarily short and, being subject to quite severe deflection, needs universal joints of considerable sophistication. Changing gear ratios – so necessary in a busy racing programme, and so blessedly easy with simple chain drive – becomes a major operation with a shaft and bevels. It is easy to be wise with hindsight, but as a matter of simple fact, all of these eccentricities of Remor's design were to disappear before the four became a success. But that is to anticipate.

For the 1951 season, English rider Les Graham, World Champion in 1949 on the 500cc AJS Porcupine, had joined MV in November 1950. Immediately he began to impose his judgement and experience on the layout of the fours. Even so, 1951 could only be called a disaster for MV with entries frequently made and not honoured. In Switzerland, the 500cc race being run in a downpour, Les Graham retired after a fall and Carlo Bandirola did well to finish fourth. It was the best result of the year, and even at the all-important Italian Grand Prix at the season's end at Monza the MVs failed to shine, with only a sixth place in the 125cc event and a wretched ninth in the 500cc race for Bandirola.

MV did in fact arrive in the Isle of Man for the TT. The four now had telescopic forks and oil damping for the rear suspension, and the engine had four carburettors, but in neither race did Graham make the least impression – his 125cc ride ending indeed within half a mile! In the Senior race he lasted little more than two laps. In both races his retirement was attributed to missed gearchanges.

For 1952 Remor revised the bore and stroke to 50×56mm (scarcely worth the trouble one would have thought) and at Graham's insistence converted the transmission of the 500cc four to chain drive. The four was also fitted with singularly hideous pivoted swinging arm front forks made under Earles patents, which did absolutely nothing for its appearance and probably little more for the roadholding and steering. They did, however, make it extremely easy to experiment with spring and damper settings.

At the Swiss Grand Prix Bandirola finished third behind the two AJS Porcupines of Jack Brett and Bill Doran after Geoff Duke retired his Norton whilst in the lead. Graham retired when he could not restart his engine after a pit stop. Nevertheless, observers agreed that the winter's development had improved the MV's speed and acceleration. They had certainly worked wonders for the little 125cc machine! At last it found both speed and reliability, and at the TT, Cecil Sandford, recruited at the last minute by Les Graham, led from start to finish off the three-lap race to beat Carlo Ubbiali's Mondial and lap at over 76 mph. In the Senior race Les Graham did almost as well, lying second to Geoff Duke until the Norton's clutch expired, and then leading from the other Norton rider Reg Armstrong. However, Graham was to slow a little on the last lap and finished second. Had the race lasted another half mile he would have won, because quite literally, as Reg Armstrong took the flag, his Norton shed its exposed primary chain!

Cecil Sandford now went on to win at the Dutch TT, take a third in Germany and score another win in Ulster. He retired after only two laps at Monza, but

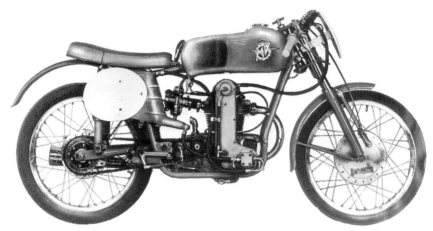

As sold to the paying customers: the sohc 125cc MV single that won many lesser events all over Europe.

The factory 125cc of 1953 now with telescopic front forks. It changed little over the years.

Ubbiali, his nearest rival for the 125cc Championship, did not, by finishing second, gain enough points to catch the British rider, who now won the titles for himself and MV. In Spain three weeks later Enrico Mendogini won again on the Morini as he had at Monza, but Les Graham was second and Cecil Sandford third; a satisfactory result emphasizing the tremendous turnaround of MV's fortunes in the 125cc class.

What, meanwhile, of the 500cc four? In Holland Graham retired with engine trouble, and again in Belgium. In Germany both Bandirola and Graham had plug trouble and made pit stops. Bandirola retired, but Graham pulled back to finish fourth. At the Ulster, Graham was joined by Bill Lomas. Alas for Graham, after raising the lap record to 105.94 mph he lost the tread from his rear tyre and retired. Bill Lomas showed his mettle by finishing third behind Cromie McCandless on the Gilera and Rod Coleman on the AJS Porcupine. At the very important Grand Prix des Nations at Monza, Les Graham and MV got it right, built up a huge and commanding lead and for once nothing went wrong.

The Surtees years: the 500cc 'fours' rarely used any sort of streamlining.

This was a taste of how the MV should have gone all year, and Les Graham won by one minute, ahead of Umberto Masetti's Gilera, at 101.29 mph and having lapped at 109.09 mph. Bandirola finished fourth behind Nello Pagani's Gilera. Then at the final Grand Prix of 1952 in Spain, Graham won just as convincingly to beat Masetti once again. All the more astonishing, because for twenty laps the big MV was on three cylinders with one of the plug leads adrift! Considering the earlier troubles, to have finished second in the World Championship to Umberto Masetti and the Gilera was no mean achievement, and MV looked to have the following season made, especially as Cecil Sandford was to be joined by the brilliant Carlo Ubbiali in the 125cc class. Alas, it did not work out!

1957 Junior TT. John Surtees was in trouble – note the smokey exhaust.

In 1953 the Classic rounds opened with the TT. The Junior was the first race to be run, and Les Graham was entered on a 350cc four, virtually the same as the larger-capacity bike except for the bore and stroke. In practice Graham had made the fastest lap at 90.75 mph, but in the race he was in trouble from the start and only completed two laps. In the 125cc event Ubbiali retired, but Les Graham rode to a brilliant win ahead of Werner Haas on the NSU Rennfox and Cecil Sandford was third. There were also seven privately owned 125cc MVs amongst the twelve finishers. Poor Les did not have long to enjoy his first, long-awaited, TT victory. The next day, chasing Geoff Duke on the Norton, he lost control at the foot of Bray Hill and was killed instantly. His death sent shockwaves through the racing world, for he was universally liked and respected and had been racing since pre-war days. He was, at 43 years of age, something of a father figure to many younger riders. He was also on terms of personal friendship with Count Domenico Agusta, who took his death very hard, and who withdrew the fours from the Championship rounds. No cause for the accident was ever pinpointed, despite considerable research undertaken by the factory.

In the 125cc class, MV did retain the Constructor's title in 1953, but the individual title was won with ease by NSU's Werner Haas. At the end of the year, Piero Remor, that enigmatic and mysterious figure, left MV to disappear forever from racing and to work for the Motom company, makers of mopeds and those curious little utility vehicles peculiar to Italy. The racer shop now answered to Arturo Magni, who was to stay in charge to the very end of MV's racing career.

For 1954, MV gave rides on 350cc versions of the four, as well as 500cc, to Bill Lomas and Dickie Dale in the Isle of Man. Dale finished seventh in the Senior, Lomas retiring after three laps. In the Junior, the positions were reversed, with Lomas finishing seventh and Dale retiring on the last lap. The 350cc fours had proved disappointingly slow and not particularly reliable. In the 125cc race in the Island, victory again went to Werner Haas on the NSU. The rest of the season was lacklustre indeed for MV. The 125cc class was dominated totally by Werner Haas and Rupert Hollaus on the NSU Rennfoxes, and after a few more nondescript placings in the 500cc class, the fours did not shine again until Monza in September, when Bandirola finished third and Dickie Dale fourth behind the Gileras of Geoff Duke and Umberto Masetti. The world's titles being settled, the last Classic of 1954 in Spain was not treated very seriously by the other contenders and Dickie Dale was able to win the 500cc race and Nello Pagani was third.

Count Agusta now approached the very forceful (reckless was the word some people used) Norton rider Ray Amm, Junior and Senior TT winner in 1953 and in 1954 winner of the controversially shortened Senior race. But Amm was never to finish a race for MV. At the non-championship meeting at Imola in April he fell from the 350cc four and was killed when he struck a roadside post. The wonder is that MV did not withdraw from the 350cc and 500cc classes, for in addition to the 125cc class, which was still very important to them, they now planned to expand into the 250cc class. However, with their regular Italian riders they soldiered on, though with indifferent results. No entries were made in the Junior and Senior TTs. In the 250cc TT, Bill Lomas (who in the larger classes was signed to Moto Guzzi) gave the new 204cc MV a surprise win, beating Cecil Sandford on a Guzzi. In the 125cc race, NSU having withdrawn from racing, Carlo Ubbiali and Swiss rider Luigi Taveri finished first and second for MV. In fact 1955 was an outstandingly good year for MV in the 125cc class, for they won every single Classic round, Ubbiali taking the Individual Championship and MV the Constructor's title.

For 1956 Domenico Agusta once again signed a British star, brilliant young Norton rider John Surtees. It was a shrewd move, for even more than Les Graham had been, Surtees was a 'thinking' rider, a natural development man as well as a very fine road racer. By now the four was making an honest 65 hp at 10,500 rpm, and suggestions by Surtees led to an improved torque curve. As Geoff Duke had

The 250cc twin of 1956 in the Isle of Man. It was practised but not raced that year.

Agostini on his way to second place behind Mike Hailwood (Honda) in the 'Diamond Jubilee' Junior TT of 1967.

done at Gilera, he persuaded MV to 'Nortonize' the frame a little, and he firmly rejected the Earles front forks that had been a feature since Les Graham's time. At the TT Surtees suffered the cruel disappointment of running out of fuel in the Junior race on the last lap whilst in the lead. In the Senior race he led from start to finish and won comfortably, not at record speed, for the weather was not kind, but convincingly enough. Geoff Duke, of course was suspended by the FIM for the first half of the season, or the race might have been considerably enlivened. Carlo Ubbiali scored a double in the 125cc and 250cc races on the Clypse circuit. Thereafter, despite a nasty spill in the 350cc event at the German Grand Prix, which broke his arm, Surtees accumulated enough points to win the 500cc title for himself and MV, and so did Ubbiali in the 125cc and 250cc classes.

By now, the little 125 was distinctly long in the tooth, and in 1957 MV were caught napping by a comeback from Mondial in both 125cc and 250cc classes, Tarquinio Provini and Cecil Sandford, now riding for Morini, respectively winning the individual Championships. At the TT Surtees and the MV were simply overwhelmed by Bob McIntyre and the Gilera. In the Junior race Surtees had to stop twice at the pits to change plugs and finished fourth. In the Senior race he chose to ride without a fairing because of the uncertain weather, but, in fact, the race was run in near perfect conditions, and a combination of McIntyre's greater experience, more aggressive style and the Gilera's superb full streamlining gave him victory and the first lap ever at over 100 mph. Surtees trailed home two minutes adrift.

As is common knowledge, at the end of 1957, labouring under a dreadful recession in sales, Gilera, Moto Guzzi and Morini withdrew from racing. After originally letting it be understood that they too would retire, MV changed their mind. With John Surtees and John Hartle, newly recruited for the 350cc and 500cc classes, they were to walk away with the 125cc, 250cc, 350cc and 500cc class Constructor's Championships in 1958, 1959 and 1960. In the smaller classes, challenges from Ducati and MZ were brushed aside. Between 1958 and 1960, Carlo Ubbiali won all three of the 125cc individual titles, and the 250cc individual titles in 1959 and 1960, the title for 1958 going to Tarquinio Provini. But during 1960, after a slow start, the new 125cc twins and 250cc fours from Honda had, towards the season's end, shown distinct promise of what they might achieve in the future.

During 1960 John Hartle had left MV, and at the season's end John Surtees retired to take up car racing. It was a difficult time for Count Agusta, and he must have been tempted to give up racing altogether as his rivals had done three years before. To race in all of the solo classes was formidably expensive and simply was not justified by the wretched sales figures. Now faced with the need for new designs and development if MV were to stay ahead in the 125cc and 250cc classes, the Count decided to race only in the 350cc and 500cc World Championships.

In 1960, MV had taken on young Gary Hocking, who had proved his worth in the 125cc, 250cc and 350cc classes. He was now to race the 500cc four in the World Championships, ostensibly as a private entrant – the machines bore the legend MV PRIVAT on tanks and fairings. At the TT Hocking also rode one of the 250cc twins and was fourth fastest in practice. Although he split the Hondas of Bob McIntyre and Mike Hailwood for the first lap of the 250cc race and lay third for the next lap, he then retired half-way through the race. Nor was he any luckier in the Junior and Senior races, for although in the 350cc class he led and made a new record fastest lap at 99.80 mph, a long pit stop and a sick motor in the closing stages dropped him to finish second to Phil Read's Norton. (It was very nearly third place, because on the last lap not only was Read ahead of Hocking but so was Mike Hailwood on an AJS 7R, all set to become first man ever to win four TTs in a week! Then, 14 miles from the flag, the gudgeon pin of Mike's 7R broke and cost him the race.)

In the Senior race, Hocking led comfortably for three laps, but had to make a pit stop at the end of four laps with a sticking throttle. He retired at the pits a lap later with the same problem. He comfortably won the 350cc and 500cc titles for 1961 for himself and for MV with wins in the smaller class at Holland, East Germany, Ulster and Monza. In the 500cc class he won seven Grands Prix out of ten counting for the Championship. He did not win at Monza in front of the Italian crowd because, for whatever motive, Count Agusta had invited Mike Hailwood to ride a four at the Grand Prix des Nations. Hailwood was not the man to play second fiddle to Hocking – and vice versa! Consequently the two went at it hammer and tongue and eventually Gary 'lost it' and was out of the race. This, and the Count's subsequent signing of Hailwood for 1962, soured Hocking's relationship both with Hailwood and with Count Agusta. Indeed one might say with motorcycle racing. After the 1962 TT he simply walked away from the European scene and returned to

The 500cc 3-cylinder that still reigned supreme in 1971.

Final flower of genius: the 500cc 'four' of 1974 that brought MV their last and hardest won World Championship.

Southern Rhodesia. He was killed practising for a car race meeting not long afterwards.

At the 1962 TT, however, that was in the future. The Junior race was an absolute ding-dong battle all the way between the two MV riders, and for the first time the lap record was hoisted above 100 mph by first Hocking from a standing start at 100.90 mnph, then by Hailwood at 101.58 mph. Hocking also lapped at 101.49 mph, but a supreme effort by Hailwood on the last lap gave him victory by five seconds.

The Senior race looked like being more of the same, but it was not to be. Hocking lapped successively at 103.76 mph (from a standing start!) and 105.75 mph and led Mike by fully sixteen seconds. But on the third lap, Hailwood's clutch started to slip. Forty seconds in arrears he called in at the pits, not to retire, as almost any other rider in the world would have done, but *to have the clutch plates changed*! This took the Italian mechanic fully 13 minutes – he won a round of applause from the grandstand – and Mike rejoined the race. He had no chance whatever of a place on the leaderboard, but he rode as though he had, to finish an astonishing twelfth, last man in silver replica time. Hocking meanwhile howled round to win at 103.51 mph and having made fastest lap second time around.

In the Junior race, Honda rider Tom Phillis, long-time friend of Gary Hocking's, had crashed at the frightening Laurel Bank section, losing his life. This tragedy only reinforced Hocking's disillusionment and hastened his departure. Hailwood was left to carry MV's fortunes on his own. He did so to such effect as to become the 1962 500cc World Champion. It was the first of four such titles for Mike, but when in 1966 and 1967 he rode for Honda in the 500cc class the individual title eluded him. MV went on to score, in all, 17 500cc Constructor's titles, the last being won for them in 1974 by Phil Read.

Hailwood rode both the 350cc and 500cc fours, but the 'scaled-up' 350cc Honda was always faster than the 'scaled-down' MV, and Hailwood rarely got the better of his arch-rival Jim Redman. In 1963 Mike stood up to the challenge of the Gilera revival by 'Scuderia Duke', about which it is easy to be scathing in retrospect, but which at the time appeared to pose a very real threat to MV's supremacy.

Once again, Hailwood and MV were 500cc champions. He repeated the feat in 1964. At the Grand Prix des Nations that year, Count Agusta was present, and witnessed at first hand the superb style of a young Italian rider, Giacomo Agostini, who finished a close, fighting fourth in the 250cc race behind the Yamahas of Phil Read and Mike Duff and the six-cylinder Honda of Jim Redman. After some thought the Count offered Agostini a contract for 1965. It was a decision he was never to regret. The Count's ostensible motive for signing Agostini was that MV wanted to make a head-on attack on the 350cc class with a new, slimmer, three-cylinder machine. The design of the 500cc four had not so much stagnated as become settled. Nor was there any reason for change. Mike Hailwood stated, long after he had left MV, that it was one of the best-handling motorcycles and had the best power characteristics of any that he had ever ridden. But the 350cc class, dominated for the previous three years by Honda and Jim Redman, was another matter. There the comparatively undeveloped, bulky and heavy MV four was now proving uncompetitive. It was replaced by the new slimline three-cylinder machine designed for MV by aircraft technician Ruggero Mazza. This machine was at once sensationally fast, and handled, if anything, even better than the 500cc four.

Agostini, young, ambitious, tremendously talented, slim of build, and above all *Italian* was, Count Agusta felt, an ideal rider for this radical new machine. So he proved to be. In his first season with MV, Giacomo Agostini very nearly did win the 350cc title – three wins, and two third places putting him into a position at the season's end where a win in the Japanese Grand Prix could secure the Championship. Sickeningly, in that race, Agostini was well ahead and likely to win when an ignition fault dropped him to fifth place.

The last racing MV of all: the ultimate development of the 'four' raced in 1976 and 1977.

The end of the season saw Mike Hailwood's departure. Although he never criticized the MV machinery (in strict contrast to his outspoken, not to say slanderous, remarks about the 500cc Honda), he had never very much enjoyed the ponderous, humourless attitude at MV, and he was frustrated by the lack of a ride in the 250cc class, which he had always enjoyed. He was, too, irritated by Count Agusta's obvious interest in Agostini's prospects of becoming World Champion and by the fact that, on more than one occasion, Agostini had been served by better machinery than he had. Mike therefore left to join Honda, only to encounter another set of problems! Now as Hailwood had in 1963, Giacomo Agostini in 1966 carried the major responsibility for MV's fortunes. He was to do so for the next seven years. In that time he was to win the Junior World Championship five times, the Senior six. He was to win five Junior TTs and five Seniors and to finish second in both races once.

For 1967 he raced a new three-cylinder 500cc machine that, like the 350, was considerably narrower, less bulky and lighter than the four had been, and though he did not win the Senior TT on either of the two occasions when Hailwood rode the big Honda, he had no reason to be ashamed of his performances. In 1966, when the TT was delayed until September due to a shipping strike, he had ridden there only once before. Now after winning the Junior race at 102.56 mph and lapping at 103.90 mph, he chased Hailwood home in a race punctuated by rain showers, having averaged 101.09 mph. At the 1967 TT Agostini was second on the Junior MV to Hailwood's six-cylinder Honda, but he was extremely unlucky not to win the Senior race! With a blistering standing start lap at a record-breaking 108.38 mph, Giacomo Agostini led Hailwood by nearly 12 seconds! His second lap was at 108.44 mph, his third at 108.12 mph, which included stopping to take on fuel. Hailwood stopped at the pits at the same time, and Agostini was away before him, as Mike had some trouble with his twistgrip. At the end of four out of six laps, Agostini still led, having averaged 106.72 mph to Hailwood's 106.47 mph. He was still leading more than half way round the fifth lap when his chain jumped the sprocket and broke!

With the withdrawal of Honda at the end of 1967, MV were once again un-challenged for the next six seasons. There was some competition from Benelli, but it was not sustained. The MVs were incredibly reliable, and even when there was no need, the factory managed to make them faster meeting by meeting. It was just as well that they did not rest on their laurels, because the two-stroke revolution was about to happen. But as late as 1971, Agostini was able to hold at bay the new challenge from Yamaha in general and the astonishing Finnish rider Jarno Saarinen in particular. And as late as 1972 he was to win both Junior and Senior TTs. However, the death that year of his friend Gilberto Parlotti, who crashed his 125cc Morbidelli in atrocious conditions, hardened Agostini's resolve to boycott the Isle of Man. He never rode there again. Possibly Count Domenico Agusta might have argued him out of this decision, but he was not there to do so. He had died in

The man who made it all happen: Count Domenico Agusta, just before his untimely death in 1971.

February 1971, the control of the racing department having been taken over by his brother, Count Corrado Agusta. The wonder is that Corrado Agusta allowed racing to continue at all.

Earlier, although never a huge commercial success, the MV motorcycle business had at least been self supporting, and even modestly profitable. Now, that was no longer the case, and the motorcycle side was regarded with distaste by the aero engineers, who considered that the capital involved could be more profitably involved. Nevertheless, not only did Corrado Agusta allow racing to continue, but for 1972 he sanctioned a new four-cylinder 350cc design, and retained Alberto Pagani, who had ridden in 1971, and Phil Read to support Agostini. After Jarno Saarinen had beaten Agostini in the West German and French Grands Prix in 1972, MV made a supreme effort to have the new 52 × 40.4mm 350cc four-valve four ready for Austria. It was good enough to win, and to take Agostini to yet another 350cc Championship despite the best that Saarinen and Yamaha could do. Agostini also won the 500cc title for MV, managing again to stave off any challenge from the two-strokes.

But 1973 was to start badly, with Saarinen, now equipped with a new four-cylinder 500cc Yamaha. After Saarinen had won at the Paul Ricard circuit in France, and in Austria, MV worked a minor miracle in rushing through a new 57 × 49mm 500cc four, which produced nearly 100 hp at close to 14,000 rpm. Riding this at the German Grand Prix at Hockenheim (where the long straights favoured the fastest machine) Phil Read beat Saarinen fair and square! MV's astonishing ability to extract more and more power – and reliability – had not yet deserted them. But the battle between Saarinen and MVs was not to continue. In a dreadful multiple pile-up that also cost the life of Renzo Pasolini, Saarinen was killed at the Italian Grand Prix at Monza. The 500cc race was abandoned. Strangely from this moment onwards Giacomo Agostini's star seemed to wane, and that of Phil Read to wax. The inevitable result was that the factory favoured Read at Agostini's expense, and a flare-up of tempers occurred between the two riders that equally inevitably led to Agostini leaving MV at the season's end after he had lost the 500cc individual Championship to Phil Read.

It was the end of an era, and for 1974 Giacomo Agostini 'went over to the enemy' – Yamaha – and MV at first retained only Phil Read to contest the World Championship, though eventually they also signed up-and-coming Gianfranco Bonera. At this time, the MV motorcycle racing organization was in desperate difficulties. Although the helicopter division was continually being called upon for technical assistance, they resented the fact. The motorcycle business was by now well nigh moribund, though it was to stagger on for another few profitless years. The appalling Italian industrial troubles meant that urgent jobs had to be farmed out or, quite literally, smuggled into departments that were for a time working normally. That in these conditions MV raced at all was a tribute to Corrado Agusta's spirit and determination. 1974 was to be MV's last really successful year.

The machines that Read and Gianfranco Bonera rode in 1974 were the final flowering of nearly a quarter of a century of steady conscientious development of a remarkable design. One might say that they were – out of their time – the last, the very last Classic Racing Motorcycles. They had disc brakes and light alloy wheels, but they also had treaded tyres, of sensible size, and the fairings were not plastered with hideous advertising. Nor did they abound in stupid 'gimmicks' of design, designed as much to gain some dubious 'psychological' advantage as to improve performance or handling. They were above all *honest* motorcycles.

The engines, with 57 × 49mm bore and stroke and four valves per cylinder, were recognizable as lineal descendants of the first Piero Remor engines of 1950. Ignition was still by a high-quality magneto driven by gear from the train to the camshafts, and four 30mm Dell'Orto carburettors were still used. Both front forks and the rear spring-damper units were of Ceriani manufacture.

Les Graham – 125cc MV on his way to a TT win in 1953 – his last ride before his death.

For the last time, MV and rider Phil Read took on the world. MV did not contest the TT, but they scarcely needed to do so. With wins in Belgium, Finland and Czechoslovakia, second place in Holland and thirds in Italy and Holland, Read and MV easily won the Championships, and Gianfranco Bonera proved his worth in this his first full Grand Prix season by finishing second in the individual Championships to Read. Giving some idea of how highly developed were these MVs, Read had won the Belgian Grand Prix at Spa-Francorchamps at 131.90 mph, lapping from a standing start at 130.25 mph and making fastest lap of the race at 133.34 mph!

Although MV raced again in 1975, 1976 and even in 1977, the 1974 season was the last one in which they won a Championship, and as good a time as any to leave them. The increasing involvement of MV throughout the 1970s in defence work and the consequent injection of government money – thus making the company answerable to the Civil Service – had made it difficult enough to race at all, and inevitably led to the race shop's closure. No MV motorcycles of any sort were made after 1977.

Although comparatively few of the smaller production racers were sold – their high price alone ensured that their survival rate has been high, both in England and in Italy. Mercifully, though for a time neglected, the 350cc and 500cc factory machinery was not scrapped or cannibalized to any great extent. At the end of 1986 MV sold all those machines (some sources claimed as many as 24) surplus to the requirements of their own museum. Three were sold to ex-MV rider John Surtees. The rest were acquired by America's Team Obsolete, but a condition of sale was that the bikes should remain in Italy, where they were, in 1987, being reconditioned under the supervision of Roberto Patrigniani. A subsequent exchange of lawsuits between the ex-partners of Team Obsolete has, at the time of writing, made the future of this collection uncertain. Fortunately no such misfortune has befallen the machines owned by John Surtees, and they have already been ridden in public by John himself.

MZ

More than two and a half decades on, it is not easy to convey the astonishment that ran through the world of international road racing when, in the late 1950s, a racing two-stroke appeared, from behind the Iron Curtain of all unlikely places, capable of challenging and sometimes beating the fastest racing four-strokes in the world. Such a thing was unheard of, for both the Spanish Montesa and the West German DKW had tried gallantly but unsuccessfully in post-war years. Now a make, virtually unknown outside East Germany and working with resources that were obviously painfully modest, was not only able to contest Grand Prix races but to win them!

MZ, the make in question, had started life as IFA, successors to the pre-war DKW company of Chemnitz in Saxony, which post-war was in Russian-controlled East Germany. Many of the original technicians had fled westwards to join the new DKW organization at Ingoldstadt, the old factory having been badly damaged in the war, but by 1946, IFA were producing motorcycles based naturally enough on the pre-war DKW RT125, a 55 × 58mm single-cylinder two stroke with three-speed gearbox.

This design was the basis of the Harley-Davidson Hummer, the BSA Bantam and several other 125cc lightweights of the early post-war years. IFA themselves used the RT125 as the basis of a 125cc racer, and by 1951, when they won the East German road-racing Championship, the engine was producing 9 hp at 7000 rpm. For 1952, they were joined by development engineer Walter Kaaden, who, prompted by the results obtained in Formula 3 car racing by a friend of his, Daniel Zimmermann, fitted a rotary disc valve and carburettor to the right-hand crankcase of the IFA. This valve, of spring steel 0.020 in thick was free to float a few thousandths of an inch sideways in his housing, was thus self-sealing and was automatically lubricated by the oil mixed with the petrol. Unlike a piston-controlled port, it allowed Kaaden to open the inlet early and still close it at the most favourable moment. It also opened and shut the port very rapidly, and allowed totally unrestricted flow through the whole inlet period. Power rose immediately to 11 hp at 8000 rpm, enough once again to win the East German Championship. These early IFAs were graceless, ugly machines with plunger box rear suspension, crude leading-link front forks and an awkward-looking riding position. Magneto

The very early MZ – or was it still called an IFA? Note the twin megaphone exhausts.

The 125cc MZ engine in the mid-1950s, now with top feed carburettor, single exhaust port and acoustic exhaust.

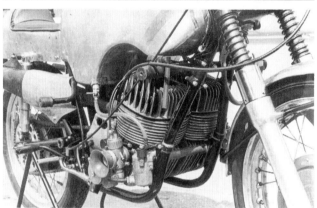

The 250cc twin in 1960, virtually two 125cc engines coupled together. Note the Norton 'Roadholder' forks!

ignition was used, and the twin exhausts were typically pre-war DKW plain pipes and megaphones emerging from the rear of the cylinder.

In 1953, IFA changed their name to MZ, Motorrad Zchopau, and were given a modest government grant to help with racing, which was still confined entirely to East Germany. Not until 1957, at the Grand Prix des Nations at Monza in Italy, did they venture abroad, and then not to any great effect, Ernst Degner, who had recently joined as a technician-rider, finishing an undistinguished seventh in the 125cc event. The machines had now become much more orthodox in appearance though they still had bottom link front forks. Inside the engine there was now a third transfer port, which not only served to cool and lubricate the crowded needle roller small end but gave a significant increase in power. There was now a single rearward-facing exhaust with plain pipe and fully tapered 'expansion box' and tailpipe. Ignition was by a double-spark magneto running at half engine speed and there was now a six-speed gearbox. Sixteen hp at 9000 rpm was claimed. In 1958, MZ appeared at the Isle of Man for the 125cc TT, at that time held on the short Clypse course. Degner and Horst Fugner finished in respectable fifth and sixth places, both averaging over 69 mph compared to Carlo Ubbiali's winning speed on the MV of 72.86 mph.

At the 1959 TT, MZ entered the 250cc event with three twins, in effect two 125cc engines side by side. Unfortunately all three retired, but they had shown a fair turn of speed. The 125cc event, however, was sensational. In addition to Degner and Fugner, MZ had entered the Swiss rider Luigi Taveri, who astonished

Before it all went wrong: in 1959 Walter Kaaden demonstrates while Ernst Degner, seated on machine, and Luigi Taveri listen.

everyone by taking an early lead and keeping it, ahead of Tarquinio Provini and Carlo Ubbiali on the MVs and Mike Hailwood on a Ducati, as well as the rest of a highly talented field. But, alas, in an evil moment Taveri had started the race wearing a new helmet, which proved too tight. Towards the end of the race he was in agony, and suffering from double vision; he slowed, letting Provini win by a mere seven seconds. Taveri made the fastest lap. Degner, who had been well in contention, retired late in the race and Fugner finished fourth, just behind Hailwood and just ahead of Ubbiali. That MZ were a force to be reckoned with was no longer in any doubt, but unfortunately the difficulties arising from living in a Socialist state prevented MZ from employing the riders they would have liked, except on the odd occasion. Nor did Kaaden have more than a derisory budget for racing and development. What he accomplished therefore was a near miracle.

The climax of MZ's success was the 1961 season. By now, with a much improved chassis, Norton front forks, superb brakes and improved weight distribution, the MZ with 25 hp at 10,800 rpm was totally competitive. Riding both the 125cc and the twin, Degner was in superb form – at the Austrian Grand Prix, he won both 125cc and 250cc races against the best that Honda could do. The 125cc race result at the German was well nigh unbelievable, with MZ riders, Degner, Alan Shepherd, Werner Brehme and Hans Fischer all finishing ahead of the Honda team, Degner was second to Phillis' Honda at Clermont Ferrand, fourth at the Belgian Grand Prix and won again at the Sachsenring. At Monza he won again, but at the Swedish Grand Prix he retired. Then, with only Argentina to go, and with the Championship almost in his grasp, Degner dropped his bombshell. In cloak-and-dagger fashion, his family were smuggled out of East Germany, whilst he made his way via Denmark to West Germany. The whole episode had been master-minded and financed by Suzuki, to whom Degner brought all his intimate knowledge of

Walter Kaaden's deepest secrets. Within weeks, Suzuki were able to attain the speed and reliability that had eluded their own technicians for years. The rest is history. For Kaaden and MZ the disaster could hardly have been more complete.

For a long time the only MZs seen outside East Germany were those loaned to English riders, first Alan Shepherd, then Derek Woodman. A high spot was Shepherd's win in the 250cc class at Daytona, but despite that and other occasional flashes of brilliance, MZ's star was eclipsed. By the time that they raced again outside East Germany they had been left far behind and they hardly raced at all after 1970, but a few MZs did find their way into private hands, usually when they were well worn and obsolete. The racing department's parsimonious funding meant that many early machines were cannibalized and parts re-worked and re-cycled, and most of the handful of bikes that still exist are from the later years. Even so, a few are seen from time to time in continental events and even in CRMC parades.

Matchless
The G45

At the 1948 Motorcycle Show, AJS and Matchless introduced new 500cc vertical twins, the engines of which had iron cylinders and heads, valve operation by transverse camshafts fore and aft with push-rods and rockers, and the unusual feature of a plain centre main bearing carried in a horizontally split centre-section that was sandwiched between the two halves of the vertically split crankcase. A sports version of the engine with light alloy cylinder head was introduced, known as the Matchless Super Clubman. With one of these engines suitably tuned and equipped with racing magneto and carburettor, and fitted into a 7R 'Boy Racer' frame, Robin Sherry rode to fourth place in the 1951 Manx Grand Prix at 87.71 mph, a most creditable performance, and a lucky one, for near the end of the race, one of the rocker pillars broke, and though the valve gear still worked the engine vibrated dreadfully.

In the 1952 TT a similar machine was ridden by well-known Australian competitor Ernie Ring, who completed four good laps before being eliminated by a fall. Then in the 1952 Manx Grand Prix, Derek Farrant with a Matchless twin won the Senior race at 88.65 mph, breaking the lap record four times.

Breaking a long silence, AMC announced that for 1953 a certain number of such 500cc racing machines would be sold under the designation of the Matchless G45; details of the engine were given in advance of the 1953 TT. Cylinder heads and barrels were in light alloy with shrunk-in iron valve seats and cylinder liners. The forged alloy steel crankshaft ran in roller main bearings and the same plain centre bearing as the G9 sports. There were special racing camshafts and the whole of the valve gear was strengthened and lightened to cope with triple valve springs. Twin Grand Prix Amal carburettors and a Lucas racing magneto completed the specification. Apart from slightly wider tyres, the rolling chassis was exactly the same as for the 350cc 7R AJS. The new G45 must have seemed an excellent idea, because at the 1953 TT no fewer than 14 were entered by some well-known names, including Derek Farrant, Arthur Wheeler, Phil Heath and up-and-coming Bob McIntyre. Alas, all the 'quick men' fell or retired, and G45s did no better than to finish in ninth, 14th and 24th places. At the 1953 Manx Grand Prix, the best result was by Manxman Derek Ennett, who finished third behind the Nortons of perennial Denis Parkinson and R. D. Keller. Other G45 riders finished eighth, 14th and 25th. All through the 1950s, G45s were sold, although in small numbers, and raced with curiously disappointing results.

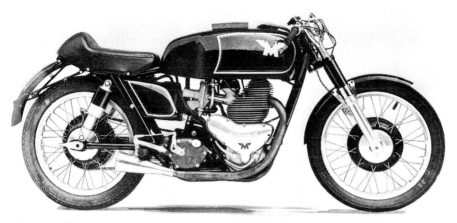

If looks could have won races! The original 500cc G45.

Frank Perris on a G45 in the 1955 Senior TT. He finished 26th.

In the 1954 TT, catastrophically wet and cut to four laps, ten G45s finished, but the highest placed was 15th. The following year, Derek Ennett finished a most creditable sixth at 92.54 mph (Geoff Duke won on the four-cylinder Gilera at 97.93 mph) just behind Bob McIntyre's rapid Norton, which averaged 93.83 mph. No G45 ever again won the Manx Grand Prix after Farrant's fairy-tale win of 1952, though many riders were well placed, and as late as 1957, George Murphy was able to finish as high as eighth in the TT behind three Italian fours, two works Guzzis and two works-supported Nortons. Behind him finished 24 Nortons, two other G45s, a privately entered 350cc Guzzi, a BSA and two 7R AJSs. The appearance in 1958 of the prototype of the G50 Matchless meant the end of the G45. It is very likely that the idea of the G45 came from outside the factory for, later, no one seemed anxious to claim credit for its conception, and development engineer Jack Williams specifically disavowed any involvement! Some confirmation of this came from Robin Sherry, who recalled that during his years of involvement with AMC, G45 development was by a quite separate group of engineers from those who worked on the 7Rs and the Porcupines.

Another explanation of the G45's orphan state is that whoever was responsible for the original idea, it was enthusiastically endorsed by H. J. Hatch, who, a late-comer to AMC, was regarded – particularly by development engineer Matt Wright – as an interloper and something of an irritant. When, in 1954, Hatch died, the pressure was off the racing department to persist with development, which was a pity. The G45 was really not fast enough or reliable enough in its relatively undeveloped form. Perhaps no amount of ordinary development could have surmounted its humble origins and the handicap of its relatively long stroke dimensions. Nevertheless, in good hands the G45 could sometimes spring a surprise. Never a very common sight in its day, the G45 has curiously proved something of a survivor, and quite a few can be seen today in CRMC parades.

The G50

Like the 7R AJS from which it was developed, the G50 Matchless was the brainchild of an ex-road-racing star, AMC Sales Director Jock West. Disappointed (and who was not?) with the record of the Matchless G45 twin, he reasoned that an overbored 7R would be lighter, handier and have less frontal area than most contenders in the 500cc class. The stroke of the 7R was 78mm, by chance the same as that of the last of Joe Craig's 500cc works Nortons. Not a bad starting point, and using a special one-off 90mm bore cylinder and a suitable piston a prototype engine was built. Cylinder and piston apart, the rest of the engine was almost all standard or modified 7R. Though the head was re-machined, standard 7R valves were used. This engine was fitted into an ordinary 7R frame and the wheels shod with slightly larger than standard tyres. Tests were very encouraging, though claims of 49 hp for the engine appear nonsensical in view of the bike's actual performance. Ridden by Australian Jack Ahearne, it finished 29th in the 1958 Senior TT, just inside Silver Replica time, at 88.71 mph. A modest speed compared to John Surtees' winning 98.63 mph on the MV, and the 95.40 mph of Bob Anderson's second-placed Norton. Nevertheless, Matchless decided to produce the G50 for 1959 with proper castings, 1½-in GP Amal carburettor and more realistic valve sizes. Now with a believable 51 hp at 7200 rpm, with small frontal area, and weighing 285 lb dry, the bike assumed a much more promising aspect. But despite the G50's well-nigh mystical reputation today, it did not immediately sell freely, and nor did it have any great impact upon racing during its production lifetime. That was brief enough. The G50 was only made for four seasons, 1959 to 1962, and less than 180 examples were produced. Development by the factory was minimal, and indeed in 1962 downright counter-productive, with the use of too large an inlet valve, a heavy and fragile forged piston and a batch of overhardened crankpins that were liable to fracture.

Not until 1964 did the G50 begin to show real promise in general road-racing terms. In the TT that year Fred Stevens finished third behind Mike Hailwood's MV and Derek Minter's Norton at a very creditable 96.40 mph. But more to the point, Matchless riders took no fewer than 15 replicas, nine silver and six bronze. Then at the Manx Grand Prix, Selwyn Griffiths gave Matchless their first win at a remarkable 96.27 mph.

It is not easy to say exactly why, two years after the factory had given up making the G50, it should have shown such an improvement, but individual tuners played a part, Ray Cowles, Tom Arter, Colin Seeley and, in America, Al Gunter and C. R. Axtell, but no one individual can lay claim to having achieved the G50s potential, and no one tuner was associated with the G50 in the way that, say, Steve Lancefield or Ray Petty were associated with Norton.

The G50 now became a very different proposition. Fortunately, just as spare parts were beginning to be a real problem, AMC finally collapsed and the patterns, jigs and tools for the G50 engine were purchased by Colin Seeley, who vigorously applied himself to satisfying the demand. Not only that, but he actually went into

Jack Williams talks to John Surtees, whilst Bruce Main-Smith listens. They were testing the very first two Matchless G50s ever made.

production with his own Seeley motorcycle, using a G50 engine, five- and six-speed gearboxes, a frame of his own design, Norton front forks and a twin front brake of formidable power. Not many Seeleys were sold, but those that were certainly gave an excellent account of themselves! Riding a Seeley G50, Dave Croxford was British 500cc road racing champion in 1967, 1968 and 1969.

Perhaps the performance that gave the G50 engine the prestige that, perhaps perversely, it enjoys today was that of Peter Williams on the Arter Matchless. This most professionally constructed 'special' used a frame (originally built for John Surtees to house a 7R engine) by Ken Sprayson of Reynolds Tubes, and was developed by Tom Arter and Peter Williams over several years, gaining a six-speed gearbox, disc brakes and cast light alloy wheels along the way. Between 1967 and 1973, Williams finished second in the TT on four occasions. He was beaten by Hailwood on the MV in 1967, by Agostini on the MV in 1970 and 1971 and by Jack Findley on the Suzuki in 1973. This last was a truly fantastic effort, and but for an oil leak, Peter Williams might well have won. Each one of his laps was at over 100 mph, his fastest at an incredible 102.74 mph, and his race average 100.62 mph. Findley's winning speed was 101.55 mph. That was the G50's last gasp, eleven years after the factory had abandoned production.

It is little realized in England that the G50 had a role in American racing in the early 1960s. To meet the requirements of the Daytona regulations, Matchless built 25 so-called G50 CSR models, which were sent over to America in February 1962.

The engines carried a belt-driven dynamo (the machines were fully street legal) and a smaller Amal carburettor, though the usual $1\frac{1}{2}$-in carburettor was supplied as an 'extra', as was a megaphone exhaust system. The chassis was a normal-

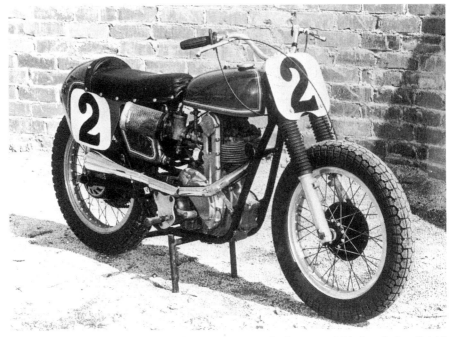

Dick Mann's TT Scrambles G50. The Americans made them go quickly long before British riders did.

Jack Williams again, AMC boss Donald Heather and G50s lined up for delivery in 1959.

appearing CSR with AMC gearbox complete with kickstart. These machines were used in all sorts of American racing with considerable success and Dick Mann used one in 1963 when he was American Champion. Mann, as much as anyone, was responsible for interesting his associates in the G50 and he contributed to work that improved the G50 engine's performance. It is not at all unlikely that this led to the general improvement noted in British performances in 1964. Few English enthusiasts realize the feedback from contributions made by American tuners in the 1960s!

When interest in racing motorcycles of the Classic era began to revive in the early 1980s, there were doubts and fears about racing a G50 in view of its rarity and the unavailability of spare parts, but such fears were quickly dispelled. The original patterns still existed, and producing spare parts, even complete engines, soon became a thriving industry!

Such was, and is, the grip of the G50 on the imagination of Classic enthusiasts that it is safe to say that a good many of the G50s now in existence never saw the light of day in the AMC racer shop! Be that as it may, G50s and G50-engined Seeleys and Mettisses are a welcome feature of the British Classic racing scene.

Montesa

The Montesa company was set up in 1944 by entrepreneur Francisco Bulto and engineer Pedro Permanyer on the basis of the latter's established Barcelona engineering business. Not that Bulto was merely a financier, for in fact he was deeply involved in the design of Montesa motorcycles. He was also an enthusiast for competition of all sorts, and Montesa, from the start, were as successful in Spanish domestic racing as they were commercially. They had begun with simple single-cylinder two-strokes of 100cc and later 125cc with three gears, rigid frames and girder front forks, but very soon carried plunger box suspension and telescopic front forks of their own individualistic design. In view of Spain's self-imposed isolation from the rest of Europe, the visit by Montesa to the 1948 Dutch TT was something of a novel event. That they finished fifth, ninth and 15th in the 125cc race, 'amongst the world's finest', as one writer says, should not be misconstrued, for the whole entry, including the Eysinks that finished first and third, and the Morinis that were second and fourth, were two-strokes. In fact the Eysinks were powered by tuned versions of the 9E Villiers engine!

Montesas did not appear outside Spain again until 1951, the occasion being the first 125cc TT in the Isle of Man. The machines were extremely well turned out and excited much interest and favourable comment. The engine, with rather long stroke dimensions of 51.5 × 60mm, had the carburettor on one side of the cylinder, the exhaust on the other, and a long plain bore exhaust pipe. At this time, Montesa claimed 11.5 hp at 9500 rpm, though this may have been an exaggeration. In the two-lap race over the Mountain circuit, veteran Spanish TT rider Jaime de Ortueta (he had ridden in the Island since the early 1930s) retired on the first lap, but his team-mates J. S. Bulto and Llobet finished fifth and sixth. Very creditable, but again it should not be lost sight of that dohc Mondials filled the first four places and that Cromie McCandless' winning speed was more than 11 mph higher than the faster of the two Montesas.

Montesa returned to the Island twice more, though, to race on the 10.7-mile Clypse course rather than over the Mountain.

In 1954 there were three entries, 'Johnny Grace' and M. C. Marques from Spain, supplemented by Norton test rider E. V. C. Hardy. Hardy hurt his arm in a practice spill, and Marques too failed to start. Grace finished seventh behind

The 1951 Montesa 125cc that raced over the Mountain course in the Isle of Man in 1951.

Hollaus' and Baltisburger's NSU Rennfoxes and four works MVs. Grace followed the TT by riding at the Ulster Grand Prix, where, in an abysmally wet and windy race, he finished eighth behind four NSUs and three MVs. Montesa's last visit to the Island was in 1956, and they were very unlucky not to win the team award, Johnny Grace retiring on lap eight of ten with clutch trouble, whilst Marcel Cama finished second at 65.24 mph, Gonzalez third at 61.13 mph and Sirera fourth at 61.03 mph. The winner was Carlo Ubbiali at 69.13 mph, so that even allowing for wet conditions, Montesa were closer to being on even terms with the four-strokes than in previous years. Everybody commented upon the minute size of the 1956

'Johnny Grace' on his 125cc Montesa in the 1955 TT.

The Montesa team in the Isle of Man 1956.

Montesa racers, which raced with 'dustbin' fairings. They still retained plunger-box rear suspension, but the engines, now with twin exhausts facing to the front and a carburettor at the rear of the cylinder, were now coupled to four-speed gearboxes. Also the subject of considerable comment was the use of what appeared to be functional silencers – certainly, the Montesas were uncannily quiet.

But those 'silencers' on the ends of long exhaust pipes in no sense supplied the acoustic function that had been apparent on Erich Wolf's 250cc DKW as early as 1952. It has to be admitted, however reluctantly, that the 125cc Montesas of 1948–1956, whilst adding interest to the Grand Prix scene, were of no very great significance in the way that the MZ was only a few years later. In any case, Montesa withdrew from racing during 1957, a decision which split not only the management but the loyalties of the workforce when 'Paco' Bulto left and formed his own company. Such key members of the Montesa competition department as Johnny Grace and Marcello Cama were only two out of a dozen who followed Bulto and assisted him in founding Bultaco.

What of the 125cc Montesas sold to private customers for racing? The simple fact is that all of those sold by the factory were for *production* racing, and the dozen or so 'Sportsman' racers sold in Great Britain were actually the creation of long-term British two-stroke enthusiast Jim Bound, who set up a tiny factory at Watford in Hertfordshire to convert Montesa 'Brios' into genuine racing models. Several of these survive today.

Morini

Alfonso Morini was, in 1924, one of the co-founders of the celebrated MM factory and in the Vintage years he raced MMs in Italian domestic events with considerable success. In 1937 he left MM to form another company under his own name making 125cc two-stroke motorcycles at Bologna. The involvement of Italy in the war prevented the Morini from earning any great reputation, but in post-war years the factory competed enthusiastically in the 125cc class of international road racing.

The stunning impact in 1948 of the overhead camshaft Mondial on the 125cc class persuaded Alfonso Morini to turn to four-strokes. Many were raced by customers and occasionally by the factory themselves. During the 1950s the 175cc single ohc Rebello was very popular, and was eventually developed into a 68 × 68mm 250cc model. Then in 1957 the factory decided to go racing with a completely new double overhead camshaft model of over-square bore and stroke at 72 × 61mm, 250cc. The camshafts were driven by a train of gears and the valves controlled by hairpin springs. The engine and gearbox castings were magnesium alloy. Primary drive to an open dry clutch was used, with a five-speed (later six-speed) gearbox. There were twin coils and sparking plugs and the claimed power output was a remarkable, but believable, 30 hp at a dizzy 10,000 rpm.

The frame was a conventional twin-loop cradle, with swinging arm rear suspension and spring damper units, Ceriani telescopic front forks and Amadori brakes – twin leading shoe at the front, single at the rear. From the start the bike was notably light and a weight of less than 240 lb was quoted. The first time that the Morini hit the headlines was at Monza in September 1958, when riders Emilio Mendogni and Giampiero Zubani humiliated the works MV twins by finishing first and second, ahead of Carlo Ubbiali, and caused Tarquinio Provini to blow up his engine in their pursuit! But despite this remarkable result and several other good results, Morini did not really achieve prominence until 1960, when they scraped together enough money to retain the legendary Provini as their sole works rider. Even then, their programme was limited, and not an unqualified success. In the season's opening event at Cesenatico, the engine appeared to be off-song, and Provini could do no better than third behind Carlo Ubbiali and Gary Hocking on the MV twins.

A week later at Imola, Ubbiali won again when Provini broke down whilst challenging for the lead. Then in Holland, Provini simply ran away from the MVs for ten laps, but fell back with a broken spring in the rear brake, after setting fastest lap. At the TT, after lying second to Gary Hocking's MV until the start of the last

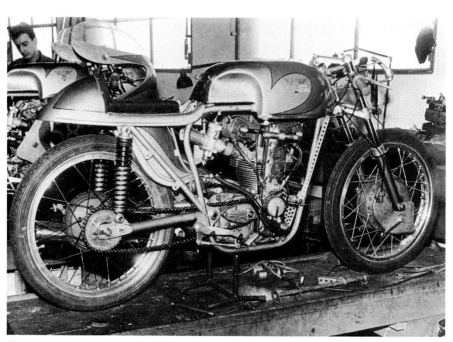

The 1959 Morini 250cc that Provini took over the following season.

Simplicity! Perhaps the most highly developed single-cylinder four-stroke engine the World has ever known. Here the engine is seen in 1960 form.

lap, Provini was passed half-way round the circuit by Ubbiali and they finished in that order. As some measure of the speed of the Italian machines at that time, Hocking averaged 93.64 mph, Ubbiali 93.13 mph and Provini 92.98 mph. The first four-cylinder Honda, ridden by Bob Brown, averaged 89.21 mph. At Spa-Francorchamps in Belgium, Provini unfortunately crashed spectacularly on the first lap! During the season, Provini fed back valuable suggestions to improve the bike, and along the way the oil was transferred to a large finned wet sump, the frame was lowered and the fairing, already a notably clean 'Dolphin' design, was improved.

The 1961 season began for Morini at Imola. Now claimed to develop 32 hp, the bike was visibly faster and Provini won the 250cc race ahead of Silvio Grassetti and Bruno Spaggiari on their single-cylinder Benellis, Hans Fischer on the MZ twin-cylinder two-stroke and Tom Phillis on the Honda four. Provini also set the fastest lap. In Spain, Provini fell whilst chasing Hocking on the MV. At Hockenheim, he was third to Takahashi and Redman on their four-cylinder Hondas in what was one of the most exciting races of his career and in France he was fourth. He did not race again until Monza in September, when he again finished fourth. Morini did not visit the TT, in 1961 or 1962. In fact, in 1962 Provini rode in the Classics only at Assen, where he was third behind the Hondas of Redman and Bob McIntyre, and at Monza in September, when he finished second to Redman and in front of the others works Hondas.

1963 was to be a very different story. With by now a fairly staggering 38 hp at 11.000 rpm, the single-cylinder Morini was faster than ever, and Provini's handling of it was phenomenal – once seen never forgotten! After early wins at Modena and Imola, Provini sensationally won the Spanish Grand Prix, beating the whole four-cylinder Honda team of Redman, Tommy Robb, Takahashi and Luigi Taveri! 'Well, yes,' said some people. 'He *could* do that on a scratcher's circuit like

Tarquinio Provini scorches to a win on the 250cc Morini at the Spanish Grand Prix in 1963.

Montjuich Park.' But even the most doubting were silenced when, three weeks later, Provini repeated the performance by winning at Hockenheim, the fastest and simplest track in Europe, 4.8-miles long and consisting of two long straights and two slowish corners.

Winning the 96-mile race at 116.26 mph, Provini also set fastest lap at 118.27 mph. Morini did not go to the TT, which was in retrospect a mistake, for on form, both man and machine could well have picked up valuable Championship points. So confident was Provini by now that when, at Assen, he was beaten by Jim Redman's Honda and Fumio Ito's Yamaha twin, he protested and caused Redman's engine to be measured! Redman was not racing at Spa, having broken his collarbone at Assen in the 125cc event after his 250cc win, but though he beat the remaining Honda riders, Provini could not catch the Yamaha two-strokes of Fumio Ito and Yosh Sunako, and had to settle for third place. At the Ulster Grand Prix, though he made the fastest lap, Provini again finished second to a recovered Redman. Then at Monza, Provini revived his and Morini's chances of world titles by beating Redman fair and square by an unarguable 14 seconds! Sensationally, lying third until, on the eleventh lap, he had to make a lengthy pit stop, was another Morini rider, the then little known Giacomo Agostini.

Morini's star was really shining after the Argentine Grand Prix in October, for once again Provini beat Redman and with four outright wins to Redman's three during the season, Redman *had* to win in Japan, the final round, if he were to beat Provini.

Indicative of the Morini's performance at this time was the fact that in the Argentine, Provini's fastest lap was, incredibly, a mere $^1/_5$ second slower than Mike Hailwood's fastest on his 500cc MV four! But at Suzuka in Japan, Provini was strangely and sadly off form due, it was said later, to fatigue and his constitutional intolerance of Japanese food. Be that as it may, he trailed into fourth place behind

Redman, Fumio Ito and Phil Read (invited out to Japan by the factory) on Yamahas. Morini had worked a near miracle, so had Provini, but that was to be the end. For 1964, Provini was with Benelli, riding their 250cc four, and Morini greatly reduced their racing activities, giving best in the Classics and supporting Giacomo Agostini in home events. At the Italian Grand Prix in 1964, he was an excellent fourth to Phil Read and Mike Duff on Yamahas and Jim Redman on the six-cylinder Honda. The rest is anti-climax. How *did* a comparatively tiny concern such as Morini manage to shake the complacency of the dominant Japanese racing teams with such a relatively unsophisticated single-cylinder machine? Not an easy question to answer. That Provini was not only one of the greatest riders of his day but also a superb development rider is part of the story, and so is the way in which the bike was continuously modified to reduce weight, drag and frontal area so as to make the most of the necessarily limited power.

Provini's knowhow assured that the handling was absolutely impeccable, which was not always the case with the machines that his rivals were riding. The engine's ultra-short stroke meant that it was compact and light at some expense in flywheel effect, and that it could safely be taken to an astronomical speed in the gears. But the main reason for the bike's phenomenal power and speed was superb design and development in the combination of porting, cylinder head design and the cams which controlled the sequence of valve events. That the Morini race shop tried both desmodromic valve gear and four valves instead of two and with neither layout found any benefit, speaks volumes for the work of development chief Ing. Biavatti and his colleagues Gino Marchesini and Dante Lambertini. Far more than the factory Nortons, the Morini deserves the accolade of the most highly developed single-cylinder racing engine ever built.

Fortunately, Morini are still in business, still making sporting motorcycles and the racing machines from the early 1960s have survived in good condition.

Moto Guzzi
1921–39

In the light of later history, it comes as quite a surprise to find out how rare were native motorcycles in Italy before the First World War. Even when peace returned, in Italy, as elsewhere in Europe, there was an upsurge of interest in motorcycles and motorcycle sport, many machines were imported, and there were ready sales to wealthy enthusiasts of the more sporting British makes like Norton, Sunbeam and AJS.

Two young enthusiasts (who had met whilst serving together in the Italian air force) had anticipated this post-war interest in two-wheeled transport and had planned to develop and produce a sporting Italian motorcycle. One of them, Carlo Guzzi, was a wonderfully intuitive engineer, but he was also logical, methodical and practical. His partner Giorgio Parodi supplied the finance and, of even more value (if that is possible), the entrepreneurial skill that kept the Guzzi concern alive in the difficult early days.

A prototype was built and tested extensively through 1920. It was a brilliant anticipation of a theme of design which would serve Guzzi for racing for 35 years. The engine and gearbox were in unit, with primary drive by gears.

To keep the bottom half of the engine robust and stiff, there was an outside flywheel, so that the crankcases were very compact, and this was further aided by the over-square bore and stroke of 88 × 82mm, 499cc. Truly astonishing for the time was the use of four overhead valves activated by a single overhead camshaft driven by shaft and bevels. This advanced unit lay horizontally in a robust double-loop cradle frame, sprung at the front with 'girder' parallel-ruler forks.

Guzzi's first visit to the Island in 1926. The 500cc model with the Parodi brothers, rider Piero Ghersi, Jimmy Simpson (in waistcoat) and the mechanic. After lapping at 68mph, Ghersi fell on lap three.

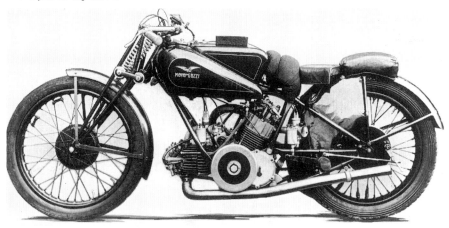

The original 1933 500cc 'Bicilindrica' with rigid frame.

Final drive was by chain, and there were large-diameter internal expanding drum brakes front and rear.

Disappointingly, when production of Moto Guzzi motorcycles began, in a tiny factory at Mandello de Lario, near Lake Como in northern Italy, the front brake had been deleted, and the advanced valve gears had been replaced by a cylinder head with a side exhaust valve and a single central inlet valve activated by a push-rod and rocker. However, in 1923, Guzzi reverted to overhead camshaft operation of first two, then four valves for a racing programme, in which some early success was achieved. Then in 1924 the name of Guzzi was considerably enhanced by a win in the Grand Prix of Europe, which that year was held at Monza. Guzzi machines finished first, second and fifth in the 500cc race.

Replicas of the winning machine, the Corsa four valve (C4V), were sold to private customers with a good record (rather as were Manx Nortons and Gilera Saturnos and indeed Guzzi Dondolinos and Albatrosses thirty years later on), the design being successively uprated year by year until 1933. However, of even more importance was the launching for the 1927 season of a 68 × 68mm 247cc racer known as the 250 TT. Nor was this designation an idle one, for such a machine had indeed been raced in the Isle of Man in the 1926 races and had done remarkably well. Except that its single overhead camshaft operated two valves instead of four, the 250 TT was very much a scaled-down version of the bigger machine.

In the 1926 Lightweight TT, rider Piero Ghersi at his and Guzzi's first visit to the Island, finished a very close second to Paddy Johnston's Cotton, and furthermore made fastest lap at an impressive 63.12 mph. Very unfortunately, Ghersi was quickly disqualified for having used a sparking plug of a make other than that declared on his entry! This may sound a harsh decision by the ACU, but it was the time of the 'bonus scandal', when fuel, oil and accessory companies were paying ever-increasing sums for wins and places, the results being used for advertising.

Unscrupulous riders would negotiate large sums with a trade representative – and then use not the product advertised but what was tried and trusted! The resulting advertising, felt the ACU, was a fraud on the public. The Guzzi team had been carefully warned in advance about the situation and though they protested volubly, the ACU stood firm. Generously they allowed Ghersi credit for his fastest (record) lap. Fortunately, disappointed though they were, Guzzi returned to the Isle of Man and continued to return. In 1935 they made history by being the first 'foreign' maker to win a TT since 1920. Not the first foreign make to win a TT – that honour went to the American firm of Indian with a resounding 1–2–3 in the 1911 Senior race – but in 1935 Guzzi won both the 250cc Lightweight race and the 500cc Senior! Rider in both events was Irishman Stanley Woods, who won the Lightweight (leading from start to finish) at 71.56 mph and with a record fastest lap at 74.19 mph. Both 250cc and 500cc machines were outstanding in having rear springing of Carlo Guzzi's design, with a triangulated swinging rear fork, controlled by compression springs lying fore and aft beneath the engine unit, and with friction dampers adjustable from the saddle. Woods' Senior mount was one of

Shock, Horror! A foreign bike wins the Senior! Stanley Woods on the spring-frame 'Bicilindrica' in 1935.

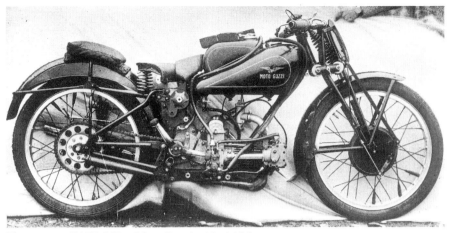

The pre-war (1937) 250cc Moto Guzzi with rigid frame.

Carlo Guzzi's 'Bicilindrica' 120-degree Vee twins, first seen in Grand Prix events in 1934. It had been an immediate success.

The cycle parts resembled those of the smaller machine, and the engine was in effect 'doubled up' from the 250cc. Though the cylinders were set at 120 degrees to one another, they fired (like a parallel twin) at 180 degress, this being achieved by a three-bearing crankshaft with four crank-webs, a centre main bearing and two offset crankpins. Guzzi claimed 47 hp at 7500 rpm – almost certainly an exaggeration – but the machine was fast, agile and, with its excellent balance, far less tiring to ride than a 500cc single. Woods won the Senior race by brilliant strategy; he knew that he and his machine were not as fast as the combination of works Norton and rider Jimmy Guthrie that he had to beat. Guthrie was number one away, starting no less than 15 minutes ahead of Woods. Over the first six laps of the seven-lap race, Woods consistently lost ground to Guthrie, so that at the end of that time he was 26 seconds behind. Furthermore, as Guthrie approached the end of lap six, a dejected-looking Guzzi pit crew had begun to check the arrangements for replenishing the fuel and oil of Woods' machine at the end of the penultimate lap. Thus it was that in an evil moment the Norton teams signalled to Guthrie to make his last lap an easy one, and not to risk a blow-in in extending his lead over a rider and machine already beaten.

Then to their considerable consternation, Woods, instead of stopping, howled down the Glencrutchery road and past the pits at full speed! Even so, Norton did not expect him to catch Guthrie on time, and when their rider took the flag, he was in fact acclaimed the winner. But they had miscalculated. In a last stupendous lap with a perilously low fuel load, Stanley Woods rode the race of a lifetime, raised the lap record by 4 mph and clawed back the 26-second deficit *and* another four seconds, to win!

In 1937, Guzzi broke another record in the Island, when their top Italian rider, the remarkable Omobono Tenni, won the Lightweight race again, the first foreign rider to win on a foreign machine. Although he also rode in the Senior race, Tenni had no such success with the Bicilindrica and retired on the fourth lap. The last few seasons of Grand Prix racing were overshadowed by the use of superchargers, notably by Gilera and BMW. Guzzi too, experimented in this area and had considerable success in 1939, including first and second places by Nello Pagani and Giovanni Sandri at, of all places, the German Grand Prix, where they beat the all-conquering blown two-stroke DKWs on their home ground.

During the late 1930s, Guzzi continued to sell 'over the counter' racing machines to their customers, notably the 250cc Albatross, a continuation of the original

TT250, and the 88 × 82mm 499cc Condor. Needless to say, a few ex-works machines finished up in private hands. None of the Bicilindricas were sold privately, with one exception. For 1937 the up-and-coming young English rider Maurice Cann (that year he won both Junior and Senior Manx Grand Prix races) bought and reconditioned an ancient 250cc Guzzi that he discovered abandoned in a builder's yard. Unknown to him, it was the machine on which Paddy Johnston had finished eighth in the 1931 Lightweight TT. Cann, a skilled engineer, made such a good job of the rebuild that he was able to use the little Guzzi to win races, and these results came to the notice of Giorgio Parodi. For whatever reason, Parodi wrote to Maurice Cann offering a Bicilindrica – at a price! Steep though it was, Cann could not turn down the chance, but though he used the machine in short-circuit events in late 1938 and rode it in the Senior TT in 1939 (he finished ninth with severe handling problems), the outbreak of war cruelly abbreviated his career. Pursuing their experiments with supercharging, Guzzi built a three-cylinder air-cooled double overhead camshaft engine machine for 1940, but it was too late to be developed and was not pursued after the war.

Of all the Italian manufacturers Guzzi were, pre-war, the boldest, they were early to visit the Isle of Man, and unlike some other factories who did so they persisted, gaining the respect of the world. Even so, they were in pre-war days curiously inconsistent, and never actually fielded a strong well-directed team. They seemed to prefer to sponsor promising riders all over Europe with a 'works' bike, a certain amount of financial assistance, and some help from factory mechanics at the major events. It was to some extent a pattern that was to emerge again in the years after the Second World War.

1946–1957

Italy entered Hitler's war late and left it early and suffered comparatively lightly – economically hardly at all. In 1946 Italian industry and in particular the motorcycle industry was rather better off than otherwise, and as after the First World War there was a huge demand for two-wheeled transport. Moto Guzzi, largest by far of the Italian makers – they employed more than 1500 at Mandello del Lario – responded with a delightful little 65cc two-stroke that sold in its tens of thousands. But they did not neglect racing, and the 68 × 68mm (247cc) Albatross and the 88 × 82mm Dondolino (an uprated version of the Condor with push-rod ohv head) were soon available to private customers. Both models featured pre-war type Guzzi suspension and both had parallel-ruler-type girder front forks at first. In 1946, the 500cc Dondolino (which translates as rocking chair) was joined by the long stroke 84 × 90mm Gambalunga (long-leg) of 499cc.

This was the first design in which a young engineer, Giulio Carcano, who had joined Moto Guzzi in 1936, played a major part. It introduced his design of bottom-link front forks that were quickly adopted for all the others models and were to be used on Guzzi racing machines for the next twenty years.

Far stiffer torsionally than telescopic forks, they reduced unsprung weight to a minimum, incorporated a natural anti-diving tendency, and used oil-damped spring struts concealed within the stanchions. Although at this time Giulio Carcano was subordinate to designer Antonio Micucci, he was eventually to become synonymous with the Moto Guzzi racing department and their successes.

Moto Guzzi were determined to re-enter international racing, and high on their list of priorities was the Isle of Man. For the first post-war TT in 1947, they sent over Giorgio Parodi, Antonio Micucci, head mechanic Moretto and two assistant mechanics. The machinery they brought – a Bicilindrica for the Senior race and a Albatross for the Lightweight, were entered by Stanley woods, the man who had given them two TT wins in one week back in 1935. Though himself retired from racing, Stanley was still keenly interested and involved. For the Senior race he entered the formidable Freddie Frith, pre-war a Norton team rider who had won the Junior in 1936, the Senior in 1937 and whose TT record was impeccable. Unfortunately Frith was not to race in the 1947 Senior. In a practice session, plagued by intermittent rain showers, he crashed heavily on the Tuesday evening at Ballacraine when the front brake momentarily locked.

With dislocated shoulder and a broken collarbone, poor Frith was eliminated from both Senior and Junior races – for the latter of which he was an odds-on favourite on his factory Velocette. Despite rumours, Stanley Woods did not attempt to substitute another rider. For the Lightweight race, Stanley had entered fellow-Dubliner Manliffe Barrington who, along with Maurice Cann on his privately entered but works assisted Albatross, dominated Lightweight practice. Although their opposition consisted almost entirely of pre-war British machinery, there was a very real danger that racing on the appalling 72-octane fuel specified, the highly developed Guzzis might break down, allowing a privateer to win, but in fact both finished, Barrington first and Cann second. Roland Pike on his home-brewed two-valve Rudge special was a distant third. There was controversy over the placings, for many believed – and with some reason – that the ACU timekeepers had inadvertently added a whole minute to Maurice Cann's last lap! The result stood, Barrington being confirmed the winner at 73.22mph, fastest lap being by Cann at 74.78mph. The Moto Guzzi contingent went home well pleased and determined to win the senior race as well in 1948.

Early in that year 'Torrens' – Arthur Bourne of *The Motorcycle* visited Mandello and was amazed to discover how for advanced the factory was on a peacetime footing, and how Italy suffered none of the rationing and shortages of materials that still prevailed in Britain, more than two years after the war's end. In particular, writing of the post-war designs, 'Torrens' raved about the 250cc racer designed by Micucci, and conceived as the basis for a family of racing machines. A 54×54mm parallel twin with two overhead camshafts driven by a train of spur gears, it offered the possibility of a 125cc single and a 500cc four all using common parts. The engine was canted forward at 30 degrees from the horizontal, in unit with the four-speed gearbox, in a typically Guzzi frame, with triangulated swinging rear fork, spring units beneath the engine and robust telescopic front forks. The brakes were enormous – larger than those fitted the year before to the 500cc Bicilindrica! 'Torrens' was given every courtesy by the enthusiastic Italians and was allowed to ride the twin on the Autostrada and on the roads near Lake Como. He was ecstatic about everything to do with it and concluded, 'Good though the single cylinder racing 250 is, I put this new 250cc twin almost in a class apart.'

Alas, for all that, the twin and the projected 125cc single and 500cc four all came to nothing in the end, when Antonio Micucci transferred to a position in charge of Guzzi's main design department at the start of 1949. Today most enthusiasts – even Moto Guzzi enthusiasts would contend that the twin was a 'failure' but many of the reasons given for its abandonment are totally specious and are, alas, part of the myth that has grown up around Moto Guzzi forty years after the event! The 250cc twin came over the 1948 Lightweight TT, as did Bicilindricas for Italian veteran Omobono Tenni and Irishman Ernie Lyons to ride in the Senior race. Stanley Woods was still in charge, and the 250cc twin was to be ridden by the previous year's winner, Manliffe Barrington. Again, Giorgio Parodi, Micucci and mechanics Felici Bettega, Carlo Agostini and Luigi Agostini were in the Island. All the machines now had a new frame designed by Micucci (and often attributed to Giulio Carcano) that carried the oil in a 4-in-diameter top tube through which the steering head passed to obtain maximum rigidity. Two-leading-shoe brakes were another innovation. On the 250cc twin, Barrington made the fastest lap in practice, and led the Lightweight race for two laps before he retired, allowing privateer Maurice Cann to win and make fastest lap.

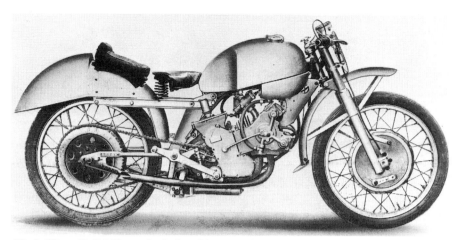

The brilliant 1948 250cc twin designed by Antonio Micucci. Foolishly discarded the following season, it could have been the basis of 125cc and 500cc machinery.

Fergus Anderson, who officially joined Guzzi the following year, cleans his Albatross in the paddock at Shaffhausen, Switzerland in 1948.

The 500cc Dondolino (little rocking chair) of 1947.

In the Senior race, Ernie Lyons got only as far as the Bungalow before falling off, but Omobono Tenni, who had frightened the Norton factory team with fastest lap in practice, stormed into an instant lead, which he held for four laps despite a lengthy pit stop on lap three. His fourth lap was the fastest of the race at 88.06 mph, but subsequent trouble with sparking plugs saw him slow badly to finish a disappointing ninth.

1949 was a year of considerable importance in the history of the Guzzi racing department, and not only because it was the year in which the World Championships for riders and constructors was instituted. In 1949 Giulio Carcano took over Antonio Miccuci's position, and Fergus Anderson, following a three-year association with Guzzi, became a member of the team. Today Fergus Anderson is often forgotten when Guzzi's great years are discussed, and he is, more than 30 years after his untimely death, in danger of being edged out of the picture and into an undeserved obscurity (that never surrounded him in life) as the legends perpetuate themselves. Fergus was born in 1909, and though his family were Scottish, he was brought up and educated in England, and spoke with no trace of a Scottish accent. He was virtually the inventor of the Continental Circus before the war and its most active member after. He rode his first race in 1932 at the Spanish Grand Prix, and thereafter made a living riding at every meeting he could attend, humping his machinery on and off trains all across Europe. By concentrating on minor events, he amassed a knowledge and skill that amounted to genius. In 1946 he was perhaps the first man to acquire a new 250cc Moto Guzzi, and begin a loose allegiance that became far firmer when the factory lost their veteran rider Omobono Tenni who was killed in the 1948 Swiss Grand Prix, only weeks after his brilliant ride in the Senior TT. Thereafter Fergus was given a 250cc Albatross and a 500cc Bicilindrica and allowed to pursue his own course. Prophetically, he often rode (and won) in minor 350cc races with the smaller machine. With the advent of the World Championships in 1949, there came a consolidation of the Moto Guzzi racing department and Anderson's acceptance as development rider, a task at which he had no equal. An extremely outspoken man, he did not suffer fools gladly, but amongst equals he was a valuable ally. In Dr Giorgio Parodi and the young Giulio Carcano he recognized equals and the three men became the firmest of friends.

It should be understood that to a large extent the racing department was the personal creation of the extremely and independently wealthy Dr Parodi, and though he was an unfailingly pleasant and generous man, it was his to do with as he

Maurice Cann's home-converted dohc Albatross that was good enough for the factory to borrow and copy!

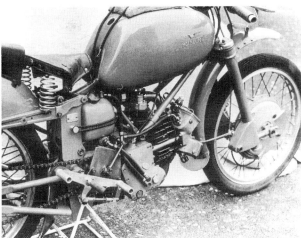

Though Guzzi did not officially race in 1950, they developed this 350cc model with five speeds. It was an absolute failure!

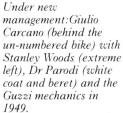

Under new management:Giulio Carcano (behind the un-numbered bike) with Stanley Woods (extreme left), Dr Parodi (white coat and beret) and the Guzzi mechanics in 1949.

pleased. Carlo Guzzi too, although adopting a lower profile than his partner, took a keen personal interest. Though the department was to some degree self-funding, and its cost could largely be written off against tax, there were occasions when Parodi used his own money to underwrite its activities: it was he who guaranteed the cost of building the Moto Guzzi wind tunnel designed by Giuseppe Guzzi, younger brother of Carlo. At the time this must have seemed an extravagance with little relevance to motorcycle production, but Parodi could afford to indulge his conviction that the wind tunnel would be of value in the future, as indeed it was. For the 1949 TT, Dr Parodi and (for the first time) Ing. Carcano were in the Island with Moretto and three other mechanics. Engaged to ride the still further-developed Bicilindrica in the Senior was British veteran Bob Foster, who had spent some time at Mandello during May. In the Lightweight race, Guzzi entered Enrico Lorenzetti and Manliffe Barrington and also gave support to several British riders who were competing on Albatrosses.

Lorenzetti and Barrington had new Gambalunghinas (little long leg), but despite the implications of the nickname, these were simply an uprated version of the Albatross with its 'square' bore and stroke. In the race Lorenzetti retired on lap three out of seven. Also Guzzi-mounted were Tommy Wood and Dickie Dale on their Albatrosses and curiously enough, both shared fastest lap at 80.44 mph. Dale retired on lap four and Tommy Wood then led the race, but Barrington passed him on the penultimate lap and they finished in that order, Barrington having averaged 77.98 mph.

In the Junior race, Italian rider Bruno Bestacchi was entered on a 350cc version of the Bicilindrica, but not too surprisingly this machine was a disappointment and was not pursued thereafter. The Senior race was yet another cruel disappointment for the Guzzi team. Bob Foster began brilliantly and on his second lap averaged 89.75 mph to take the lead from the AJS Porcupine twins of Ted Frend and Les Graham. This lead he held comfortably until half-way around the penultimate lap, when he coasted to a halt at Sulby with a sheared drive-side mainshaft.

Moto Guzzi had the consolation at the season's end of having won the first Constructor's Championship in the 250cc class, rider Bruno Ruffo having scraped to a win in the individual title. It has to be admitted that 1950 was not a very good year for the Moto Guzzi race department; no doubt, as a new organization it had to bed down, but some dubious decisions seem to have been made. Having quite rightly rejected the 350cc Bicilindrica, Carcano designed a new 78 × 73mm 349cc single with four valves and single overhead camshaft. With a five-speed gearbox, this was fitted into a Gambalunghina frame and used at Mettet by Enrico Lorenzetti. It was not as fast as Les Graham's 7R JS and eventually seized. Rebuilt, it was sent to the Isle of Man for Maurice Cann to ride, but he chose instead to use an overbored 310cc Gambalunghina, which retired with a broken valve. Both machines went back to Mandello and the 350 was abruptly abandoned. In the Lightweight TT Cann's Guzzi was no match for Dario Ambrosini's basically pre-war single-cylinder Benelli, which won the race at 78.08 mph with a new record fastest lap at 80.90 mph. Bob Foster was again the sole entry on a Bicilindrica in the Senior race, but he was never higher than sixth place and again retired on the last lap but one.

Soon after this depressing TT Moto Guzzi temporarily withdrew from Classic racing. Without doubt they were rattled at being beaten early in the season by the 250cc Benelli, which went on to win the Championship for Ambrosini and for its constructors. Probably Guzzi regretted the time spent on the aborted 350 single. The Bicilindrica now appeared badly in need of development, having been disappointingly slow at the TT. It may have been coincidence, but for the 1950 season the permitted octane rating of the fuel had been raised dramatically. Could this have caught the race department off balance? Were they distracted by the fact that the long-awaited wind tunnel was nearing completion?

Omobono Tenni at Ballaugh in the 1948 Senior TT on Antonio Micucci's redesign of the Bicilindrica. It weighed nearly 70lb less than originally.

In particular, Carcano's reluctance to develop the Bicilindrica is puzzling. Despite its 17-year history, this machine had many virtues and would appear to have offered considerable potential still for improvement. It was no wider than a single – something that ought to have recommended it to Carcano. Despite some thoughtless claims, it was far from 'overweight', scaling less than 280 lb dry, a good 50 lb less than a factory Norton. In its post-war form, handling was beyond reproach, as highlighted by its last victory in international competition, when Fergus Anderson rode it to a win at the 1951 Swiss Grand Prix in atrocious conditions.

All in all, one is left wondering why it could not have been given a new lease of life. Instead, perhaps in frustration, perhaps to demonstrate who was the ultimate boss, Giorgio Parodi chose to commission a replacement design from consulting engineering Carlo Gianini in Rome. Gianini had all those years earlier been in partnership with Piero Remor in the early days of the OPRA and Rondine adventures that led to the pre-war four-cylinder supercharged Gilera. This move would not have gone down very well with Ing. Carcano, even though the resulting in-line four did not materialize until well into 1952.

Be that as it may, Guzzi did not officially enter the TT during 1951 and Anderson and Lorenzetti were on their own in the Island. From the start, Fergus Anderson led, and at the end of the first lap had a remarkable 44-second lead over Tommy Wood, with Ambrosini surprisingly relegated to third place. A lap later, having broken the lap record at 83.70 mph, Anderson's lead had extended to 1 minute and 31 seconds! But on the third of the four laps, his engine broke its connecting rod at Ballig. Tommy Wood, riding the race of a lifetime, fended off Ambrosini's challenge on the Benelli to win at 81.39 mph, and Enrico Lorenzetti finished a good third.

Maurice Cann for once did not ride in the Lightweight. Deciding that his pre-war Bicilindrica (now fitted with many post-war parts, including Gambalunga front forks and brake) should be still good for a replica, he entered it for the Senior race. In practice, doing 120 mph flat out downhill at Glen Vine, the bottom stays of the front mudguard snapped simultaneously so that the mudguard caught the tyre and instantly acted as a self-servo brake! In the resultant spectacular crash, Cann was lucky to escape with his life, but with severe concussion and an injured hand any racing was out of the question.

At the Swiss Grand Prix, poor Ambrosini was killed during practice and a shocked Benelli family withdrew from racing. The 250cc class in Switzerland became a walkover for Guzzi, who filled the first four places. Bruno Ruffo beat Maurice Cann to win the Ulster Grand Prix and at Monza he was the first of six Guzzis to finish in line astern, thus again winning the World Championships for himself and the factory.

For 1952 the team was to concentrate on the 250cc class, the bicilindrica having finally been pensioned off. The machines had new frames with conventional swinging arm and vertical spring-damper units. Large-bore Dell'Orto racing carburettors were now carried, not on curved inlet pipes but at a steep angle on long, straight flexibly mounted tracts. During 1951, Maurice Cann had raced with an impressive double overhead camshaft cylinder head of his own design and make, which had so impressed Giorgio Parodi that he had begged the loan of it from the Leicester engineer over the winter. Thereafter the Guzzis featured double ohc heads, but early in 1952 there was a bewildering variety of dohc, sohc, four-valve and two-valve configurations to be seen before eventually the racing department settled for two valves and dohc.

At the TT Fergus Anderson won the Lightweight race at 83.82 mph, followed home by Lorenzetti and Syd Lawton on a spare factory Guzzi. Maurice Cann, who had blown up his own machine in practice, was also on a spare factory machine and finished fifth. Bruno Ruffo had made fastest lap at 84.82 mph, and led for the second and third laps, but had to stop on the last lap to change a plug, and finished sixth. With a win at Assen, second to Maurice Cann at the Ulster and a win at Monza, Enrico Lorenzetti became World Champion, and Moto Guzzi held the title for the third time in four years.

But 1953 was the last year in which Moto Guzzi were serious contenders in the Lightweight class. They had been caught up and were about to be overtaken by the German NSU twin. (Did anyone think of what might, have been had their own twin of 1948 been developed?)

The 1951 250cc with four valves and twin carburettors. 'Try anything' seemed to be the motto at the time.

End of the line for the 'Bicilindrica': the final 1950 version.

That 1954 was not another barren season for Moto Guzzi comes close to having been a lucky accident! Over the winter, Fergus Anderson had successfully argued for the resuscitation of the 310cc single that Maurice Cann had used in the TT four years earlier. He proved the value of his intuition with an astonishing victory at the International meeting at Hockenheim, and Guzzi prepared a machine of 320cc (actually at 72 × 79mm, 317cc) for Anderson's use in the Junior TT. His remarkable third place at 89.41 mph compared with the 90.52 mph of the winner, Ray Amm and the 90.44 mph of runner-up Ken Kavanagh, both works Norton mounted, had a decisive and stimulating effect upon Carcano's thinking thereafter.

The 250cc Lightweight TT was another remarkable triumph for Moto Guzzi, though most unfortunately the brilliant Bruno Ruffo did not ride, having broken his leg so badly in practice as to end his racing career there and then.

Fergus Anderson won at 84.73 mph, narrowly beating the up-and-coming young German Werner Haas on the NSU. Anderson also made fastest lap at 85.52 mph, but it was Guzzi's swan song in the 250cc class – the remainder of the season was dominated by Werner Haas and Rupert Hollaus on their twin-cylinder NSUs. Moto Guzzi's only other Classic wins that year were by Lorenzetti at Monza and Barcelona, and Haas and NSU won the Championships for 1953.

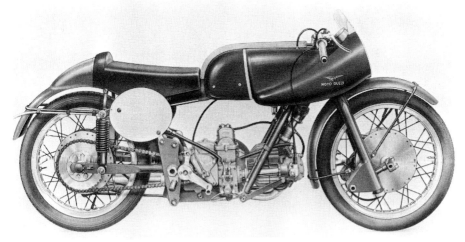

The famous Gambalunghina 250cc – 'Little long leg'. Seen here is the 1953 version.

The 350cc class was another story. By July, the race department had built entirely new bikes of 75 × 78mm (345cc) with five-speed gearboxes and rudimentary streamlining. At the Dutch Grand Prix on the 10.2-mile Van Drenthe circuit, Anderson lapped at 91.29 mph from a standing start and he and Lorenzetti led the Nortons of Ray Amm and Ken Kavanagh by 500 yards! Anderson lost time with a pit stop to adjust his clutch and later retired with a split petrol tank. He made the fastest lap at a hair-raising 96.28 mph. Lorenzetti (who also suffered from a split tank in the last few laps) won the race by 22 seconds from Ray Amm, at a speed of 93.44 mph. Pretty convincing stuff, and in Belgium, Anderson and Lorenzetti again led the Norton team home. In Switzerland, another win for Fergus, and at Monza Lorenzetti won (and made fastest lap) ahead of Anderson and new recruit Duilio Agostini. In the 250cc event, Lorenzetti won again, beating Werner Haas and lapping at an amazing 100.17 mph, but this was not enough to offset results earlier in the season! At Monza, Moto Guzzi were joined by Ken Kavanagh, who was to replace Bruno Ruffo in World Championship events.

Fergus Anderson's surprise 350cc Championship had been won more by lucky intuition on his part than by any logical, deep-laid, long-term scheme. Carcano was bright enough to carry the winning formula a step further, and the last event of the season, the Spanish Grand Prix, gave him a chance to test the theory that was coming together in his mind. Moto Guzzi overran the 250cc event in the absence of NSU, Lorenzetti, Kavanagh and Anderson leading home another four Moto Guzzi riders, including Rupert Hollaus, having something of a busman's holiday! There was no 350cc class, but instead all three Guzzi riders were entered in the 500cc race. That this was run in relentlessly pouring rain hampered efforts by the riders of Nortons, MVs and Gileras to use their superior power around the little 2.4-mile circuit, and though Lorenzetti and Kavanagh eventually retired, the 350cc Guzzis dominated the race. Anderson led from start to finish – at half-

As originally raced. The shaft-drive in-line four ridden here by Fergus Anderson into seventh place in the 1953 Belgian Grand Prix.

distance he had a 56-second lead! He was able to slow down quite deliberately and still finish well ahead of the four-cylinder MV of Carlo Bandirola and the four-cylinder Gileras of Dickie Dale, Giuseppe Colnago and Nello Pagani. Another precedent had been set, to be consolidated over the winter months.

With this victory there disappeared any lingering hopes that Guzzis might pursue development of the Gianini-designed in-line four that had been commissioned late in 1950. Built, as well as designed, in Rome, the prototype had been delivered to Mandello del Lario in 1952. The in-line four is now often written off as a 'flop', and as with the 250cc twin of 1948 various specious reasons for its 'failure' have been advanced. In fact the main reason for its low profile was the syndrome of 'Not Invented Here' and the sad fact that Giorgio Parodi's health was in decline in 1953 and 1954 (he died in mid-1955) and consequently he did not exert his authority as he might have done at an earlier time.

As it was delivered, Giulio Carcano claimed that the engine was 'good – but not that good' and that the frame was 'useless, too heavy, too high, totally inefficient.' His redesign of the frame was brilliant, and led to the clever 'space-frames' used on the single-cylinder machines of 1954 and 1955. The use, too, of a rudimentary 'dustbin' fairing anticipated later developments. The in-line four, naturally enough, was liquid-cooled and used shaft final drive. Its advantages were its strikingly slim frontal profile, its low build as redesigned by Carcano and by repute a very flexible power delivery from a low speed. With twin overhead camshafts operating two valves per cylinder, the distinctly oversquare 56×50mm 493cc engine was straightforward in concept, but complicated in its detail design. Because of Gianini's insistence upon using one-piece connecting rods and one-piece big end cages, the crankshaft used horribly expensive Hirth couplings in its assembly. Its valves seated directly on the valve seats in the light alloy head, the seats being work-hardened by obduration within a few seconds of the engine's being started.

The most unorthodox feature of the engine was its carburation, or rather, lack of it. A system of cam-timed air blasts from a tiny Roots paddle-blower, concealed within the gearbox, atomized fuel fed continuously to jets in the individual inlet pipes (the surplus was scavenged and fed back to the petrol tank) by a gear-type pump. This system seems to have worked very well indeed. Disadvantages were chiefly concerned with the use of an engine speed clutch, which made for slow gear changes, and shaft-drive which with 60-odd bhp on tap led to peculiar handling when accelerating away from slow corners. No truly successful racing motorcycle has used shaft-drive. But to convert to chain-drive would not have been difficult. The in-line four was first seen in public at Monza during practice at the end of 1952. In May 1953 at Hockenheim, admittedly not the most demanding of circuits, Enrico Lorenzetti won the 500cc race and Fergus Anderson made fastest lap. A few more half-hearted appearances and the innovative machine was shelved. Anderson practised with one at the 1954 TT, but rode a single in the race. In February 1954 Moto Guzzi announced their plans for the year; they were for single-cylinder machines in 250cc, 350cc and 500cc capacities, all of them with two-valve heads, double overhead camshafts and five-speed gearboxes. The 250cc stayed at 68×68mm, the 500cc was the familiar 86×82mm bore and stroke, but the 350cc engine was well oversquare at 80×69.5mm. All were carried in the so-called 'Bailey Bridge' space-frames devised by Carcano to be used in conjunction with new 'dustbin' fairings designed around wind tunnel testing. All carried their fuel in tanks suspended below the top tubes of the space frames. At Hockenheim early in May, Anderson won the 350cc race and Ken Kavanagh the 500cc. Anderson rode an in-line four, but retired with a puncture. At the time, Fergus appears to have been something of a lone voice in wanting to pursue the in-line four, although in later years he admitted that its shaft-drive had given him some interesting moments!

As developed. The in line four in 1954 guise with dustbin nose fairing. Note the fuel injection 'trumpets'.

The space-frame single layout. Note the cylindrical fuel tank slung below the top frame tubes.

The 1954 TT was a downright disaster for Guzzi, their sole result being a fifth place for Fergus Anderson behind a string of NSUs in the Lightweight race, run on the Clypse course. Both Anderson and Kavanagh retired in the Junior and Senior races, neither having made much impression in either race.

In Belgium it was a happier story, with Kavanagh and Anderson first and second in the 350cc race and Kavanagh second to Geoff Duke in the 500cc event. In Holland in the 350cc race their positions were reversed, whilst again Kavanagh finished second to Geoff Duke in the 500cc class.

Wins in Switzerland, at Monza and in Spain in the 350cc class brought the Championships to Fergus Anderson and Guzzi for a second time. Now, with incredible insensitivity, the FIM chose to suspend Fergus Anderson's licence indefinitely! The 'reprehensible conduct' of which he was accused, and over which he was given no chance to defend himself, was that in his occasional pages of 'Continental Chatter' in *The Motorcycle*, he had aired the odd mild criticism of some aspects of the FIM's conduct of affairs. Moto Guzzi's immediate response was to show their confidence in Fergus by making him Team Manager for the 1955

*Another view of the
space frame 350cc of
1954.*

*From one extreme to the other. Dropping the space frame theme, Carcano reverted to
Micucci's large diameter top tube and extensively redesigned the front forks.*

season. But so outraged was general opinion by the FIM's heavy-handed behaviour
that Anderson's licence was in fact restored. For 1955, further refinement of the
bikes took place, though efforts were concentrated upon the 350cc and 500cc at the
expense of the 250cc machinery: new light alloy cylinders had hard chrome bores;
frames were even lower and slimmer; and the streamlining even more wind-
cheating. Above all the bikes were feather-light. Although only 35 hp at 7800 rpm
was claimed for the 350, its speed was phenomenal. Since his licence had been
restored, it had been Fergus Anderson's intention to ride as well as to manage the
Guzzi team, and indeed he did so at Mettet in Belgium in May and won both 350cc
and 500cc races.

But during practice at the TT the brilliant young Bill Lomas had a severe
disagreement with AMC, and Anderson, who knew a good rider when he saw one,
signed Bill there and then. It was a sensational debut, for after a slow start in the
350cc race, Bill went on to take the lead on lap five out of seven, won at a record
speed of 92.33 mph and his last lap was another record at 94.13 mph. Another new
Guzzi signing, Cecil Sandford, was third behind Bob McIntyre's Norton, riding a
1953 bike with 1954 streamlining. Duilio Agostini, strange to the Island, was
eighth at 87.84 mph. Ken Kavanagh retired on the third lap, but in the Senior he

made amends by finishing third to the Gilera of Geoff Duke and Reg Armstrong at a remarkable 95.16 mph. Bill Lomas finished fifth at 91.12 mph.

In Holland, Kavanagh, Lomas and Dale were 1–2–3 in the 350cc class, but did not compete in the 500cc race. With wins at the German Grand Prix, the Ulster Grand Prix and at Monza, Bill Lomas became World Champion in the 350cc class. One would have thought it an occasion for rejoicing, but, alas, for Fergus Anderson it was not. At this distance in time the details are not clear, but at some time during the season he must have been under an intolerable strain to resign, as he now did in a fairly bitter frame of mind. And to resign not only as team manager, but from any connection with Mandello del Lario, where, as he freely confirmed, he had spent the ten happiest years of his life. Perhaps he was more upset than he realized by the death of his old friend Giorgio Parodi and Carlo Guzzi, who might have provided a sympathetic ear for Fergus' grievances, and might perhaps have intervened on his behalf, was at the time deeply immersed in the design of a new road-going model, the Lodola. Be that as it may, Fergus shook the dust of Mandello from his feet. He still intended to ride on the Continent and could have joined DKW, but instead chose to go with BMW.

After a very indifferent ride at Imola and a much better one at Mettet, where he finished third, poor Fergus was killed competing at Florette with the BMW. He had made fastest lap of the 500cc race whilst chasing John Surtees' MV four, but then apparently eased off. According to contemporary reports, 'between the right-left bends in the village of Bujet, the tail of the BMW swung out on a patch of wet tar'. Later commentators have suggested that the cylinder head touched the ground. Whatever the reason, Anderson fell heavily, the bike struck the straw bales surrounding a steel telegraph pole, demolishing them. Anderson in turn hit the now unprotected pole and was instantly killed. The whole world of motorcycle racing mourned his death.

For 1956, Carcano chose to revert to a frame using the large-diameter top tube first introduced by Antonio Micucci eight years earlier. Now, still carried by a double-frame loop, the engines were suspended rather than cradled. Girling dampers with rebound springs were now carried outside the front fork stanchions. At the rear, the swinging arm, controlled also by Girling units, pivoted on a sturdy casting which was integral with the gearbox. The engines were little altered from those used in 1955.

Its final fling. The 350cc Moto Guzzi in its final year, 1957.

Officially riding for Moto Guzzi during 1956 were Bill Lomas, Ken Kavanagh and Dickie Dale. By now, however, Guzzi were seeing the 500cc single for the stop-gap that it was, so for that matter was the 350cc single, even though two more World Championships lay in the future, but the 350 had the subtle advantage that the opposition were racing scaled-down 500s, and their bulk and weight were in strict contrast to the handiness and tiny frontal area of the Guzzis.

The 500cc four-cylinder machines weighed little more, if any, than the 350cc, and in the 500cc class the single-cylinder Guzzi did not quite enjoy the edge it did as a 350. Nor was the 500cc model as reliable as it could have been. It was all very well Giulio Carcano comparing a 500cc Norton connecting rod to something out of a diesel engine, but that rod had evolved the hard way!

Carcano had no illusions that he would eventually have to travel the multi-cylinder road, but he was not the man to copy, and a transverse four would make a mockery of all his thinking.

He could scarcely revert to the in-line concept and he rejected a twin as unlikely to produce sufficient power. The idea of a Vee-four, used by AJS before the war and by Honda in the 1980s, does not seem to have occurred to him, nor does that of a transverse air-cooled three or water-cooled Vee-six, all of which would have been options. Instead, he conceived a design that went from one extreme to the other and must have given the race mechanics recurring nightmares. This was the transverse, water-cooled Vee-*eight*. He argued that such an engine would employ such tiny bores and strokes (44 × 41mm) as to be scarcely more bulky than a twin, and, of course, he was correct. The engine's size and weight, which often appear formidable, are put in perspective by a photograph of one being carried around by Bill Lomas!

The cylinders were set at 90 degress, an angle which gives good primary balance. The one-piece crankshaft was machined out of the solid in one plane like a conventional four-cylinder crankshaft and the connecting rods employed split big ends and split light alloy roller cages, which proved unreliable in use. A change was made to a crankshaft built up by the use of horribly expensive Hirth couplings (as had been used on the in-line four) so that one-piece rods and bearing cages could be used.

Carcano took advantage of the change to have a two-plane crank, which improved the secondary balance of the engine considerably. Two valves per cylinder

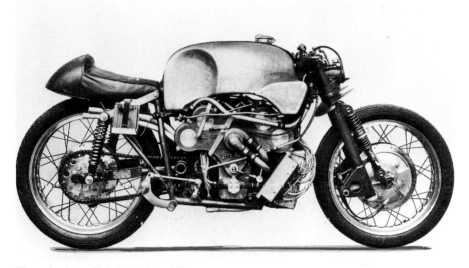

The quite incredible Moto Guzzi V8.

seated directly on the head as they had in the in-line four. There were eight separate exhaust pipes and eight tiny racing Dell'Orto carburettors. The two overhead camshafts on each bank of cylinders were driven by trains of spur gears. The contact make-and-break mechanisms for each bank, used in conjunction with battery and coil ignition were driven from the left-hand ends of the camshafts and the water pump from the right. Another legacy from the in-line four was the use of cylinder liners that screwed into the cylinder head casting and ran in contact with the cooling water. Primary drive to the gearbox with large, exposed dry clutch was by gears. The gearbox itself could contain four or five gear ratios as circumstances demanded. The engine was first tested during April 1955, and soon discovered to have a far better spread of power than had been hoped for. A peak of 62 hp at 12,500 rpm was claimed, which does not sound unreasonable.

The engine was fitted into something that could be called a scaled-up version of the 350 frame, though the engine was, on the Vee-8, carried between twin cradle loops rather than suspended. Tests took place at Monza at the end of 1954 (Guzzi made no secret of the Vee-8's existence) and was ridden in practice for the 1955 Belgian Grand Prix by Ken Kavanagh, when he experienced the first of many crankshaft failures. The bike did not appear again until, appropriately enough, 1 April, 1956, when Ken Kavanagh rode it in the Coppa d'Oro race. He retired after nine laps with what was said to be overheating, but was probably more big end bearing trouble. Bill Lomas practised for the Dutch Grand Prix at the start of July on the Vee-8 and made fastest lap, but again a big end failed, and he rode a single in the race. Ken Kavanagh on the other 'Eight' lasted for only four laps. The bike showed its huge promise at the German Grand Prix three weeks later, when Lomas made fastest lap at 95.38 mph in a furious duel around the 7-mile Solitude circuit with Geoff Duke on his Gilera. But again, afer four laps, the Guzzi retired with what was said to be a split water hose. And so it went on . . . !

Fortunately the 350cc class was kinder to Guzzi in 1956. Ken Kavanagh won the Junior TT, Bill Lomas won in Holland, in Germany and at the Ulster, and between them the team amassed enough points for Moto Guzzi to win the Constructor's Championship. Lomas was individual 350cc Champion for the second time. Lomas, unfortunately crashed at Monza in September and broke his wrist whilst fighting to fend off Libero Liberati on his new four-cylinder Gilera. However, he was soon fit enough to take part in tests of the revised 500cc Vee-8 at Monza. These were followed by tests at Montlhéry which is hard to understand – and in England, which is plain bizarre! Accompanied by mechanic Pietro Pomi, Lomas rode the Vee-8 at practice sessions at Oulton Park and Snetterton. 'The purpose of the programme', said *The Motorcycle*, 'is to perfect the steering and general handling.' One would have thought that there were better times and places to accomplish this than at a wind-and-rain-swept British circuit in November!

At the same time, it was announced that for 1957 Guzzi would support only Lomas, Dale and Keith Campbell. Ken Kavanagh, Duilio Agostini and Giovanni Rocchi were to be dropped.

In view of later events, one wonders if the farcical test series in the depths of an English winter were not symptoms of the malaise that was to take Moto Guzzi to the brink of disaster not so much later. Nothing of this filtered through early in 1957. Now Carcano revised the 350cc engine, with flexibility and torque at comparatively low rpm as a goal. Back went the bore and stroke to 75 × 79mm, and smaller inlet valves were used to speed up the mean speed of the gas flow. The streamlining was improved still further and the weight was reduced to a staggering 220 lb. With 38 hp at 8500 rmp, the 350cc single was still competitive. At the start of 1957, Motor Guzzi added young Giuseppe Colnago to the team. Just as well, because at Imola in April Bill Lomas crashed badly, breaking his shoulder, and did not ride again in 1957 or indeed ever again as a factory rider. The Vee-8 was out again. At Syracuse in Sicily, Colnago gave it its first win (albeit in a non-Grand Prix

Mechanic's nightmare indeed. Eight of everything!

Bill Lomas shows that the Vee-8 engine was in reality quite small and light for all its formidable complexity.

151

event) and lapped at 95.81 mph. At Imola Dickie Dale won and made fastest lap and at the German Grand Prix finished fourth to Liberati and Bob McIntyre on Gilera fours.

Dale finished a poor fourth at 94.89 mph in the famous Golden Jubilee TT, for the eight laps of which Bob McIntyre on the dustbin-faired Gilera four averaged a staggering 98.89 mph and lapped at 101.12 mph. Dale had been beaten by two Gileras and an MV. This as much as anything exposes the pretensions of the Vee-8. But why go on? That was to all intents and purposes the end of the Vee-8. With Lomas out of contention, Keith Campbell proved himself to be a worthy contestant for the 350cc title. He finished second to McIntyre in the Junior TT, won the Dutch, the Belgian and the Ulster races and became individual champion for 1957.

The 1957 Ulster Grand Prix was Guzzi's last Classic race. In September there came the dramatic joint announcement from the various Italian manufacturers, including Moto Guzzi, that they were withdrawing from racing. The money – in the midst of a European slump in motorcycle sales – had run out. The Guzzi racing department was disbanded. Fortunately, Guzzi were able to fight back in the commercial market place with Carlo Guzzi's last masterpiece, the little 175cc Lodola, and with Lino Tonti's brilliant development of the transverse V7 in all its various guises.

The Guzzi company had a strong, individualistic attitude and preserved its history. The Moto Guzzi museum is an example to any manufacturer, and contains examples, in working order, of all the machines ever raced. That apart, Guzzis were such fascinating machines that few racers have been scrapped, and at continental events they are to be seen in profusion.

NSU
The Rennfox and Rennmax

In December 1950, Germany was readmitted by the FIM to international road racing. Without delay, NSU announced that for 1951 they would contest the 500cc class with a four-cylinder machine. This, an entirely new design by technician Albert Roder, appeared at the end of April 1951 at the annual national meeting at Eilenreide near Hanover. It was ridden by Heiner Fleischmann, but soon retired. This NSU was a heavy, bulky machine with unorthodox trailing-link front forks, using rubber suspension fore and aft. The transverse engine, with bore and stroke of 54 × 54mm, had twin overhead camshafts, four separate carburettors and four exhausts with short megaphones. Thereafter, despite much experimental work, NSU experienced an inordinate amount of trouble with the four, in particular an appalling high-frequency vibration possibly linked to insufficiently stiff crankcase castings. Whatever the cause, Fleischmann's best placing in the season was third behind the BMWs of Georg Meier and Walter Zeller at Feldburg. At the season's end NSU decided to abandon the machine, giving as a face-saver the explanation that they had decided only to race in classes in which they sold machines for the road. This they believed would be good advertising for the forthcoming 125cc Fox and 250cc Max models, although the racing bikes bore little if any resemblance to the roadsters!

That NSU themselves had their doubts about the 500cc four from the start is indicated by the appearance very early in 1951 at the Schotten meeting of a single-cylinder 54 × 54mm 125cc double overhead camshaft racing machine of notably neat appearance and sophistication. Though it was said to be a step in developing the four, it appeared to be very much a design in its own right. Its frame resembled that of the little Fox production machine with a pressed-steel backbone, pressed-steel bottom link front forks and swinging arm rear suspension. The engine had an inclined cylinder with a steep downdraught for its 22mm (later 26mm) racing carburettor. Magneto ignition was used and the twin camshafts were driven by a single vertical shaft, bevels and spur gears. This 125cc racer appeared several times in practice at German national meetings and was judged to be very fast indeed. Ridden by Otto Daikar, it won the first race in which it was actually entered, but the best result in an international event during 1951 was second place to H. P. Müller's 125cc DKW at the German Grand Prix at Solitude in August.

In overall charge of the development programme was the formidable Dr Walter Fröde, who chose to base the twin upon an experimental sports engine that had been taken to the testing stage and then abandoned. Obviously it was desirable to have as much commonality of components as possible between the two engines, but the layout of the twin was to some degree dictated by the crankcase casting, which meant that a chain primary drive, four-speed gearbox, and a separate shaft and bevel drive to each camshaft were used. Both engines had simple pressed-up crankshafts, that of the twin with crankpins at 360 degrees. Light alloy cylinders with pressed-in iron liners and heads with cast-in iron valve seats were used and the valves were controlled by hairpin springs. The 125cc engine had a 26mm carburettor, the 250cc two 24mm carburettors, later increased in size to 25mm. A magneto was retained on the 125cc engine, whereas the 250cc twin used battery and coil ignition. The 125cc machine kept its pressed steel frame and forks, but the 250cc model used a steel tube frame and telescopic front forks. The names Rennfox and Rennmax now became official.

1952 was to be a year of development, largely devoted to sorting out teething troubles, of which, as might be expected with engines revving to 9000 rpm and more, there were quite a few. Nevertheless, both machines, ridden by Bill Lomas and Werner Haas, did well in German National events.

'They're away!' Rennmaxes at the start of the Grand Prix des Nations at Monza, 1953. For once they were not all-conquering – Enrico Lorenzetti won on a Moto Guzzi.

153

The original 4-speed Rennmax, showing the telescopic forks and small front brake used at that time.

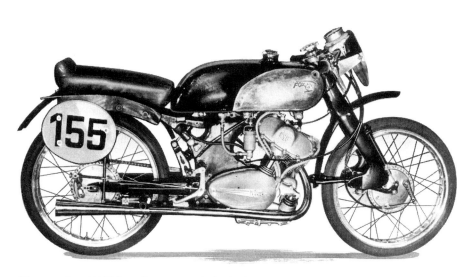

The very first NSU Rennfox seen early in 1951.

The 1953 Rennmax with pressed steel frame and forks.

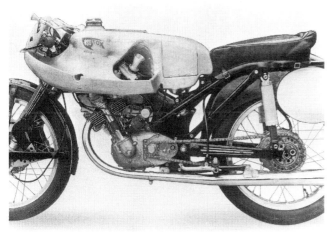

Unstreamlined Rennfox 1953.

Bill Lomas won the non-Championship 250cc race at Hamburg in August, and, although Lomas' 250cc machine broke down in the German Grand Prix, Werner Haas won the 125cc race convincingly. Then at the Grand Prix des Nations at Monza in September, Haas served notice on the Moto Guzzi factory that henceforth they were not going to have it all their own way! He harried Enrico Lorenzetti all the way to the flag to finish a close second in the 250cc race beating the redoubtable Fergus Anderson. Roberto Colombo, on the other NSU, finished fifth.

For 1953, the 250cc machine also featured a pressed steel frame and bottom link forks that resembled in appearance (if not in fact) the frame of the road-going Max. Winter development, including larger carburettors, now raised the power of the single to 15 hp at 10,500 rpm and that of the twin to 30 hp at 10,000 rpm. For 1953, NSU were confident of success and their confidence was justified. Werner Haas went on to win the Riders' Championship in both 125cc and 250cc classes. At the TT he finished second in the 125cc event to Les Graham on the MV and in the

250cc race, again, second to Fergus Anderson on the Guzzi. Bill Lomas did not ride in the TT, having broken his wrist in practice, and he left NSU soon afterwards. His place was taken by Irishman Reg Armstrong, just in time to win the Ulster Grand Prix.

Immediately after the TT, NSU revealed a new 125cc single-cylinder engine which had actually been in the Island and used in practice, though not in the race. Ridden by Haas, it was victorious on its first outing at the Dutch TT. Strangely, it had a single overhead camshaft layout. Bore and stroke were altered to 55.9 × 50.8mm, the vertical shaft and bevel drive to the camshaft was now on the left of the engine, the magneto was replaced by coil ignition and there were six speeds in the new gearbox. Power output was alleged to be 16 hp at 11,000 rpm. Later the design reverted to double overhead camshafts, and bore and stroke were altered to a radical 58 × 47.3mm, which raised the power to 18 hp at 11,500 rpm. This engine was standard for 1954. Werner Haas won the Riders' Championship in both 125cc and 250cc classes for 1953, and NSU won the Constructor's Championship in the 250cc class. They were level with MV in the 125cc class on points, but MV took the title under the regulations. So closely matched had been the two teams' results throughout the season that the FIM were forced to compare their aggregate times for the various wins and places! MV's aggregate was 6hrs 11mins 51.93secs, NSU's 6hrs 12mins 28.02secs, a total difference of only 36.09 secs!

For 1954, the 250cc engine was redesigned, with a new crankcase casting that permitted six gears. Gone was the chain primary transmission, and the camshafts were now driven by a single vertical shaft driving the inlet camshaft by bevels with a train of spur gears to the exhaust camshaft. The cylinder heads were new, with a very narrow included valve angle. The carburettor size was raised to 28mm. The heart of the engine was a horrendously expensive crankshaft with central spur gear

Rennfox with the curious streamlining that was first known as the 'Dolphin'. This is Robert Hollaus winning the 1954 Ultra Lightweight TT on the Clypse circuit.

drive to the gearbox between the two inner main bearings and made in five pieces bolted together by aircraft engine-style Hirth couplings. The nature of these was such that the final grinding of the journals did not take place until after trial assembly of the complete crankshaft. Such sophistication was probably quite unnecessary, but Dr Fröde was taking no chances – even the camshafts were made in two parts and united by Oldham couplings to combat torsional vibration. The 1954 season was a total triumph for NSU, who won *every* race in the 125cc and 250cc class that they contested. Rupert Hollaus won the 125cc TT (held on the Clypse course) and Werner Haas won the 250cc race over the Mountain circuit at over 90 mph – over 5 mph faster than the year before! In line astern behind him came team-mates Hollaus, Reg Armstrong and H. P. Müller, relegating Fergus Anderson on the leading Guzzi to fifth! Hollaus won the 125cc title and Haas the 250cc title for 1954, and though no Constructor's title was awarded, NSU would obviously have been first in each class – the rest nowhere. Alas, the wonderful season ended tragically, when 20-year-old Rupert Hollaus was killed in practice for the GP des Nations at Monza. NSU withdrew and never officially raced again. They had proved that a scientific, technological approach could gain, in a few brief years, what other manufacturers had taken decades to achieve. With power outputs of around 160 hp per litre at 11,500 rpm, the 1954 machines were unsurpassed until, in the early 1960s, Honda, self-confessed admirers of NSU, overtook them with four-cylinder machines. Today, happily, many of the works NSUs survive both in private hands and in museums and are to be seen in demonstrations and regularity events on the continent.

The NSU Sportmax

During 1954 and 1955 NSU breathed some much-needed life into the 250cc class in international road racing with the series production Sportmax, which was to remain competitive until the early 1960s. As early as October 1953 a prototype, differing in some ways from the production machines, was ridden into tenth place in the Spanish Grand Prix by Kurt Knopf. For 1954 NSU made a small number, difficult at this time to verify the precise number, of Sportmaxes, which were sold to selected German riders. The bottom link forks and molybdenum steel alloy pressed frames closely resembled those of the 250cc Rennmax twin. Like the Rennmax, the Sportmax carried 5½ pints of oil in the spine of the frame. Eighteen-inch alloy rims carried 2.75 in front and 3 in rear racing tyres. The 200mm two-leading-shoe front brake strangely enough earned a poor reputation from owners, many of whom substituted brakes by Norton or Oldhani. At the rear, there

A youthful John Surtees on his Sportmax. Note the extra-large front brake.

Stripped Maxes converted for racing, showing the pressed steel frame.

D. Wright practices for the 1955 Lightweight TT on his Sportmax.

was a 190mm single leading shoe brake. The 69 × 66mm 247cc single ohc engine, the camshaft driven by two eccentrics and connecting rods, externally closely resembled the standard Max except for its 30mm Amal carburettor. But, in fact, many engine and gearbox components were specially manufactured from superior materials. The engine gave 28 hp at 9000 rpm – at that time enough to see off anything but a good works machine. Although almost all the riders in 1954 contested German events exclusively, Georg Braun scored an impressive second place to Rupert Hollaus at the wretchedly wet Swiss Grand Prix at Bremgarten, finishing ahead of H. P. Müller on a Rennmax after Werner Haas had fallen on the first lap. Privateers Knopf and Stein also finished on Sportmaxes.

For 1955 NSU made a considerably larger batch of machines, once again for 'selected' riders, who included Hans Baltisberger, Georg Braun, H. P. Müller, Pierre Monneret, Reg Armstrong, John Surtees and Werner Haas. Haas, who had business interests of growing importance, decided however to retire before the 1955 season began.

The 1955 Sportmax had a far better 260mm two-leading-shoe front brake, and the engine now produced nearly 30 hp. On the Continent the Sportmax dominated the 250cc class, and indeed H. P. Müller won the Rider's Championship for 1955, but only after a controversial decision at the FIM Congress upheld a protest about Bill Lomas having refuelled his MV at the Dutch TT without stopping his engine.

In all about forty Sportmaxes had been made, but a good many more engines were supplied as 'spares' during 1955. Kits of parts to convert ordinary Max engines were also sold, and, in fact, between 1955 and about 1962 a good many hybrid Sportmaxes, racer or semi-racer specification engines in modified standard Max frames, appeared, diluting the value (still a high one) of the genuine article. Sportmaxes were owned and ridden successfully in the late 1950s by a good many top flight British and Continental men, including Sammy Miller and Mike Hailwood.

Three times whilst the Lightweight TT was held on the Clypse course Sportmax riders finished in third place: in 1955, H. P. Müller; in 1956 Hans Baltisberger and in 1958 Mike Hailwood. The best performance on the Mountain circuit was Dan Shorey's eighth in 1961, in which year the race was absolutely dominated by works machines from Japan. At National and Club racing levels, of course, the Sportmax remained competitive until 1963, when the Greeves Silverstone made its appearance.

Survival rate is high and, especially on the Continent, genuine Sportmaxes, and some of the hybrids, are rallied, raced and paraded. Still a very impressive example of what could be achieved with a comparatively simple single-cylinder four-stroke engine.

Norton
The Manx

After Alec Bennett's Senior TT victory in 1927, Norton surprised nobody by offering a TT Replica model at the Olympia show that year. This, the 79 × 100mm 490cc CS1 (Camshaft one), was joined a year later by the 71 × 85mm CJ (Camshaft Junior) of 348cc. Both machines, particularly the CS1, were immediately successful in private hands, and as the factory made improvements and alterations to the works machines so these were passed on to the cash-paying customers. Thus the CS1 and CJ benefited to the extent of full cradle frames, better brakes, four-speed gearboxes with foot change, and even the improved ohc engine designed by Craig and Carroll. So successful were these machines that, in 1933, Norton offered pure racing versions, the so-called International Models 40 (348cc) and 30 (490cc), production of the CS1 and CJ continuing as sports machines.

The impact of Norton's policy on racing in the 1930s is best illustrated by the fact that between 1931 and 1938 *every* Senior Manx Grand Prix and four of the Junior races were won by Norton riders! The relative lack of success of the 350cc model reflected the well-established presence in the Junior class of the KTT Velocette, but significantly in the last two years before the war, 1937 and 1938, Nortons filled the first six places in the Junior event!

Post-war, the machines were designated the Model 40 Manx (348cc) and Model 30 Manx (490cc), both engines now featuring bronze-skulled light alloy cylinder heads and light alloy cylinders with iron liners. The long-stroke engine dimensions, however, remained unaltered. Plunger box rear suspension and Norton's new hydraulically damped Roadholder forks were fitted as standard. Not many new Manx Nortons could have been made and sold in 1946, but it was still a nasty shock for Norton admirers when the Senior Manx Grand Prix was won not by a Norton but by Irish farmer Ernie Lyons on a push-rod Triumph twin! To further sap the confidence of Norton owners, this result was repeated by Manxman Don Crossley in 1948 (though by a narrow margin), but thereafter Nortons won the Senior Manx almost as though by right. In the Junior class, it was not until 1950 that the 7R AJS scored a win over the Nortons, the rider again being Don Crossley.

In 1950, Norton introduced the new Featherbed frame for the works team, and this was offered for sale for the 1951 season. The rear sub-frame carrying seat and anchorage for the suspension units was bolted to the main frame. This led to a mysterious spate of broken suspension damper rods as the sub-frame vibrated in resonance with high-frequency imbalances in the engine. Remedied on the works machines in 1952, it was not until 1954 that the sub-frame on the Manx Norton was welded integral with the main frame.

As early as 1949 the Manx was offered with a double ohc head cast in RR56 and with inserted iron valve seats, but not until 1954 were the archaic long-stroke

The original Walter Moore-designed ohc 500cc Norton, the CS1 model of 1927.

Notice anything different? The interim experimental Norton, with Arthur Carroll's crankcases, but still with Walter Moore's head and cambox.

The International model of 1933 as sold to the Clubman to go racing.

161

The 500cc Manx Norton in its final post war guise. One of the last batch from Bracebridge Street in 1961.

dimensions modified in the light of modern thinking to the near-square figures of 76 × 76.7mm for the 348cc model 40 and 86 × 85.62mm for the 498cc model 30. Each year, detail improvements were faithfully incorporated as they proved themselves on the works machines, but not until Joe Craig had retired, his place being later taken by Doug Hele, were any further fundamental changes undertaken, and those were mainly concerned with reliability. Since 1953, Norton had belonged to AMC, and in 1961 the parent company decided that making racing motorcycles was a distraction. A few Manx Nortons were assembled in 1962, but that was the end, or very nearly so. In fact, as late as 1967, sidecar racer John Tickle attempted to revive the Manx Norton under his own name, but without real success.

Nortons had made the Manx models in batches of 80–100 of each model each season, but sold them only to riders of proven ability.

In the great days, the idea of winning a TT with a privately owned machine had been a mere dream (although in 1961 when Gary Hocking's lone MV fell by the wayside in the Senior race, Mike Hailwood on a Bill Lacey-tuned Norton made that dream come true), but the Manx Grand Prix was another affair. Between 1946 and 1972, 27 racing seasons, a Norton rider won the Junior race 13 times and the Senior race 17. Many, many a rider made his name and his way to better things with a Manx Norton, and throughout the whole Classic era Nortons were the mainstay of racing at every level, and of the Continental Circus in particular. As late as 1968, Norton riders won both the Junior and Senior Manx Grand Prix races. Happily, a Manx Norton was not something that was lightly tossed aside for scrap, and very many have survived. Happily, too, interest in them is such that a healthy infrastructure of firms catering from the Manx Norton owner has arisen alongside the Classic movement. Today many Manx Nortons, often superbly restored, are to be seen at Classic events all over the world.

The Factory Machines

The first overhead camshaft Norton racing engine was designed by Walter Moore for the 1927 Senior TT with traditional Norton bore and stroke of 79 × 100mm, 490cc. The race went well and Alec Bennett won at 68.41 mph, and before he retired, Stanley Woods made fastest lap at 70.90 mph; the engine, joined in 1928 by a 71 × 85mm 350 version, thereafter proved disappointing at the TT though reasonably successful elsewhere. After Walter Moore left Norton in 1930, Joe

Craig, ex-team rider and since 1929 in charge of the racing department, drastically revised the layout of the engine, ably assisted in this task by designer draughtsman Arthur Carrol. Norton never looked back. At the 1931 TT, Tim Hunt won both Junior and Senior races, and made fastest lap in the Junior. Jimmy Guthrie was second in the Junior and Senior, Stanley Woods was third in the Senior, and Jimmy Simpson made fastest lap. From then until the outbreak of war, only twice did Norton *not* win the Senior TT: in 1935 when, with a ride that has passed into motorcycling legend, Stanley Woods on the Bicilindrica Vee-twin Guzzi beat Jimmy Guthrie's Norton by a mere four seconds after breaking the lap record on the final lap; and in 1939, when the Norton team did not officially enter and the race was won by the supercharged BMW twin of Georg Meier.

Over the years, the factory Nortons had been progressively developed by Joe Craig. The early iron cylinder had given way to a light alloy barrel and fins with shrunk-in iron liner. The iron head gave way to one of aluminium bronze, and then one of RR56 light alloy with a bronze 'skull', which embraced the valve seats. By 1937, the stroke of both engines had been shortened, the 350cc engine being 75.9 × 77mm and the 500cc 82 × 94.3mm. There were twin overhead camshafts, the valves were controlled by exposed hairpin springs, and the exhaust valve had a hollow stem filled with metallic sodium to assist cooling. Many castings were of magnesium alloy, considerably lighter than aluminium. An exhaust pipe and megaphone were well tuned to take advantage of extreme overlap valve timings and inertia effects in the inlet tract and cylinder. With a compression ratio of slightly over 11 to 1 and running on 50/50 petrol/benzole mixture of about 85-octane rating, the 500cc engine as used in the 1938 TT (where Harold Daniell won at 89.11 mph and lapped at a staggering 91 mph) developed more than 52 hp at 6500 rpm. The 350cc engine the same year gave 37 hp at 6750 rpm.

In 1937, the bikes had gained rear springing, although of crude plunger box pattern – and in 1938 telescopic front forks, though perhaps not caring to infringe BMW patents Norton did not fit these with oil damping. Large conical hubs which incorporated the brakes were cast in magnesium, and the four-speed gearboxes, though little changed over the years, were immensely strong and trouble-free. Those pre-war machines have been described at some length because they were quite literally the same machines with which Norton began racing again in 1947.

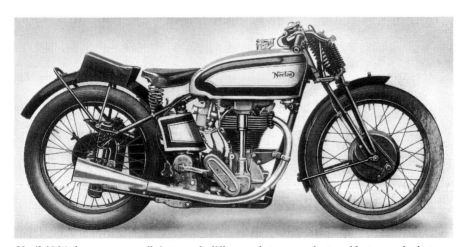

Until 1936 there was not all that *much difference between a factory Norton and what was sold to the racing clubman. The 1936 dohc 500cc altered all that. It had rear springing too.*

Post-war, Norton started to get left behind. This 1949 500cc doesn't look so different to that of 1939!

Joe Craig had left Norton in 1939, joining first BSA and then AMC, and whilst at the latter had supervised the design and construction of the supercharged twin-cylinder racing motorcycle that post-war was to emerge, without its supercharger, as the E90 AJS 'Porcupine'. As late as December 1946 it was publicly stated that Craig was to stay with AJS, but in January 1947 he was back at Bracebridge Street,

Inspired! The original 'Featherbed' of 1950 – the works team here seen off to the Island – changed Norton's fading fortunes and transformed the meaning of the word 'handling'.

Birmingham, as 'Technical Director'. The best that could be done for the 1947 TT was a facelift for the pre-war bikes; the front forks were given hydraulic damping and small Newton struts were also used to damp the rear suspension. The front brakes were altered to two-leading-shoe configuration.

But as regards the engines, the FICM having ruled that petrol only, and that of no higher than 75-octane rating, should be used for racing, only a backward step could be taken. A shocked Joe Craig found that for this fuel, which he called 'little better than paraffin', he had to lower the compression ratio of the 500cc engine to a miserable 7 to 1! Of course, everybody was in the same boat. The resulting loss of power was reflected in speeds at the TT. The Senior race was won by Norton's Harold Daniell, with Irishman Artie Bell backing him in second place, but the running speed was over 6 mph down on Daniell's speed in 1938, and the fastest lap by about the same amount. In the Junior race, Norton's team of Daniell, Bell and Ken Bills all fell by the wayside, presenting the race to Velocette riders, who finished in the first four places.

The immediate post-war years were not happy ones for Norton, for not only did they experience a lot of engine trouble because of the low octane petrol, but they were in continual difficulties with broken frames. In retrospect, this was almost certainly because, seeking to lighten the bikes, they used Reynolds 531 alloy steel tubing, which was not suitable for Norton's crude hearthbrazing style of frame building. Nevertheless, in 1948 Artie Bell was third in the Junior TT and won the Senior race. In 1949, Bell was again third in the Junior, and Daniell won the Senior. In the Senior Clubman's TT, a race for machines sold to the public, victory went to a young Norton employee on a 500cc 'International' model. Geoff Duke, until then better known as a trials rider, went on to win the 1949 Manx Grand Prix.

1950 was altogether a happier year for Norton. In the first place they had a brand new frame, the 'Featherbed', so called by Harold Daniell after his first experience of it. This had been developed, designed and built by two Belfast brothers, Rex and Cromie McCandless, who had a long and successful association with racing in Northern Ireland.

The first frames were tested in the Isle of Man over the winter of 1949 and met with an enthusiastic response from the riders. Later, the Featherbed frame was to be bronze-welded from 531 tube by the Reynolds Tube Company, but all the frames for 1950 were made by Rex McCandless. For 1950, Geoff Duke joined Daniell and Bell in the works team, a most formidable trio. And to add a further sparkle to Joe Craig's eye, the permitted octane rating of the fuel was lifted for the 1950 season. And a wonderful season it was, with Norton winning the Senior World Championship for Constructors and taking first, second and third place and fastest lap in both the Senior and Junior TTs.

It was in 1950 that in the Grand Prix rounds the four-cylinder Gilera and MV machines began to serve notice that they could not be ignored, but, by and large, Norton were able to hold their own. They had, as always, the best riders in Europe. The machines were not as fast as the fours, but they were not that much slower, and being lighter, they had better acceleration, and braked better. They handled better and above all they were more reliable. Not until 1955, when Norton withdrew from racing, was a four-cylinder machine to win the TT. By that time too, Guzzi's ultra lightweight horizontal-engined singles had a grip on the Junior class that was not loosened until they too withdrew from racing. But in 1951, with Geoff Duke winning both 350cc and 500cc Riders' titles, and Norton the Constructors' in the World Championship, Joe Craig seemed to be able to walk on water! At the TT Geoff Duke, Johnny Lockett and Jack Brett finished 1-2-3 in the Junior race.

The Senior result was a mild surprise in that Nortons did *not* finish first, second and third, Duke and Cromie McCandless being separated by Bill Doran on the E95 AJS Porcupine in an unexpected second place.

In 1952 and 1953, Norton still continued to win at the TT; in the former year,

Geoff Duke and the 1950 Featherbed – made for each other.

Les Graham on the MV four was unable to do better than to split the Senior Nortons of Reg Armstrong and Rhodesian Ray Amm. In the Junior race, Geoff Duke won and Reg Armstrong was second. For 1953, both Geoff Duke and Reg Armstrong left Norton to join Gilera, and the writing was on the wall as far as the Grand Prix events were concerned. But once again Ray Amm saved the day for Norton at the TT, winning both Junior and Senior races. To be sure, in the Senior, Duke led for three laps on the Gilera, but he then fell and was eliminated. Ray Amm then took the lead and went on to win at a record speed of 93.85 mph, having made fastest lap at 97.41 mph, ahead of Jack Brett on another Norton. Reg Armstrong on the Gilera finished third.

It was in 1953 that Norton were taken over by AMC, and early in 1954 it was announced that the Norton works team would not contest the Grands Prix. At this time the engines were at the very peak of their development by Joe Craig, the 350cc, being of 78 × 73mm and developing 38 hp; the 500cc, 90 × 74.8mm, 54 hp. These figures may not appear very impressive alongside those claimed for 1938, but of course they do not reveal the shape of the all-important torque curve, nor the fact that the engines were remarkably flexible and controllable on short circuits. In their final incarnation, Craig's engines had shortened connecting rods and bobweight crankshafts with an outside flywheel as much to reduce the height of the engine as anything else. Carefully controlled squish areas were machined on the piston crown and cylinder head to give a compression ratio in each case of around 10.5 to 1. Both valves were sodium cooled and the exhaust valve guide was also cooled by surplus oil from the cambox, which was drained back to the crankcase via a small light alloy radiator.

By now Norton had to concede that they had been overhauled and left behind by Gilera's four in the 500cc class and Guzzi's horizontal single in the 350cc class. Their best riders had left them to ride Italian machinery. Could Norton still prevail at the Isle of Man? Under normal circumstances, probably not.

In the 350cc race, having built up a huge 58-second lead over Ken Kavanagh's Guzzi in four laps, Ray Amm retired with a sheared drive-side mainshaft. Kava-

Keeping them going. The Norton depot in the Isle of Man at TT time.

nagh also retired, and the shortened five-lap race was won by New Zealander Rod Coleman on the three-valve factory AJS with Derek Farrant second on a similar model (it was the only time in the Classic era that AJS were to win a TT). Bob Keeler on a Norton was third. Ray Amm had made fastest lap at a remarkable 94.61 mph.

The Senior TT caused considerable controversy. Bad weather caused the race to be postponed twice, and the start was at noon. For two laps, Duke on the Gilera four narrowly led Ram Amm's Norton, and indeed, except for the first lap, every one of Amm's laps was considerably faster than the times recorded by Duke. At the end of lap two, Duke had a mere two-second lead, and was probably already in deficit to Amm when the third lap began and Duke called at the pits to refuel. Whether, in a seven-lap race, Duke could have caught and passed Amm is an ever open question, but in fact the deteriorating weather caused the stewards to stop the race at the end of the fourth lap. Amm won, a full minute and six seconds ahead of Geoff Duke, whose last lap was 38 seconds slower than Amm's, which is in itself part of the controversy. Was the Gilera in mechanical trouble? Was the Norton's handling in the wet that much better than the Gilera's? Be that as it may, Ray Amm on the Norton won the TT and set fastest lap at 89.92 mph on his final tour.

It was the end of an era, the Norton factory's last TT victory. A factory team was announced for 1955 consisting of Jack Brett, John Hartle and John Surtees (Ray Amm had accepted an offer from MV to ride their 500cc four), but within weeks the AMC management changed their minds and closed down the Norton racing department. Joe Craig, to whom his work had been his life, retired, remarried and went to live with his Dutch wife in Holland. He died of a heart attack in 1957. The racing department was in fact later re-opened, and development of the Manx engine was pushed forward by Doug Hele in the late 1950s, but though the benefit

Works Norton 1952 – note the small-diameter rear wheel and the special inverted suspension units.

of these improvements was passed on to private purchasers of Manx Nortons, the factory merely gave a very limited degree of support to a few favoured riders.

For the 1957 Senior TT Doug Hele built a new 500cc engine incorporating all the recent improvements to camshaft drive and valve gear and with a bore and stroke of 93 × 73.5mm. With this engine, up-and-coming Australian Bob Brown finished third in the Senior TT behind the four-cylinder Gilera of Bob McIntyre and the four-cylinder MV of John Surtees. Hele also experimented with desmodromic valve gear, but it was never used in earnest. In 1962 AMC closed down the Norton factory at Bracebridge Street, Birmingham, moving the operation to their own factory in London. Sales of the Manx Norton to private customers ceased in 1963.

Post-war works Nortons had, against all the odds, won the Senior TT every year that they had been entered, eight years in succession, and six times a Norton had made fastest lap. In the Junior race, Norton entries had won four times and made five fastest laps. It was a record of which anyone could be justly proud.

Nortons at Daytona Beach

The famous Daytona Beach races were run from 1937 to 1954 under Class 'C' rules of the American Motorcycle Association. In essence these rules called for machines 'of Stock design, as manufactured, catalogued and sold for general motorcycle use', going on to stipulate the octane rating of the fuel and the maximum compression ratio allowed. Capacities were equated at 750cc for side-valve engines and 500cc for those with overhead valves. The circuit, which altered slightly from time to time according to the state of the beach itself, was about 4 miles around, two miles of straight and the banked turns being on the beach itself, the remainder being on a narrow, bumpy sand-swept tarmacadam road running parallel to the beach. The beach races were a gloriously American celebration of speed, freedom and motorcycling, unique in the world, and quite unlike anything known in Europe. An atmosphere of carnival prevailed, with social events and with Main Street officially closed for lighthearted (and sometimes not so lighthearted) drag contests in the evenings.

What could be more alien to this archetypically American event than the Manx Norton, developed by decades of European road racing and specifically by the

Nortons in the Paddock at Daytona in circa 1949.

Nortons 1 – 2 – 4 in 1950, L-R Bill Matthews, Dick Klamfoth and Bill Tuman. Francis Beart in dark glasses.

rigorous disciplines of the Isle of Man TT? And yet, for a few years between 1948 and 1953, Norton were to make a tremendous impression and to win the races four times in succession. But a little-remembered fact is that 1948, when Steve Lancefield helped American Norton riders to finish first and second in the 100-mile Amateur race and second in the 200-mile race, was not Daytona's first experience of the overhead camshaft Norton. That victory was not reported in the British motorcycle Press, for in 1941 all sporting activity in Britain was at a standstill due to the war, and who cared, anyway, about some weird sort of sand racing in faraway Daytona, Florida? Nevertheless, in 1941, the last year that the 200-mile race was run before America's entry into the war, it was won, and won handsomely, by Billy Matthews of Ontario, Canada, who, against the advice of his own Canadian sponsors, entered the Beach races at his own expense. His machine was a 500cc 'International' model with single ohc engine of 500cc, a kickstart (as required by the regulations), girder front forks and plunger box rear suspension. The Norton was far lighter than any of the 45 cubic inch American twins, developed about the same power, and had the benefit of a four-speed gearbox with foot gear-change and far better handling and steering.

Matthews himself was surprised that the AMA (admittedly the creature of Harley-Davidson) accepted his entry at all, and could only conclude that it was because of ignorance of the Norton's record on the one hand and lack of imagin-

Charlie Ulevich at the North turn in the 1950 Daytona.

Don Evans and Tuner Clarence Czysz with the Norton they used to win the 100 mile race in 1948 and 1949.

ation on the other! Be that as it may, he entered, practised and won. Not unil 1948 did Nortons appear again at the beach, this time at the request of the American importer.

Steve Lancefield, famous Norton tuner and brother-in-law to Norton team rider Harold Daniell, spent several weeks in America looking after the bikes running at Daytona. They were in essence, standard Manx Nortons, but fitted with gearboxes with kickstarters, necessitating a wide jump between 10–1 bottom and 6–1 second gear. Lancefield found the specialized nature of Daytona racing bewildering, but acknowledged that the AMA had a perfect right to make rules to suit the peculiar conditions. 'I have heard it said in Britain that the AMA rules regarding compression ratio and fuels are unfair and unreasonable,' he said afterwards. 'I find it difficult to subscribe to that view', and went on to explain just how 'unfair and unreasonable' American entrants might find the regulations in Europe racing.

Steve found it difficult to balance the equation of a 7.5 to 1 compression ratio, 85-octane fuel, and the peculiarities of the atmospheric conditions at Daytona. He also discovered that the light alloy rims used for road racing was unsuitable for the beach, sand packing itself in the gutters formed by the construction of the rim to either side of the spokes and making the wheels unbalanced. Steel rims which did not collect sand had to be substituted. But the obstacles were overcome and though they did not win, Nortons, ridden by Don Evans and Dick Klamfoth, were first and second in the Novice race, and second in the 200 mile race to Floyd Emde on a 45 cubic-inch Indian was none other than 1941 victor Billy Matthews from Canada. Indeed, had it not been for lack of crowd control costing Matthews time at his refuelling stop, he might very well have won, as he was only 18 seconds in arrears at the flag.

For 1949, Norton took the decision to employ Francis Beart to do the job that Lancefield had done the year before. This time there was no doubt at all about the results. Dick Klamfoth, Bill Matthews and Tex Luse finished 1-2-3 in the 200-mile race and Norton riders were first and second in the Amateur event.

With Beart again in charge, 1950 was another Norton victory, Bill Matthews reversing 1949's positions by beating Klamfoth, with Tom McDermott on a BSA third and another Norton rider in fourth place. By now, Francis Beart must have found it almost monotonous to oversee Norton victories at Daytona, for in 1951 Klamfoth again won the 200-miler with Bobby Hill second.

The 100-mile race was won on a Norton by Bob Michael. With the first seven places in the 200-mile race occupied by British Nortons, Triumphs and BSAs, it was humiliating that the first Harley-Davidson should finish no higher than eighth place!

Norton were to win at Daytona one more time in the 200-mile race in 1952. Again, it was Dick Klamfoth, with Cliff Farwell second and Bob Michael fourth. Almost unbelievably, the first Harley to finish was in 17th place, one of only two Harleys to finish; Nortons, Triumphs and BSAs had simply dominated the whole event. But it was to be Norton's last big result at Daytona, for at last Harley-Davidson struck back! They had for some time been forced to acknowledge that veteran private tuner Tom Sifton was able to obtain more power and speed from the 45 cubic inch engine than were they themselves. In a private deal, Sifton went to work for the factory, the result being the legendary KR model, new for 1953. It was enough to restore Harley's battered pride, and at the 200-mile race that year, Paul Goldsmith at last beat the Nortons to win at a record 94.45 mph. The 100-mile race was won by Johnny Miller on a Norton.

And that really was the end for the Manx Norton at the beach and in any case the regulations had been changed, effectively outlawing the Manx models. No more support was forthcoming from the factory, and in 1954, Norton did not figure at all in the results. Even three times winner on a Norton, Dick Klamfoth, rode a BSA!

Ossa

The Ossa company was started in the late 1940s by ex-road racer and industrialist Manuel Giro, and Ossa motorcycles were always quite a bit better made and finished than other Spanish bikes. In the early 1960s, Manuel Giro's son, Eduardo, joined the company as a designer, with considerable practical experience and a degree in mechanical engineering to his credit. Soon after his arrival, and directly under his influence, Ossa began to take part in Endurance racing in the 175cc and 250cc class. At their first attempt in the 1965 Barcelona 24 hours race, they took first and second places in the 175cc class with what were virtually standard machines, apart from higher compression ratios and larger carburettors. There were many more wins and places, and soon the 60 × 60.9mm engine was enlarged to 70 × 60mm (230cc) to even greater effect. Perhaps the most notable results were an *outright* win in the 1967 24 hour races at Barcelona and Trevor Burgess' win of the 250cc class in the production TT in the Isle of Man the following year.

In the late 1960s Eduardo Giro designed and built a full 250cc engine of 70 × 65mm bore and stroke, largely from standard 230cc parts. It used a rotary disc valve on the side of the crankcase, had a standard four-speed gearbox and was fitted into a standard roadster frame. Though several prototypes were seen in public, they were not raced, for there was a long way to go before such an engine could be truly competitive. Development was promising, but even so the bike's first appearance at the Spanish Grand Prix in 1967 was premature and Carlos Giro could do no better than sixth place. Back to the drawing board and the dynamometer – and a radical new machine emerged for 1968. Engaged to ride it was Spanish 250cc champion Santiago Herrero.

The bike was quite revolutionary, with a light alloy monocoque which contained the fuel, and from which the engine and five-speed gearbox unit was suspended. The engine was air-cooled with truly enormous fins on cylinder and head. The exhaust system was equally oversized and the effect was to make a machine, intrinsically small, appear quite tiny. On the right-hand side of the crankcase was a specially made 42mm Amal carburettor attached to the disc valve chamber. On the left, the exposed generator for the transistorized ignition and a massive dry-plate clutch. Suspension and brakes were unremarkable. The new machine's first couple of outings ended in mechanical failure, though in the Spanish Grand Prix, Carlos Giro riding a second bike did take fourth place. At the 1968 Lightweight TT, Herrero, on his first visit (and aiming to finish rather than to make a sensation), did well to take seventh place. He then went on to sixth place in Holland, fifth in Belgium and third at Monza.

1969 was even more encouraging. The engine was claimed to be producing 42 hp at 9000 rpm, a figure that sounds modest enough for the results achieved. The Telesco front forks had given way to Italian-made Cerianis, and a large Ceriani two-leading-shoe front brake was fitted. Coupled gas-spring rear units were tried, but were eventually replaced by ordinary springs. Water cooling (with a very low-volume system and water pump) was tried but not adopted.

At Jarama, Herrero won with ease, and he did so again at the French Grand Prix at Le Mans. Quite remarkably, he finished a fine third in the Junior TT behind the 4-cylinder Benelli of Kel Carruthers and the Suzuki twin of Frank Perris. At Assen he was again third behind Pasolini and Carruthers on the Benellis, and he won at the Belgian Grand Prix at Spa. He was second to Pasolini at the Sachsenring, and in Belgium he fell, remounted and still finished sixth. At this point he was in the lead for the 250cc World Championship ahead of Carruthers, but though the title was not to be decided until the last round, Herrero's chances took a tumble when he crashed at the Ulster Grand Prix injuring his left arm. He had a mere three weeks to recover, and indeed rode at Imola in early September, still in plaster, to finish fifth. Then in Yugoslavia, he again crashed, and the title went to Carruthers. It had been

The light alloy monocoque, enormous fins and large exhaust are clearly visible in this view of the Ossa.

'Santi' on his way to third place at the 1968 Italian Grand Prix on the disc-valve Ossa.

a brilliant and gallant try, and had attracted tremendous attention and interest.

1970, again, began well with a win at Alicante. A spill at Rimini and a broken piston ring at the Nurburgring were disappointing, but at Le Mans, 'Santi' finished second, and in Yugoslavia he won once again. For the Lightweight TT he was highly tipped, and the bike was decidedly faster in practice, attaining 137.9 mph past the Highlander, 4.6 mph faster than the year before.

In the race, the Ossa was never higher than fourth, and on the last lap, near the 13th milestone, Herrero and Stan Woods collided and the Spanish rider received fatal injuries.

The family firm of Ossa were shocked to the core. All interest in road racing ceased immediately, never to be revived.

Like many other Spanish manufacturers, Ossa suffered from the political up-heaval following the death of Franco and by 1984 the firm was moribund, and today the actual fate of the several versions of the disc-valve single-cylinder racer are not known, although no doubt they will in time emerge again.

Royal Enfield GP 5

In 1963, the 250cc class of road racing in Britain was jerked into life by the startling advent of the Greeves Silverstone two-stroke. Several other firms, Cotton amongst them, tried to imitate Greeves' success using the recently announced Villiers Starmaker engine unit, but Villiers had been premature, for the Starmaker was full of design faults and grossly underdeveloped, and none were raced effectively until 1964. One man who could have made a worthwhile contribution, Hermann Meier, was working at the Lube factory in Bilbao, Spain. Returning to England in early 1964, he was working for Scott Motorcycles in Birmingham on their air-cooled 350cc twin-cylinder racing engine when he was approached by Geoff Duke with an offer from the Royal Enfield factory. Enfield managing director Leo Davenport was well able to see the potential of the revival of interest in the 250cc class. Enfield themselves had tested a Villiers Starmaker engine in a neat frame built for them by Ken Sprayson of Reynolds Tubes. Test rider John Hartle was enthusiastic about the frame, but by no means so about the engine! Meier's brief was to design a single-cylinder engine that could both be sold to private owners and, developed to a greater degree, raced by a team of factory riders.

Royal Enfield had tested the 'Starmaker' engine on the dynamometer and after careful adjustment had obtained a best reading of 29 hp. Could Meier guarantee an increase of 10 per cent over this figure? He was quite certain that he could, and on the understanding that he would have a free hand with the layout, he joined Royal Enfield. But to his dismay, he soon discovered that he would be forced for 'policy' reasons to use the Alpha crankshaft assembly made by an associated company in the same group as Royal Enfield. As the Alpha assembly had a stroke of 72mm, whereas Meier had envisaged a much shorter stroke, this meant lowering the target crankshaft speed considerably – specifically from approximately 9000 rpm to closer to 8000 rpm. Even so, with the design he had in mind, Meier was still confident of success.

Crankcases of Meier's design were supplied by Alpha bearings and bolted up to an Albion five-speed gearbox by four long studs. Crankcases and gearbox were spaced apart to allow air to cool the crankcases. The rather lengthy duplex primary chain was enclosed in an oil bath. The most original feature of the engine was the transfer porting which embodied two auxiliary transfer ports behind the main ports, fed from corresponding ports milled in the pistons. Battery and coil ignition and a $1\frac{1}{2}$in diameter Amal Grand Prix Mk II carburettor were used. Testing of early engines gave a power output of 34 hp at 8000 rpm with a compression ratio of 12 to 1; this power output was later raised substantially on the dynamometer.

Geoff Duke was anxious and impatient to run a machine in the 1964 Manx Grand Prix, and an experienced rider (and a resident of the Isle of Man), Denis Craine, was engaged to give the Royal Enfield its debut. Alas, the five-speed Albion gearbox broke immediately and Craine's race was over almost before it began. As it was common paddock gossip that Greeves had experienced diabolical trouble with the same gearbox earlier in the season, one wonders whether the Royal Enfield team were not just a little remote from the action!

Hermann Meier (left)
and Charlie Rogers work
on the GP5 prototype.

For 1965, Gordon Keith (who had won the 1964 Manx Grand Prix on a Greeves) and Triumph tester Percy Tait were engaged to ride the Royal Enfield, now known as the GP (Grand Prix) 5. New Albion gearboxes were obtained and the bikes were fitted with 'pointless' electronic ignition. Dyno testing now gave 36 hp at 8000 rpm with exemplary reliability, but at the track the bikes seemed as though under a curse.

At Mallory Park, having gone well in practice, Gordon Keith had his engine lock on the starting line. The cause? – a tiny piece of steel that had been carelessly dropped into the crankcase on assembly and eventually jammed between flywheels and crankcase! Enfield entered Tait and Keith for the 1965 Lightweight TT with equally heartbreaking results. Tait's bike was completely burned out in practice, and though a spare was available, both he and Gordon Keith were eliminated early on by trivial mechancial failures. At the Hutchinson 100 meeting at Silverstone in August, Tait's machine held together long enough for him to finish in third place, behind the factory Yamahas of Phil Read and Mike Duff, at an average speed by no means badly down on that of the winner.

Unfortunately the Enfield management was by now becoming heartily sick of the project, and decided that the 1965 Manx Grand Prix would make it or break it. Neil Kelly, like Craine the year before, a Manxman and with Manx Grand Prix experience, was engaged to ride. The GP5 had by now gone into production and besides Kelly there were seven private entries for the race.

The winner was Denis Craine on a Greeves at a new record speed of 88.37 mph, with a fastest lap of 89.48 mph. On the last lap, Neil Kelly, on the Enfield, was in third place behind Brian Warburton on a TDIB Yamaha. At Ramsey, Kelly was a mere two seconds in arrears. Alas, on the mountain climb, his clutch failed and he was out! Nor did any of the private entries finish, with the exception of S. C.

It looked good, but the GP5's record was abysmal.

Russell, 53rd and last at 52.3 mph! Scarcely the sort of result that the Royal Enfield factory might have wished for, and it came as no surprise to many people that Royal Enfield's retirement from racing was uncompromisingly announced on the front page of the issue of *Motor Cycle News* that carried the report of the race!

It had been a naïve venture embarked upon a year too late by a management that had no experience of road racing – or indeed, latterly, of any sort of competition. The fact that the company were by 1965 in financial difficulties was another nail in the coffin of the GP5. Including the very few machines sold to private customers, between a dozen and 20 machines (estimates vary considerably) had been assembled. A surprising number have survived and, in various degrees of originality, are raced and paraded in CRMC events.

The Starmaker Racers

Both the Cotton Telstar and the DMW Hornet road racers of the mid-1960s were designed around the Villiers 'Starmaker', a brand new competition engine that, so confidently named, made its first appearance at the 1962 motorcycle show. Though Villiers had at the time a near monopoly of supplying two-stroke engines to British lightweight manufacturers, they had for many years resolutely refused to consider any sort of racing. But the upsurge of interest in 250cc Motocross had meant the growth in the late 1950s of a whole new industry of makers of conversion sets for Villiers engines.

One of these, made by Greeves, a small independent motorcycle manufacturer, had been good enough to win the Coupe d'Europe, effectively the 250cc Motocross World Championship of 1960 and 1961. Not only was this poor publicity for Villiers, but it appeared to them that there were extra sales to be made for a genuine competition and super sports engine. The Starmaker was the result. At 68 × 68mm (247cc), it had a fashionably square bore/stroke ratio. It had full circle flywheels with integrally forged mainshafts running in roller main bearings and a caged needle roller big end ran on the pressed-up crankpin.

The crankcase was liberally finned for both cooling and rigidity. So were the light alloy cylinder head and the cylinder barrel with cast-in austenitic liner and machined ports. A duplex primary chain drove the bolted-on four-speed gearbox through a robust metal-to-metal plate-clutch which used a Hausermann diaphragm pressure spring. Ignition was by battery and coil. The carburation arrangements were unorthodox, there being two 1 $^1/_{16}$ in Amal carburettors on a Y-shaped manifold. One carburettor was allowed to open fully before, by use of a complicated junction box mechanism, the other carburettor began to open. The exhaust system, for which great things were claimed, was a peculiar flat affair with baffles and two small, short outlet pipes. Another feature was the torroidal combustion chamber allegedly based on diesel engine practice, which, it was claimed, promoted turbulence in the compressed charge. Perhaps it did, but the fact that the sparking plug was remote from the torroid meant that any advantage was completely wiped out. The simple fact was that at the time of the Starmaker's launch, the Villiers company had done little or no testing. The engine having been conceived as a Motocross unit did not help its prospects for road racing, but over the next twelve months the company encountered all sorts of trouble, and only a tiny handful of engines were supplied.

Royal Enfield tried a Starmaker in a road-racing prototype and decided that they could do better themselves. Greeves dismissed the engine after one look at it. Only Cotton and DMW soldiered on. Both the Telstar and the Hornet were conventional enough motorcycles. The Cotton used Armstrong leading link front forks with the spring-damper units concealed in the stanchions. The DMW used their own make of Metal Profile telescopic forks with a single central spring-damper unit. It also used DMW's own design of Girling-type brakes with a wedging action of the operating cams. The Cotton used proprietary British hub brakes fore and aft. Both machines were nicely made and finished and attracted a lot of interest, but their failure to appear on the track cost them firm sales that inevitably went to Greeves. During 1963 Derek Minter, at that time arguably the best rider in Britain, appeared a few times on a factory-prepared Telstar, but after what seemed a promising debut at Mallory Park at the end of March, when he finished second to Mike Hailwood on his Ducati, he did little more, because in May he crashed his Manx Norton at Brands Hatch and was out of racing for a considerable time. Even

The Villiers Starmaker engined-Cotton Telstar which in the hands of Derek Minter went very well. This restored example has the six-speed gearbox.

The DMW Hornet offered with alternative 9-inch twin leading shoe brake at the front.

so, his experiences with the Cotton led him to tell the company in no uncertain terms how poor the engine was.

This led to Villiers implementing an urgent development programme, which was overlooked by two-stroke technician Peter Inchley. Out went the twin carburettors in favour of a $1^{1}/_{2}$-in Amal GPII instrument, out went the torroidal combustion chamber to be replaced by a wide squish band and central chamber, and out went the ill-conceived exhaust. Over the months Inchley raised the power to a respectable 31 hp at 8000 rpm, and considerably improved its reliability. Even so, Cotton's apparent success in 1964 – Derek Minter and Bill Ivy rode works-prepared machines – was something of a sham where the machines sold to customers were concerned. Minter, it is true, won the ACU Star for 1964, but it was more by default and Minter's brilliant riding than by any great superiority of machinery. In 1965, after a further winter's work by Peter Inchley, the Starmaker-engined Cotton performed much more convincingly, with early wins at Mallory Park, Brands Hatch and Oulton Park for Minter and a win at Snetterton for Bill Ivy.

Inchley himself was also riding a Starmaker-engined machine, the Villiers special, which made use of a Bultaco TSS frame and running gear. A new feature for 1965 was a six-speed gearbox which had been designed by John Favill and Bernard Hooper before they left Villiers at the end of 1964. These were fitted to Inchley's 'Special' and to the machines ridden by Ivy and Minter, and were in theory available to private owners. At the TT there were six Cottons entered, but Bill Ivy was offered a ride by Yamaha in the 250cc race. Apart from the Swiss rider Weiss, the entries by Minter, John Kidson, Chris Conn and Kevin Cass look suspiciously like factory-supported machines, because none of these riders appeared elsewhere on Cottons. The only finisher was Derek Minter, ninth at 84.32 mph. Immediately behind him was Jack Findlay on the only DMW in the race, once again works supported, at 83.87 mph.

At the Manx Grand Prix, there were nine Cottons entered and four DMWs, but there were no fewer than 25 Greeves, one of which, ridden by Dennis Craine, won the Lightweight race at 88.37 mph. Best result by a Starmaker-engined machine was A. F. Dickinson's eighth on his DMW. Two more DMWs and one Cotton finished within replica time.

Towards the season's end, Minter turned his back on Cotton and his bike was ridden to a couple of second places by Dave Degens. The likelihood is that Minter abandoned his 250cc ride when he realized that he could not win the ACU Star, which went to Dave Simmonds on an ex-works Honda twin.

However, he was back on the Cotton for 1966, and scored several leaderboard places in the early races. However, the surprise of the season was Inchley's 'Special', which not only performed well all season on the short circuits, but finished third in the Lightweight TT at 91.49 mph behind the works Hondas of Mike Hailwood and Stuart Graham. At the Manx Grand Prix, P. R. Hunter finished 15th on a DMW, the only Starmaker-engined machine to finish. Cruelly enough, John Wetherall, after making fastest lap on a Cotton at 89.02 mph, retired on the last lap. Entered by Frank Higley, the machine was, though such things were forbidden, almost certainly a works entry in disguise. By late 1966, Villiers were bankrupt. The Starmaker engine had, by and large, been an expensive fiasco, selling in heartbreakingly small numbers even for Motocross. The collapse of AMC, whose James and Francis Barnett machines were Villiers' largest users, was the final blow. Villiers was bought out by Denis Poore's Manganese Bronze Holdings, who had earlier bought AMC, and it was announced in November 1966 that a road racer using the Starmaker engine would, under the AMC name of AJS, be sold in 1967. Prototypes were built, Peter Inchley raced one in the early part of the season without any great success, and he retired at the TT. End of story.

The new Yamaha TD1C made the Starmaker – and all the other singles – look painfully slow. How many Starmaker-engined racers were sold is very hard to discover, but at an educated guess the total could scarcely have been 50, most of those being Cottons.

A surprising number have survived and, restored, are quite a familiar sight in CRMC parades and races.

Suzuki

The Suzuki company of Hammamatsu had been successful makers of textile machinery for nearly forty years when, in 1952, in response to the tremendous domestic demand for cheap transport, they diversified into making simple motorized bicycles. Three years later they introduced a proper motorcycle, the 125cc three-speed Colleda two-stroke. The Colleda's bore and stroke of 52 × 58mm almost certainly indicates that, like so many others, Suzuki had taken a long hard look at a DKW RT125 before embarking on their design. From the Colleda, they evolved a racing machine for the 1955 Asama plains meeting, run over four laps of an 11.9-mile dirt and cinder circuit. The Colleda RB (Racing Bike) had telescopic front forks and swinging arm rear suspension, and the engine was a tuned version of the ordinary Colleda with a piston-controlled inlet port. Five bikes were entered for the meeting, but the race was a triumph for Yamaha and their 125cc YA1 racer – their riders taking the first four places. Two of the Suzukis retired and the rest could do no better than fifth, sixth and seventh. Not too disastrous one would have thought – everyone has to start somewhere – but so disgusted were the Suzuki management that they abandoned racing for the next three seasons.

Then, stimulated by the domestic successes of Honda and Yamaha, they decided to make a serious effort to compete. As chief racing designer they engaged Take-

The Suzuki Colleda RB of 1959 as raced at Asama plains.

hanu Okano, a 49-year-old professor of aeronautical engineering, who was to be assisted by Masanao Shimizu, who had prepared the original 1955 Colleda RBs. The 1959 racers looked the part with large single leading-shoe brakes, conventional suspension fore and aft and sturdy-looking twin-loop cradle frames. The engines, still using piston-controlled induction, now had bore and stroke of 56 × 50.6mm with 22mm Mikuni carburettor and magneto ignition. Three bikes were entered for the 1959 Asama meeting, but Suzuki were no more successful than before, only one rider finishing, in fifth place behind a quartet of Hondas. But instead of withdrawing once again, Shunzo Suzuki, the company's president, decided that they would sink or swim – and that in 1960 they would actually contest the 125cc TT in the Isle of Man! Following this extraordinary decision, considering their meagre results to date, Suzuki sent their technicians Matsumiya and Maruyama to the Isle of Man, where they met up with ACU representative Angus Herbert, Shell race manager Lew Ellis and ex-World Champion Geoff Duke. Between them, they made a very thorough assessment of what was entailed in racing in the TT, which in 1960 was run once again on the 37.75-mile Mountain circuit rather than on the comparatively easy 10.79-mile Clypse course.

Even confronted with the documentation and ciné films assembled by Matsumiya and Maruyama, one senses in retrospect that the embryonic race department really had no real idea just how demanding the TT was going to be!

The new machine, designed throughout by Professor Okano, was the 125cc 44 × 41mm air-cooled twin cylinder RT60, still featuring piston-controlled induction. Except for some insignificant details, the frame and cycle parts very much resembled those of the 1959 Colleda RB. A four-speed gearbox with an open dry-plate clutch was almost certainly inadequate for the Isle of Man, especially since the engine had a desperately narrow power band. Assisted by Shell Petroleum both in Japan and in England, Suzuki arrived in the Isle of Man at the end of May. There were three riders, Michio Ichino, Toshio Matsumoto and a man who was to remain a member of the Suzuki works team longer than most, Mitsuo Itoh. There was also a veritable host of managers and mechanics.

An early misfortune was that because of a misunderstanding, the Suzukis were not entered as Suzuki at all, but instead as 'Colledas'! More serious was that very early on Itoh fell heavily at the Bungalow, hurting his knee badly enough to spend the rest of his TT visit in a bed at Noble's Hospital in Douglas. In his place, Suzuki recruited Liverpool rider Ray Fay, no super star, but a steady rider who knew his way around the Mountain circuit. Throughout practice, Suzuki were continually

Professor Osaka's RT60 125cc twin of 1960. Three finished in the TT, 15th, 16th and 18th.

Stealing MZ's ideas already – disc valve induction on the 1961 125cc twin.

The timing gears that Suzuki blamed for so much of their trouble in 1961.

in trouble with holed pistons and seizures. Nothing in their assessments and calculations had prepared them for the *reality* of the Isle of Man, and though their two-stroke twins had a meagre 13 hp compared with the 23 hp of the Honda four-strokes (never mind the 21 hp of the single-cylinder two stroke MZs), they were forced to lower the already modest 8.8 to 1 compression ratio in the hope that at least the bikes might finish. This they did, but their performance was most unimpressive. Thirty-three machines started and 22 finished. The Italian MV four-stroke singles were first, second and third, and the MZs of John Heplmann and Hugh Anderson fourth and fifth. Hondas filled the next five places, three Ducatis and Pagani's MV the next four. Suzukis trailed home in 15th, 16th and 18th places – Matsumoto in 15th place just scraping into Bronze Replica time. But at least they had *finished* and no one in the team could ever again have any illusions about the nature of European racing in general and the TT in particular!

During their stay in the Island, the Suzuki team had been lodged at the Fernleigh Hotel, where Walter Kaaden and his East German MZ riders and mechanics also stayed. Kaaden did his best to make sure that none of the Suzuki personnel got a good look at the MZ machines, but total secrecy was almost impossible to maintain. And, of course, MZ could make no secret of the most obvious feature of their engines, the rotary disc induction valve. For 1961 Professor Okano designed two new machines, the 44×41mm 125cc twin cylinder RT61 and the 56×50.5mm 250cc, twin-cylinder RV61. Both were air-cooled and both used rotary disc valve induction. Both too had six-speed gearboxes with external dry clutches, but the frames remained surprisingly similar to those of the year before, or come to that, of the original Colleda RB! For the 125cc, 15 hp at 10,000 rpm, for the 250cc, 28 hp at 11,000 rpm were claimed.

By this time, Suzuki had come to the same conclusion as Honda: if they were to make an impact on European racing then they must, however reluctantly, recruit 'European' riders. Whatever the reason, these nominally European riders were usually what were then called 'Colonials', and Paddy Driver, who was Suzuki's first choice, was no exception, being a South African. Though Paddy did a lot of test riding and was entered by Suzuki in both 125cc and 250cc TT events, he was never happy with the small two-strokes and after some disappointing rides, by his standards at any rate, he drifted away. But for 1961, Suzuki's most promising rider was New Zealander Hugh Anderson, well known for excellent rides on MZ, AJS and Matchless machinery and chosen by the shrewd Lew Ellis of Shell Petroleum to join Suzuki at the TT. Once again Suzuki's riders and mechanics stayed at the same hotel as the MZ team.

If they had had a bad practice period in 1960, they had an even worse one in 1961! The reason given for the unreliability of both 125cc and 250cc machines was trouble with the train of three gears that drove the magnetos. Too-tight meshing led to broken teeth, too slack and the alteration in ignition timing caused seizures and holed pistons. But this excuse was a pretty feeble one, and the real problem was almost certainly the abysmally inept exhaust system designs and general ignorance of the finer points of two-stroke technology. (At the time, and for some years after, Suzuki *road* machines were startlingly inferior in many respects to those of Yamaha or even the British Villiers!) Be that as it may, Suzuki were in desperate trouble. With seven machines entered in each race, they were forced to cut down to four in the 125cc event, thus depriving Alastair King, Paddy Driver and Hugh Anderson of their rides. In fact, on race day only three Japanese riders, Itoh, Ichino and Masuda, faced the starting flag. All three were out of the race within three laps! The 250cc race was a little better for Suzuki, but only by contrast! Three machines retired on the first lap, another on the fourth. Only Anderson and Ichino finished, in tenth and 12th places. Anderson, at a race speed of 82.53 mph, more than 15 mph down on Hailwood's winning speed on the four-cylinder Honda, just scraped into Bronze Replica time, the last finisher to do so. He had been headed by five

Hondas, Fumio Ito's Yamaha, a privately entered Moto Guzzi and two six-year-old privately entered NSU Sportmaxes!

It was a very bad day for Suzuki, and indeed for Shell Petroleum, who were publicly backing them. Some fairly desperate measures were contemplated, involving calling in various European two-stroke experts to 'rescue' Suzuki. The rescue, when it came, was from an unlikely direction. In their two expeditions to the Isle of Man, Suzuki technician 'Jimmy' Matsumiya had done his best to learn the secrets of MZ's speed and reliability, and had gone out of his way to be friendly to rider technician Ernst Degner, who, if the truth be told, had quite independently and without any prompting, long since wondered if he could escape from the Eastern zone and sell his skills and talents in the free world. As is often the case in such situations, neither side would make the first move! But at the Dutch TT Degner, Matsumiya and Shunzo Suzuki had a secret meeting that was to have far-reaching consequences.

A great deal was at stake on both sides. Degner was terrified of being found out by his political 'minders', something that would have meant the end of his career and everything he had worked for. He was in the lead in the 125cc World Championship with a good chance of winning. He was, moreover, a brilliant development rider and an asset to any racing organization. Above all he was the intimate associate of Walter Kaaden and had worked closely with him since 1957. In East German terms he had a very good job with many fringe benefits. He now proposed to take enormous risks and make considerable sacrifices. If Suzuki wanted his services then he demanded security (in every sense of the word) and commensurate rewards. Let there be no mistake about *that*. Professor Okano, who was present, protested at one point about Degner's demands. In terms about as close to bluntness as one Japanese was capable of using to another of similar rank,

The TT winning 50cc RM62 designed and ridden by Ernst Degner.

Nothing like so successful, though a huge step forward for Suzuki – Degner's Japanese copy of the MZ, the RT62.

Shunzo Suzuki begged the Professor not to interfere. For Suzuki, this was a life and death affair, almost literally so! To continue to race, doing as badly as they had done to date, was visibly to fail. But to withdraw was almost worse. Suzuki conceded to Degner's demands and an agreement was reached.

Though an informal contract between Degner and Suzuki was drawn up and signed, this was the time of escalating tension between East and West Berlin, and the building of the Berlin wall. In a real-life scenario as crudely dramatic as any spy story, Suzuki undertook to smuggle Degner's wife and two small sons out of East Germany, to be re-united with him in England after the Swedish Grand Prix.

That the plot succeeded is history. The embarrassment and damage done to MZ was catastrophic. Degner knew priceless secrets, which were now at the disposal of a company with the wealth to exploit them, a company far more powerful than MZ. Inept though Suzuki sometimes proved over the next half-dozen seasons, the sheer numbers that they were able to bring to bear ensured that their racing programme brought them tremendous publicity. MZ on the other hand were now regarded as a political risk by the East German government and for several years were restricted in venturing abroad.

What did Degner *really* contribute to Suzuki's racing programme for 1962 and the years that followed? It is not an easy question to answer. Despite his conspicuous failure to take Suzuki to success, Professor Okano continued to stand over racing development and, by some riders' accounts, to exert a baneful influence over many aspects of otherwise promising designs. Though Suzuki were between 1962

The very troublesome 250cc twin of 1962 abandoned later in the season.

The 250cc RZ64 'square-four' modified for 1964, but still with thermo-syphon cooling.

and 1967 to claim six World Championships (to Honda's fifteen and Yamaha's three), four of them were in the 50cc class. Degner certainly lifted Suzuki's racing endeavours bodily out of the no-hope slot that they had occupied in 1960 and 1961, but he was, after all, the Sorcerer's Apprentice, not the Wizard himself. Though his contributions gave an instant and welcome leap upwards in power output and speed, it is difficult now to assess how far his influence extended after that initial breakthrough.

For 1962 he certainly had a major part to play, and Suzuki abandoned the 125cc twin for a single-cylinder of 54 × 54mm, the RT62, that was virtually a copy of the 1961 MZ. The corresponding RV62 250cc twin used the same dimensions. The 125cc unit had seven gears and the 250cc six gears. Both machines had entirely new frames very much after the style of the 'Featherbed' Norton. The 40 × 39.5mm 50cc eight-speed RM62 employed a similar frame suitably scaled down. All three engines of course had disc valve induction and, through Degner's inside knowledge, far superior porting, including the vital third transfer port, to anything that Suzuki had previously achieved for themselves. In another respect the machines showed a great advance. MZ had been late starters in the development of acoustic exhaust pipes, 'expansion chambers' in popular parlance, and even by 1961 had not reached the sureness of touch that they were to show later in the decade. Even so they were eons in advance of Suzuki, whose ludicrous exhaust systems in 1960 and 1961 betrayed a total lack of comprehension of the physics involved.

Degner, though probably not a party to Walter Kaaden's mathematical calculations, had a working knowledge of the relative proportions and rates of taper necessary to 'tune' a system to the engine's speed and porting, and the exhausts that he drew up and that hours upon hours of dynamometer testing refined were as big a breakthrough as any other aspect of the new machines. Both front-facing and rear-facing exhausts were tried, and though dynamometer tests were inconclusive, Degner firmly believed that the rear-facing port gave better acceleration. It had been an article of faith with Walter Kaaden that this was so, due to the angularity of the connecting rod pressing the piston against the rear wall of the cylinder so that there was a better seal between the piston rings and the exhaust port. By the time of the Ulster Grand Prix early in August, the front-facing pipes on some of the bikes were dropped in favour of the rearward-facing pipe that Degner had used all along.

Amongst other MZ spare parts which Degner brought with him to Suzuki were pistons made of high-silicon-content aluminium alloy and oval-turned, two elementary facets of two-stroke technology that seem to have previously been unknown at Suzuki!

Looking back on the 1962 season it is apparent that, though the Suzuki racing machinery was unquestionably far better than before, it was still inferior in the 125cc class to Honda and MZ and in the 250cc class to Yamaha. The 250cc twin was also painfully unreliable and prone to seizing and was all but abandoned as the season went on. Nor was the 125cc single the unqualified success that Suzuki may have expected. Nevertheless, a respectable number of leaderboard places throughout the season, culminating in a win at the Argentine Grand Prix for Hugh Anderson, resulted in Suzuki coming second to Honda in the 125cc World Championship for constructors, an achievement that, on 1961's performance would have been unthinkable.

The really astonishing success was in the newly introduced 50cc class. Since 50cc racing had first sprung into prominence (in Great Britain of all unlikely places), it had progressed from being a bit of harmless fun (with races won at an average speed of 50 mph or so) to extremely serious competition for the FIM's Coupe d'Europe in 1961 with factory participation and support from half a dozen manufacturers. The West German Kreidler factory and their rider Hans Georg Anscheidt had dominated the European Championship rounds and were now looking forward to doing the same with the World Championship. Well appreciating the need for multi-speed gearboxes, Kreidler provided their riders with no less than twelve!

Based in Paris (later to move to Holland), the Suzuki team of Anderson, Degner, Perris, Itoh, Ichino, Seichi Suzuki and Morishito went first to the Spanish and then to the French Grand Prix. At the former event, Suzuki were in dire trouble, and the only result was a poor seventh place for Ichino in the 50cc race. By the time that they reached Clermont Ferrand a week later, the Suzuki riders and mechanics were beginning to appreciate Degner's point that carburation in an actual race differed radically from what served perfectly well on the dynamometer! Nevertheless, Perris for one had three machines seize on him. Degner finished fifth in the 125cc race, and Suzuki, Itoh and Degner were fifth, sixth and seventh in the 50cc event. So far the little RM62 had given no sign of what was soon to turn into a sensational performance.

Because the 50cc TT eventually turned into an ill-supported farce, it is often believed to have been of little interest when it was initiated, but such was far from the case, and the motorcycle press gave it enthusiastic and sympathetic coverage.

Practice showed that Degner's persistence with carburation and gearing was beginning to pay, and the RM62s were visibly faster than the Honda and Kreidler factory entries around the Island. Honda indeed were forced to cable home for ten-speed gearboxes to replace the eight with which they had been confident at the season's beginning. Incredibly, these were made, flown to Europe and fitted in time for the race! Kreidler were in trouble with high-speed handling despite the sophistication of their frames and suspension. The Suzukis on the other hand were fast, they handled and they were reliable. The two-lap race was a walkover for Degner, who averaged a mind-boggling 75.12 mph to finish well ahead of two Hondas and a Kreidler. Itoh was fifth, Ichino sixth and Suzuki eighth.

The 250cc twins proved so unreliable in practice that they were not raced. Nor did the 125cc single cover itself with glory, only Degner finishing in a disappointing eighth place. The RM62 maintained its form throughout the rest of the season, winning four more of the Grands Prix, with a wealth of other good leaderboard positions.

At the Ulster, Degner fell heavily in the 125cc race and badly injured his knee, causing him to miss the East German round, although whether he would have

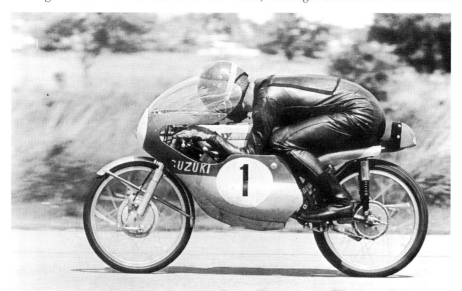

Hugh Anderson rides the RM65, the first of the 50cc twins, to fastest lap and second place at the 1965 Dutch TT.

dared ride there in any case is *most* unlikely, for he was reluctant to venture even to Finland as being too close to the Iron Curtain for comfort. Despite this, the season's performances had been enough for Degner to win the Rider's title, and for Suzuki to win the first of the four World Championships that they were to hold in the 50cc class between 1962 and 1968. In the 125cc class Suzuki won only one Grand Prix (Anderson in the Argentine), but accumulated enough points to finish second in the Constructor's Championship.

For 1963 the 50cc machine remained much the same as far as the cycle parts were concerned, but the engine was now given a rear-facing exhaust, the carburettor size went up to 24mm and a nine-speed gearbox was fitted. Eleven horsepower at 13,000 rpm was claimed for the RM63, a 50 per cent increase over the power output in 1962, when a 22mm carburettor had been used. The RT62 could probably have been developed considerably for 1963, but instead an entirely new 43 × 42.6mm twin was designed and built in two forms, the RT63 with rear-facing exhaust ports and the RT63X with front-facing ports.

As had happened the previous year, it was the rearward-facing exhausts that were eventually used, though Degner used the RT63X to win the non-championship United States Grand Prix in February. Suzuki did not contest the 250cc class for 1963, having the good sense not to stretch the riders and mechanics too far when their chances in the 50cc and 125cc classes appeared to be very bright. In the 50cc class, Honda had at least temporarily withdrawn, and in the 125cc class their new fours were to prove no match for the Suzuki two-stroke twins. It was in 1963 that Austrian rider Bertie Schneider joined the team. Though never in the same class as Degner, Anderson and Perris, he rode well and accumulated enough points in the 125cc class to finish fifth in the World Championship. His best result was his win in the 125cc race at the Belgian Grand Prix.

1963 was a year of outstanding success for the Suzuki team and the company won both 50cc and 125cc Constructor's Championships by a mile. Hugh Anderson was individual champion in both classes. Right at the season's end, at the Japanese Grand Prix at Suzuka, the factory wheeled out three top secret machines for Perris, Anderson and Degner to ride in the 250cc class.

They might have been wiser to keep the advantage of surprise for the start of the next season (and had they done so Ernst Degner would have been spared an horrific accident), but one supposes that Suzuki wanted to put on a show in front of their home crowd as a climax to a successful year.

The model was the ill-fated four-cylinder water-cooled RZ63, the so-called 'square' four. On the first lap of the 250cc race Degner fell heavily, momentarily losing consciousness. When he came to, and went to pick up his machine, the fuel tank exploded in his face, inflicting dreadful burns. At this moment, Frank Perris arrived on the scene and dragged Degner to the side of the track. After that, Anderson's ninth place in the race was only of academic interest. Degner's injuries and subsequent plastic surgery kept him away from the track for most of the 1964 season. The square four should have been invincible, but in fact it was little short of a disaster. In effect two 43 × 42.6mm twins were coupled together by an idler gear and water-cooled. The intrinsically lengthy, bulky and heavy engine was fitted into a stretched version of the 125cc frame, which lacked rigidity and handled in downright dangerous fashion. Weight distribution was highly suspect, and though the frame was successively altered, it never inspired confidence in the riders. Furthermore, it had some irritating tricks, resulting from the fact that the water cooling depended upon thermo-syphon effect. This meant in any case that a larger radiator and total volume (and weight) of water had to be carried than would have been the case had a pump been used. But it also meant that the water temperature fluctuated considerably. If the radiator was large enough to prevent overheating at full demand, then a few seconds of riding on a trailing throttle would allow the temperature to drop enough to upset the carburation! This may well have been connected, too, with the square four's vicious propensity to seize without warning, a trait that caused Australian rider Jack Ahearn, who joined Suzuki for the 1964 TT, to nickname the bike 'Whispering Death'. In the 250cc race, Ahearn's bike seized on the third lap at Glen Helen whilst he was in a good sixth place and he was lucky to escape from a nasty situation.

The four's record in 1964 was a pathetic one, and did Suzuki's reputation no good at all, as it was seen to fail in public over and over again. With Degner out of action through most of 1964, Anderson again won the 50cc World Championship on the RM64 50cc single, but the 125cc twin was now struggling to stay with the vastly improved Hondas, which, for example, finished in first, second and third places at the TT, whilst Perris, Schneider and Anderson all retired. In fact, in 1964 Suzuki only had outright wins at the East German Grand Prix (Anderson), the Ulster (Anderson again) and the Japanese Grand Prix (Degner). In the last event, Degner rode a water-cooled prototype, the 125cc RT64A, in effect the precursor of the RT65.

For 1965, the square four was extensively redesigned, the engine being shortened by coupling the two crankshafts directly together, which enabled the use of a shorter frame. A water pump allowed the use of a smaller radiator and less volume of fluid, and largely cured the problem of unstable water temperatures. But the machine was little used in 1965. Bertie Schneider had either left Suzuki or been sacked – stories vary. Hugh Anderson did not ride it, Jack Ahearn (though he had vowed never again to do so) rode at Rouen and once again crashed! Even now, the forty-year-old Australian was prepared to ride the square four in the TT alongside Frank Perris. But fate took a hand, and his machine seized once again in the last evening practice, and Jack was lucky to escape with his life from a crash that left him too concussed and bruised to start in the race, even had he been so inclined. Frank Perris, nothing daunted, came to the line and, despite having to change a plug, was rewarded with an excellent third place in the 250cc race behind Jim Redman's Honda six and Mike Duff's Yamaha Vee-four. The only other results of any note were Yoshimi Katayama's fourth at the Dutch TT and his fourth and Perris' fifth at Assen. Then much to Perris' disgust, Suzuki decided to abandon the four, despite his conviction that most of its problems were solved. His feeling was that, having persevered with it at the ever-present risk of losing his life, he should have been allowed to challenge Yamaha's new Vee-four fair and square. Yamaha themselves were to experience alarming handling problems in 1966 – Suzuki had largely put theirs behind them, and in retrospect Perris felt that Suzuki stood an excellent chance of winning the 250cc World Championship. However, it was not to be. The Belgian Grand Prix of July 1965 was to be the last appearance of the Suzuki square four.

To combat the menace of Honda's fast and reliable twin-cylinder 50cc machine in 1965, Suzuki had designed and built the remarkable RK65 water-cooled 32.5 × 30mm 50cc twin with its twelve-speed gearbox. Alleged to produce 16 hp at 16,500 rpm, this was housed as a stressed member in a new 'open' frame of dural tube, which with its dural tube swinging arm rear suspension kept the weight down to 130 lb – no more than the single-cylinder air-cooled engine and steel tube frame of the 1964 machinery. However, after Degner, Anderson, Ichino and Koshiro had finished in line astern at Daytona, the new twin went on to a disappointing season.

At the West German Grand Prix, Ralph Bryans and Luigi Taveri on the Hondas were first and second. At the Spanish round, Anderson won, but at Rouen, the two Honda riders again finished first and second. In the Isle of Man Taveri again won the 50cc event ahead of Anderson and Degner. Very plainly, though Suzuki had thought a 12-speed 50cc twin would put them ahead, they were in grave danger of losing the 50cc title! This was indeed to be the case. Degner won at Assen but the Hondas had enough points to win the Constructor's title and Ralph Bryans took the Championship. Fortunately, the 125cc class was another matter.

The 'square-four's' finest hour – Frank Perris on his way to third place in the 1965 Lightweight TT.

Throughout the early part of the season came a succession of wins by Anderson with Degner or Perris in second and third places. The TT was something of a disappointment, for though Hugh Anderson twice broke the 125cc lap record, leaving it at 96.02 mph, he had lost vital minutes during the first lap, having to change a plug whilst in the lead, and heroic efforts could not better fifth place at the finish. After that, an almost unbroken run of wins brought the Championship to Suzuki and to Anderson, who, out of 12 events had won seven.

But looked at a little more closely, Suzuki's affairs were not quite in fairy-tale order at the season's end. A certain coolness and rivalry between Frank Perris and Hugh Anderson had arisen, perhaps when, Anderson being out of action with injuries, Perris had won the East German Grand Prix. This had tempted Anderson to ride too soon in the Czechoslovakian event with his leg still in plaster. In his determination to beat Perris, he crashed again, giving Perris an easy win. Degner had crashed heavily in the rain at Monza, shattering his thigh, and was doomed to spend nine months in hospital, never again to ride for Suzuki except in the 1966 TT, held that year in September after a seamen's strike had caused postponement from the regular date. He finished fourth behind the Hondas of Bryans and Taveri and Anderson's Suzuki and then formally retired.

Although in fact both Perris and Anderson were to sign again with Suzuki for 1966, this was by no means certain at the 1965 season's end, and with Kreidler's withdrawal from the 50cc class no secret, Suzuki offered their star rider, Hans Georg Anscheidt, a place in the team. Travelling to Japan at Suzuki's expense, he finished fourth at Suzuka and was signed on. He was to win the individual 50cc Championship in his first season for Suzuki, though the Constructors' title went to Honda once again. In fact, Anscheidt won the 50cc title for three consecutive years, 1966, 1967 and, after Suzuki had withdrawn from racing, in 1968.

The RK remained substantially the same through those years, though the gearbox contained fourteen ratios instead of twelve, and the power output was eventually lifted to 18 hp at 17,500 rpm. The final RK67 version had a smaller radiator assisted by a water pump instead of the thermo-syphon system which had proved satisfactory on the earlier versions. The 125cc machinery for 1966 differed from that of the previous season only in the use of a dural-tube frame and swinging arm. Unlike the 50cc machine, the 125cc had a full twin-loop frame and did not use

All that machinery for only 50cc – the RK67 exposed.

The RK67 engine in close up.

191

the engine-gearbox unit as a stressed component. Unfortunately for Suzuki, Honda chose to launch their remarkable five-cylinder 125cc racer for the 1966 season and in that year Suzuki scored not a single win, allowing Honda and Luigi Taveri to walk away with the title.

1967 was to be Suzuki's final year in European Grand Prix racing, not that anyone realized that at the season's start. Both Anderson and Perris had retired at the end of 1966, and Suzuki had signed on Stuart Graham on Anderson's advice. Graham had ridden brilliantly for Honda in 1966, but now they withdrew from the 50cc and 125cc classes. Normally this would have made Suzuki's task an easy one. There was now no credible opposition in the 50cc class, and Yamaha were thought likely to be racing their rather elderly RA97 twins – their new RA31 Vee-four had been withdrawn after practice at the 1966 Ulster Grand Prix. But, in fact, any problems that Yamaha may have had then had been well and truly solved by early 1967. For Suzuki, Graham and Yoshimi Katayama were on ten-speed RT67 twins now fitted with water pumps and smaller radiators, for which 35 hp at 14,000 rpm was claimed. It was not enough to hold the Yamahas at bay. Bill Ivy's performance on the Vee-four was quite phenomenal, and brought him – and Yamaha – well-deserved Championships. Early in the season, as it became obvious that the Yamahas were both fast and reliable, the Suzuki racing department did the obvious thing and set about designing a Vee-four of their own. This, the RS67, had bore and stroke of 35.5 × 31.5mm and water cooling by pump. The gearbox contained no less than twelve speeds. Forty-two hp at 16,500 rpm was claimed, which should have been enough to stay with the Yamahas in 1968, but the RS67's only public appearance was at the 1967 Japanese Grand Prix. There Stuart Graham made a poor start, and near the end of the race one of his exhausts broke, but he finished a good second to Bill Ivy.

But in early 1968, Honda announced that they would not contend the World Championship in 1968, and Suzuki almost immediately followed suit. Because Anscheidt and Graham had signed contracts for the 1968 season they were each given a bike, Anscheidt a 50cc and Graham a 125cc, complete in both cases with spares so that they could race them as privateers. Anscheidt, facing negligible opposition, was able to retain his 50cc title.

Very, very few Suzuki racing machines survive today. It was always a rigid factory policy during the years that they were racing that old machines should be destroyed and this was fanatically adhered to. So that there should be no resurrection of these machines, they were almost always given the oxy-acetylene cutter and sledgehammer treatment before being buried in the foundations of new factory buildings. This is sober fact.

The Suzuki factory themselves have only an RM63 50cc single, an RK66 50cc twin and one of the Vee-four racers that were built for the 1968 season. Officially another half a dozen machines have survived, including the 50cc twin and 125cc twin given to Anscheidt in 1968 and the 125cc given to Stuart Graham.

Unofficially, quite a few machines were liberated and stolen and subsequently went underground in the 1960s (most of them in Holland) and some have never surfaced. So if some Dutchman tells you that he has a queer old moped in his garden shed it could be worth a look! But by and large, the few, very few surviving Suzukis are in private hands and in museums.

Triumph Grand Prix

The 500cc twin-cylinder Triumph 'Grand Prix' had a short life and, alas, not a very successful one, lasting only from early 1948 to the end of 1953. The origin of the model lay with the factory 'special' built for the 1946 Manx Grand Prix by renowned tuner Freddie Clarke, using Tiger 100 parts and the light alloy cylinder and head from a wartime generator unit. With this machine fitted with one of Edward Turner's experimental spring hubs, Irish rider Ernie Lyons rode a sensational race in truly appalling conditions to a surprise victory over all the established Norton stars. Why then, did Triumph wait 18 months before offering the Grand Prix for sale? In his book, *Whatever happened to the British Motorcycle Industry?* Bert Hopwood claimed that the whole plot was hatched behind Edward Turner's back, whilst he was away on an American tour, and that he was furious about the whole thing. On the other hand Ernie Lyons told the present writer that Turner not only knew all about it, but gave Freddie Clarke a free hand!

Its late appearance is not quite such a mystery if one takes into account how, at the time, Triumph were overwhelmed with demand for road bikes from the USA, and recall that Freddie Clarke left Triumph to join AMC in January 1947. Even after 18 months, Lyons' MGP victory was fresh enough in people's minds for riders of the calibre of such past TT winners as Freddie Frith, Bob Foster and Ken Bills to enter Triumphs in the 1948 Senior TT along with such well-thought-of privateers as Albert Moule, Norman Croft and Vic Willoughby. Alas, all retired but for Croft, who finished 12th at 76.05 mph. Ken Bills had lain fifth on lap four, and Albert Moule had worked up to sixth on lap six before retiring, but it was a disappointing result.

Manxman Don Crossley did better in the 1948 Senior Manx Grand Prix, leading from start to finish to win at 80.62 mph, despite a desperate last-lap challenge from Charlie Salt on a Norton. Triumph riders also finished fourth and fifth and, in all, there were six within Replica time.

In the 1949 Senior TT 14 Grand Prix models were entered, all of them by 'Clubman' riders. Remarkably S. H. Jenson and C. A. Stevens came home fifth and sixth at 83.17 mph and 82.90 mph. Several riders did reasonably well in short-circuit racing – Percy Tait for one – and almost alone, M. D. Whitworth

Beautifully restored, this 500cc Grand Prix Triumph looks just as it did when new.

(with factory support) campaigned with some success on the Continental Circus, before losing his life at the 1950 Belgian Grand Prix.

In 1950, high-octane petrol became available and, at a stroke, racing speeds were lifted dramatically, the winner's speed in the Senior TT being more than 5 mph faster than the year before. It is arguable that the possibility of high-compression ratios favoured the big single Nortons more than it did the Triumph twins. Be that as it may, in the TT that year no Grand Prix Triumph rider reached the leader-board, and the only finisher was Tommy McEwan in 13th place at 83.39 mph. The Grand Prix model was then dropped, and replaced in the catalogue by the Tiger 100C, nothing more than a Tiger 100 with a race kit. This sold well in America, but very few were seen or raced in England.

The Triumph Grand Prix looked superb and sounded delightful, but had neither the speed nor the stamina of the Norton. Quite a few survive or have been built up as replicas, though few are seen in Classic racing.

Velocette

In 1949 Freddie Firth won the newly instituted 350cc World Championship titles for himself and Velocette, and Bob Foster repeated the feat in 1950. Both men were respected veterans who had won TT races before the war, and both were near the end of their careers. The same could have been said of Velocette themselves, who had started racing 350cc overhead camshaft single-cylinder four-strokes in 1925 and who closed their race shop at the end of 1952. Velocette's first TT win was in 1926, and they won again in 1928 and 1929. Thereafter though wonderfully successful elsewhere, they did not again win a TT until 1938.

In 1929 they offered a racing machine for private owners, the model KTT, and through all the years that this was developed, it bore a very close resemblance to the machines raced by the factory. Some idea of its popularity in the early days can be gained from race reports of the time. In the 1930 Junior Manx Grand Prix for instance the first *eight* riders home were all on Velocettes. For 1936 Velocette retained the brilliant Stanley Woods as their number one rider. Woods improved the machines by moving the engine and gearbox further forward in the frame and persuading the company to adopt rear springing. This was achieved with a simple pivoted rear fork controlled by oil-damped upright units using air as a springing medium. This sprung frame was offered to private owners with the advent of the Mk 8 KTT of 1937. In 1938 and again in 1939 Stanley Woods won the Junior TT with what was in effect a factory prepared Mk 8 Velocette. From 1948 to 1950 the Mk 8 was again in production, but as Velocette were deeply committed to the production of the revolutionary LE commuter bike, they did little or no post-war development on the Mk 8 KTT.

As with all of the model K series from the beginning, the engine had bore and stroke of 74 × 81mm, 349cc. The single overhead camshaft was driven by vertical shaft and bevels and operated the valves through rockers. Hairpin springs were used and the valve gear was fully enclosed. The pressed-up crankshaft ran in taper roller main bearings and there was a caged needle roller big end. Oil was fed by a double gear pump to the big end, to the contact point of cams and rockers and to the top pair of bevel gears driving the camshaft. The oil drained back into the crankcase sump and was then recirculated via the dry sump oil tank. Magneto ignition and an Amal racing carburettor were used. Pre-war, on 50/50 petrol/benzole, 27 hp at 6500 rpm was quoted, and as fuel of a lower octane rating was specified post-war until 1950, it is unlikely that this figure was significantly bettered. The post-war Mk 8

The legendary Freddie Frith on his Velocette in 1949. He won every round of that year's 350cc World Championship.

The post war KTT Velocette as sold to paying customers.

Works Velocette for the 1952 Junior TT – the last year they raced.

retained the pre-war frame, even to the 'girder' front forks. When racing first resumed post-war it was with pre-war machinery and in the 1947 Junior TT Velocettes ridden by Bob Foster, David Whitworth and Jock Weddell finished first, second and third.

The following year Freddie Frith won and Foster was second. But with the advent of the championships in 1949 Velocette prepared a number of very special machines with double overhead camshaft engines using magnesium castings. Many of the cycle parts too were of lighter construction and these special machines had a remarkable performance. There were only five championship rounds, at the TT, the Swiss, Belgian and Ulster Grands Prix and the Grand Prix des Nations at Monza. Freddie Frith convincingly won every round to take the Championship. However, at the Manx Grand Prix that year, the best-placed Velocette was that of Cecil Sandford in fifth place, headed by the Nortons of Cromie McCandless and Geoff Duke and, significantly, by the 7R AJSs of Don Crossley and Peter Romaine.

Having won the Championship, Freddie Frith retired, and for 1950, his place as number one Velocette rider was taken by Bob Foster. At the TT Bob retired on the first lap, but thereafter showed his and the double overhead camshaft Velocette's remarkable form with a win in Belgium ahead of Artie Bell and Geoff Duke on works Nortons, and another (ahead of Duke) in Holland. At the Swiss Grand Prix Foster, along with several others, fell in a first lap incident caused by rain and an appalling road surface, but he remounted and finished second to Les Graham on a factory 7R AJS. Then with a win in the Ulster Grand Prix he clinched the title for the second year running.

By now Velocette were well into production with the road-going model LE and production of the Mk 8 had all but ceased. The credible alternative to a 40mm Manx Norton, for the private owner, had now become the 7R AJS. Under the circumstances, one wonders why for 1951 Velocette chose to race at all, and even more why they should choose to race in the 250cc class! Nevertheless, they built three 68 × 68.5mm racers with the engines housed in rather inept new frames fitted with telescopic front forks of Velocette design. Five-speed gearboxes were used, and one 350cc machine on the same lines was built to be ridden by Bob

Foster. However, the 1951 season was an almost complete washout, and so was an even more reduced effort in 1952. The end of a proud tradition had arrived.

Today, a large number of Velocette racers survive in private hands and are sometimes seen in parades and even in races. Many of the special factory machines have been traced and restored by arch Velocette enthusiast Ivan Rhodes, and give pleasure to many people every year.

Yamaha
YDS1R-TD1C

When, in 1954, the Nippon Gakki company, based in Hammamatsu, decided to apply their Yamaha musical instrument trademark to a lightweight motorcycle, it was to a German machine first seen nearly 20 years earlier that they turned for inspiration. In this they were in good company, for the simple DKW RT125 two-stroke, designed in 1935 by Martin Weber, had been (and continued to be) a best-seller in its own right and post-war had been the basis of at least half a dozen other makes of motorcycle, most notably the Harley-Davidson Hummer and Britain's ubiquitous BSA Bantam. Yamaha's version, the YA1, was actually an improvement on the original, having primary drive by gears instead of chain and with four gears in the gearbox instead of three. Despite fierce competition within the Japanese industry, the YA1 straightaway captured a viable portion of the domestic market and made Yamaha motorcycles a profitable operation. To race was, in the mid-1950s, the cheapest and most obvious way of advertising in Japan, and Yamaha took tuned YA1s to the Fuji and Asama meetings in 1955.

Success rewarded their efforts, and the result was an immediate and gratifying rise in sales. So successful was the YS1 that Yamaha decided that they must offer another model, a 250cc twin. They could well have simply doubled-up the existing 125cc engine, but they did not, choosing instead to acquire another German motorcycle for study. This was an MB250 Adler, a machine of notable refinement, elegant design and superb engineering. At the time, Adler enjoyed a wonderful reputation in competition, not only in events such as the International Six Days Trial but also in domestic German road racing, and it is likely that this weighed heavily with Yamaha. The Yamaha YD1 that appeared on the Japanese market for the 1957 season was no slavish copy of the Adler. In view of subsequent history, it is ironic that the Yamaha designers identified and eliminated a poor feature of the German design – use of an engine speed clutch located outboard of the primary drive gear on the left-hand crank mainshaft. The YD1 engine was straightforward enough, with vertically split crankcases and unit four-speed gearbox. There were two separate full-circle flywheel assemblies, bolted together, with a splined centre-section embracing a labyrinth gas seal between the two crankcases.

The 180-degree crank assembly ran in four ball bearing races and the outer shafts ran in conventional garter seals. In the small ends of the connecting rods were phosphor bronze plain bearings, in the big ends, crowded rollers. Mainshafts and crankpins were pressed-up with interference fits. The right-hand mainshaft carried a 6-volt alternator and the twin ignition make and break. The iron cylinders were deeply spigoted into the crankcases, so much so that the inlet tracts for the single carburettor were formed within the crankcase castings. Domed pistons and light alloy heads with central sparking plugs provided at least a token squish band. The frame was pressed steel, rather heavy but not at all unattractively styled, with deeply valanced mudguards and pressed-steel enclosure for the rear chain. There

How it all began – Fumio Ito races on the dirt section at Catalina Island in 1958.

were large cast alloy full-width hubs with adequate brakes, and suspension was by conventional telescopic forks at the front, swinging arm and spring units at the rear. Again, the YD1 was an immediate success, and again Yamaha planned to race tuned versions in Japanese competitions. But the bikes that were first raced at Asama in 1957 differed considerably from the road-going model.

Twin carburettors and racing exhausts were used, and the engines highly tuned. Recognizing that the pressed-steel frame was too heavy and cumbersome for racing, a new steel tube frame was built and damped rear units fitted. At Asama, once again Yamaha were gratifyingly successful, taking the first three places in the 250cc race, much to the disgust of Honda! Again, sales of road bikes rose accordingly, but by now Yamaha had their eyes on the American market, and for 1958 decided to send their star rider, 'wild man' Fumio Ito, to the Catalina Grand Prix, a part-road, part-dirt race held on Catalina Island. The same frame design was used, but Ito at first experimented with replacing the rear suspension units with solid struts! The engine featured a different bore and stroke, and was oversquare at 56 × 50mm. It was a configuration that was to last a dozen years. The Catalina bike had twin carburettors and high-level exhausts, and indeed resembled a Motocross machine more than a road racer. Unfortunately, the exuberant Ito, whilst well placed, cast the machine away, and though he did all he could to recover, he could manage no better than sixth place. But the bike had been shown to be fast, rugged and reliable, and Yamaha were well pleased.

For 1959, Yamaha took a great step forward with the delightful YDS1 road machine, which with one exception (and that an unlucky one) showed no trace of its German ancestry. The frame was to the same pattern as the Catalina racer, but much heavier, and with stouter front forks and oil-damped rear spring units. The engine was completely new. Bore and stroke were 56 × 50mm, and the use of a new five-speed gearbox meant that the crankcase and gearbox castings (still split vertically) were revised, and no longer embraced the inlet tracts. The cylinders were still cast iron, but well designed and cooled. The styling of the YS1 was frankly stunning, and though not as light as it looked, its performance was a revelation for the time. The one part of the design that was in fact a reversion to the MB250 Adler of three years earlier was the use of an engine speed clutch, hung outboard of the primary drive gear on the end of the left-hand crank mainshaft. On the road-going YDS1, this was no particular drawback, and probably contributed its mite to the engine's smoothness and torque. But it does not require a degree in mechanical engineering to appreciate that with a *racing* motorcycle, turning at up to 10,000 rpm, the change in momentum of such a considerable mass (attendant upon too-enthusiastic a start, or a missed gearchange) could result in the snapping of the engine shaft like the proverbial carrot! Through the life of the Yamaha 'production' racers, until the TD1C of 1967, this clutch was to be a miserably weak point requiring constant attention.

For 1959, Yamaha offered the YDS1R, a race kit to fit the standard YDS1 consisting of racing seat, tank, mudguards, clip-ons, light alloy cylinder with cast-in iron liners, 27mm racing carburettors and racing exhausts. Racing machines of 250cc that could be purchased by the ordinary 'clubman' racer at that time were few and far between either in Europe or in America. To sell the YDS1R in the States should have been excellent advertising for Yamaha, and helped sales of the road bikes, instead the race-kitted bikes were a disaster, none too reliable mechanically, and horribly prone to seizure and holes in the crowns of the pistons. Nor were they fast! In fact they were slow enough not to expose the handling deficiencies that a better performance would inevitably have shown up! The major villain of the piece where 'thermal reliability' was concerned was the quite ludicrous exhaust systems, which were nothing more or less than a straightforward copy of the pipes, developed years before in Germany, for the RS250 Adler, and which, unmatched to the rest of the engine, in effect weakened the mixture at high rpm and caused detonation.

Yamaha chose to interpret this failing as being due to a poor heat-path between the cast-in iron liner and the light alloy cylinder. Had that been so, then the most sensible expedient would have been to have used 'pressed-in' iron liners, fine-machining the mating faces and using a high-temperature shrink-fit. Yamaha, however, experimented with chrome plating and anodizing of the light alloy cylinders, doing away entirely with the iron liners. According to author Collin McKellar in his book *Yamaha Two-Stroke Twins*, they 'coated the cylinders with nylon' in 1962. If they did, then they would havee been bitterly disappointed, as nylon melts at quite low temperatures, as anyone can prove for himself! Even Teflon (PTFE) would not maintain the necessary mechanical properties inside the

Sonny Angel's YDS1R with Norton front brake.

Possibly the first racing Yamaha into England – an early TDIA.

The TD1B still came with kickstart and carburettors that were far too small.

cylinder of a racing two-stroke. This passage, in an otherwise quite superb book, remains an enigma.

No YDS1Rs were sold in Europe, but in 1960 Californian rider Sonny Angel came to England to take part in a few short-circuit meetings and, more importantly, to compete in the Lightweight TT in the Isle of Man. The motorcycle press took considerable interest in this previously unheard of racing motorcycle, but its performance turned out to be very disappointing. Reporting the race meeting at Silverstone on 28 May, *The Motorcycle* commented: 'By lap four of the 250cc event, Mike Hailwood on his Ducati had lapped Sonny Angel on his five-speed, Japanese-built Yamaha twin.' And another machine to add to Sonny's discomfiture by lapping him was an Ariel Arrow, tuned by Herman Meier and ridden by M. P. O'Rourke that finished fourth behind Hailwood and two NSU Sportmax riders.

The TT was even more of a fiasco, for poor Sonny did not even qualify. Writing in *Motorcycling*, Phil Irving said: 'The Yamaha 250cc twin, like the Suzukis, suffered continually from burned and seized pistons and did not give a very good account of itself.' Though the ACU offered to waive qualification, Sonny Angel did not start. At this time, good though their road bikes undoubtedly were, Yamaha showed almost no intelligent understanding of how the racing two-stroke engine really worked. Thus, when the factory-built TD1 replaced the race-kitted YDS1R in 1962, it was *still* fitted with the exhausts designed for the RS250 Adler! And though the pipes fitted to the TD1A had tapered reverse cones rather than the parabolic 'cones' of the TD1, the pipes were plainly far too short. In effect, exhausts that would have become effective at 10,500 rpm were fitted to an engine that was strangled by inadequate carburettors and an inlet timing move suitable for about 8000 rpm. The result was a racing motorcycle that was 'all show and no go' – plenty of rpm but no real performance. Despite claims for the TD1 and TD1A of 32 hp at 9500 rpm, it is very unlikely that they developed much more than 27 hp. The TD1 and TD1A now employed a pressed-in iron liner, and though this did improve thermal reliability, it was not a complete cure.

In 1963 there were only three Yamahas in Britain and they made absolutely no impression. Not until 1964 did a few bold spirits work out for themselves why the bikes were so disappointing. And disappointing they were. Several other riders since Sonny Angel had entered Yamahas in the TT. One of the very few finishers had been R. W. Boughhey, who, in 1964, finished fifth, but that year there were only eight finishers, and Boughhey's speed of less than 80 mph (with a fastest lap of 80.91 mph) put the result into perspective, when contrasted with the winning average of 91.45 mph! So did the results of that year's freshly reintroduced Lightweight Manx Grand Prix, won at a most impressive 86.19 mph by Rhodesian Gordon Keith on a single-cylinder Greeves Silverstone two-stroke. Aermacchis were second, third and fourth, the first Yamaha being fifth, five mph down on the Greeves winning speed. Nevertheless, it was during 1964 that Northerner Brian Warburton scored the first ever win by a Yamaha in Britain at the July meeting at

Brian Warburton hustles a TD1B to second place in the 1965 Manx Grand Prix.

Don Padgett on a TD1C in the 1967 Manx Grand Prix. He finished third.

Aintree, beating the Greeves of Bill Crozier and John Shacklady. He thereafter had many more good results, and significantly nearly (but not quite) beat Dennis Graine's Greeves in the 1965 Lightweight Manx Grand Prix. It was in July that Reg Everett riding a Yamaha tuned by London dealer Ted Broad won his 250cc race at Snetterton, the first of many excellent results. Reg, in fact, went on to become one of the most successful Yamaha riders of the Classic years, others who readily spring to mind being Don Padgett and Derek Chatterton. But during 1965 and 1966, though the number of Yamahas increased all the time, a TD1B was no guarantee of a win or even a good place in British short-circuit racing. The dubious reliability of the engine speed clutch, and the still existing discrepancy between inlet and exhaust timing meant that even for the 1966 season the rider of a Greeves, Cotton, Bultaco or Aermacchi stood as good a chance of winning races as did a Yamaha owner.

Apologists for Yamahas of this time often claim that their relative lack of success was due to poor handling, but at the time none of the more successful riders complained about this. What they wanted was more power! This they got with the appearance of the TD1C. Sooner or later, Yamaha had to get it right, and the wonder is that it had taken so long. To be sure, the TD series were developed by quite a different team from that responsible for the RD series of works racers, but one is entitled to think that if it was possible for British and American amateur tuners to effect improvements, the job could have been done so much more easily in Japan!

Be that as it may, the TD1C settled any argument. It had its clutch mounted where it always should have been, on the end of the gearbox mainshaft. The cylinders now had their bores hard chrome plated by a licenced process and the plating did not chip or peel as it had on earlier engines.

The TD1C was fast and far more reliable than any previous Yamaha. Despite sometimes scathing comments passed on its handling by testers today, the impres-

Yamaha TD1C engine forks and wheels in a special frame, raced at Daytona. American tuners had a lot to do with making the TD1C perform.

sion at the time was that it was better in every respect than earlier TDs and as good as any bike that could be bought. The vast improvement in performance came about because at long last, by using a bigger inlet port, longer inlet timing and new exhausts, the inlet and exhaust sides of the engine's breathing no longer fought one another, but were in harmony at the same speed. A minor feature, seemingly insignificant at the time, was the use of auxiliary transfer passages, one each side of the inlet port and fed via ports in the piston skirt that opened just after the main transfer ports. Looking at these, merely the depth of a few millimetres, it would have been easy to say, as some people did, that they were too small and restricted to perform any useful function. Easy, but quite wrong, and these insignificant-looking ports foreshadowed a whole new area of future development in racing two-strokes.

As it had been with the Greeves Silverstone in 1963, the results of a few events early in 1967 made it painfully apparent that anything other than a TD1C Yamaha was going to struggle in the 250cc class in British racing and this became even more the case as the season went by. Brian Ball won the Lightweight Manx Grand Prix. The race was run in horrible wet and windy conditions and was cut to four laps, but Ball averaged 83.73 mph. Four Yamahas finished in Replica time, and another seven finished.

By 1968, the Yamaha 'takeover' was so total that Greeves, whose Silverstone models had sold steadily and won races at all levels for five seasons, simply withdrew from what had become a quite unequal contest. Such was the measure of the Yamaha TD1C. Subsequent development of the 350cc TR2 and the water-cooled TZ models is outside this directory's scope, but during the 1970s Yamaha production racers came to dominate every class of racing.

Not as many TD series racers survive as might have been expected. Nor are they particularly prominent in CRMC racing, although one highly modified TD1C owned by Arthur Pine was so successful that it was eventually barred! Several very nicely restored and original TD Yamahas are aired in CRMC parades.

The Works Racers

The origins and early history of the 125cc single-cylinder Yamaha YA1 and twin-cylinder 250cc YD1, and the racing versions developed from them, are told in the section of this directory devoted to the Yamaha TD series. Essentially stripped, modified and tuned versions of the road bikes, both models did well in Japanese domestic racing – what there was of it – and the so-called Catalina 250cc twin was a definite evolutionary step in the development of the YDS1 road bike and the TD1 racer.

However, in 1960, Yamaha set up a Race Development department of greater importance, and considerably more success, than the section responsible for the TD 'customer' racers. This Department was headed through the vital years by a young doctor of Aeronautical engineering, Makayasu Nakamura, who in a few years had risen to the post of chief designer to Showa, a motorcycle company taken over by Yamaha in 1959. Nakamura had been tremendously impressed by the development in Europe of the MZ two-stroke, and had become a firm advocate of the rotary disc induction valve in particular, and the approach of MZ's Walter Kaaden in general.

With Yamaha's decision to contest the World Championships, albeit in a limited way to begin with, Nakamura asked for and was given one year to come up with competitive 125cc and 250cc machines. The outcome was the 56×50mm, 125cc RA91 and the 56×50mm RD48, both entirely new and purpose-built designs with sensible commonality of components. Both engines had disc valve induction, the single-cylinder RA91 having a valve and carburettor on either side of the crankcase (a feature which was copied in 1962 by West German firm Kreidler for their 50cc Grand Prix racer). Both engines had vertically split crankcases and simple pressed-up crankshafts with caged needle roller big ends. Though general lubrication was by oil in the petrol, the big end bearings were supplied with extra oil via drillings in the crankshaft fed by a pump mounted on the gearbox. Six-speed gearboxes and external dry clutches were used, the gearboxes and external dry clutches were used, the gearboxes being in unit with the crankcases. The light alloy cylinders had iron liners pressed into place to a high interference. High-silicon content pistons carried one thin steel piston ring with hard chrome plating on the bearing edge. Such rings had been used successfully by DKW several years earlier and they were almost unbreakable. Unfortunately they could not be used in a chrome bore as rapid wear resulted. In time Yamaha's RD section were to solve

Fumio Ito races to sixth place in the 1961 Lightweight TT. Did the fairing help or hinder?

Yamaha's first really competitive RD56 of 1963 seen here in the Island. Fumio Ito finished second to Redman's Honda by 0.27 seconds!

Fumio Ito (right) with Don Vesco after the US Grand Prix of 1963.

even this problem. The exhaust pipes showed the least sure touch of any point of the design, although this too would be remedied in time.

Both RA91 and RD48 shared the same frame, to the same design, but made from better-quality, lighter-gauge tubing, as the YDS1. Oil-damped telescopic front forks and rear suspension units were used, and the single leading-shoe brakes were a close copy of proprietary Italian Cerianis. Both machines were fitted with huge Dolphin fairings with exaggerated 'blisters' which concealed the riders' arms excellent aerodynamically, but any advantage must have been lost by the unnecessarily large frontal area. It was in 1961 that Yamaha made their first limited foray into European Grand Prix racing with the RA91 and the RD48. 1961 was the year in which Europe, especially Britain, lost any illusions that may have existed earlier about the capabilities of Japanese motorcycle engineers. Honda had raced at the TT in 1959 and 1960 and acquitted themselves honourably, though their twin-cylinder 125cc and four-cylinder 250cc machines had been no match for the highly developed European machines and their experienced riders.

In 1959, racing on the short Clypse course, Japanese riders of 125cc Honda twins had finished sixth, seventh, eighth and 11th. In 1960, on the much more demanding Mountain circuit, they had finished sixth, seventh, eighth, ninth and tenth in the 125cc race, and in the 250cc fours had finished fourth, fifth and sixth in their race.

The Press and the public were quite rightly impressed and were disposed to take Japanese machines, even Japanese two-strokes, seriously. The 1960 fiasco of poor Sonny Angel's YDS1R was forgotten. First reports said that Yamaha were sending a 'twelve-man team of riders', but this was a misunderstanding, and in fact Yamaha's team conprised their star rider Fumio Ito backed by H. Oishi, O. Masuko, T. Noguchi and Y. Sunako. All were to ride both 125cc and 250cc machines and under the circumstances they acquitted themselves extremely well. By later standards, Yamaha's claim of 18 hp for the RA91 and 35 hp for the RD48 seemed modest and realistic, and such power, especially in the hands of comparatively inexperienced riders could scarcely challenge the Hondas or even the highly developed European machines of the time.

Yamaha's European debut was at the French Grand Prix at Clermont Ferrand. In the 125cc race Noguchi finished eighth. In the 250cc race Ito was eighth, and Noguchi tenth, and no doubt their feelings were that they had done well to have any finishers at all!

Then they went on to a far more demanding test in the Isle of Man, where the 125cc race was of three laps and the 250cc race of five laps of the still-punishing $37\frac{3}{4}$-mile Mountain circuit.

In the 250cc event, Ito was within sight of the leaderboard throughout the whole race, but one by one his team-mates retired. Ito did extremely well to finish in sixth place, although to keep matters in perspective, his speed of 87 mph was 11 mph down on Hailwood's winning speed, and would not in fact have won the 125cc event! Almost forgotten now, the little RA91s proved more reliable and relatively faster, with Ito finishing 11th, Oishi 12th and Noguchi 17th in the 125cc race, all of them, be it emphasized, within Silver Replica time. In view of the RA91's bulk and weight, this was a better result than it appears.

At Assen in Holland, Ito scored another sixth place in the 250cc race with Noguchi eighth, and in the 125cc event Sunako was ninth, Ito tenth. The final round of Yamah's 1961 season was at Spa-Francorchamps in Belgium. Ito finished fifth and Sunako sixth in the 250cc class, Sunako and Oishi 13th and 14th in the 125cc race.

Yamaha had added interest to the Grand Prix scene and won a lot of friends, and were cordially invited to stay in Europe for the remainder of the season, but at the end of July they returned to Japan. They had not driven all before them – neither had Honda in 1959 or 1960 – but they had nothing to be ashamed of, and could

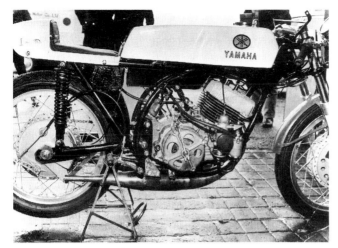

The 1964 RD56 appears lower and neater than the previous year's model.

Almost the end of the line for the twin in 1965.

reasonably expect to return in 1962 with machinery substantially improved in the light of experience. But in fact, in their absence, things had not gone well with Yamaha. An ill-considered attempt to meet Honda head on in the domestic 50cc 'step through' market and the launch of a disastrously bad scooter at almost the same time backfired badly and brought the company close to insolvency. Fortunately, drastic measures rescued Yamaha, but racing was a luxury that had to be foregone for 1962. Even so, the RD section were not idle. Dr Nakamura had his eyes firmly fixed on the future, and (at the expense of the RD91) development of the 250cc twin was intensified.

The high speeds of European circuits and especially of the Isle of Man had exposed the limitations of a frame that was after all basically three years old, and suspension that derived from road bike components. A new frame was built, lighter and stiffer, with full twin loops, designed after the fashion of the Norton 'featherbed' with ample gusseting in the area where the front tubes crossed the tank rails. Suspension, front and rear, was improved considerably, but strangely, single-leading-shoe brakes were retained.

The engine was entirely new, with a seven-speed gearbox driven by a central gear between the two crankcases. The carburettors were increased in size and the inlet timings extended. The cylinders were now light alloy castings with chrome bores and the pistons were fitted with very narrow cast iron rings. The third transfer ports, previously vestigial, were now of generous size and fed direct from the crankcase. Vastly improved exhaust systems now made their appearance, seeming to indicate that the RD section had carried out some vital, fundamental research. Power at 11,000 rpm was still modestly claimed at 40 hp. Gone was the monster fairing, replaced by extremely graceful streamlining of much reduced frontal area (and with detachable belly-pan) that would have been a credit to any Italian designer.

This machine, now known as the RD56, was ready in plenty of time for the 1962 Japanese Grand Prix at Suzuka; in a very close-fought race, Fumio Ito was third behind the Hondas of Jim Redman and Tommy Robb. A Honda win was almost taken for granted, and third place by another Japanese make, with a Japanese rider, was excellent publicity. Over the winter, the RD56 was further refined, the carburettor size increased and the magneto replaced by coil ignition. Power was increased to the level – and perhaps beyond – of the four-cylinder Honda. The improved RD56's first appearance outside Japan was at the United States Grand Prix at Daytona, Florida, and in the absence of Honda, Ito made short work of the 250cc event. The sensation, however, was Don Vesco's win in the *Senior* race, overcoming a formidable array of talent mounted on 500cc Manx Nortons and G50 Matchlesses! 'This brilliant performance should put every participant in Inter-

Technician Hasegawa (left) and Bill Ivy in 1966 with the RA97 twin.

Getting the heat away
was not easy on short
circuits – this special
brake was fitted to Bill
Ivy's bike as an
experiment.

The extremely bulky, heavy engine of the 1966 RD05 250cc.

209

national racing on their guard for 1963,' wrote one British journalist – a true prophet!

Following this giant-killing act, Ito obtained permission to attack the lap record on the 2½-mile banked oval track and was successful, turning in a fastest lap of 131.2 mph!

In Europe, Yamaha team riders Ito, Sunako and Hasegawa were joined in the Isle of Man by Englishman Tony Godfrey, chosen for his expert knowledge of the Mountain circuit. But Ito showed his quality by lapping in practice at 93.04 mph, whilst Godfrey for all his experience did only 89.42 mph. Yamaha had entered the 125cc race, but long before they left Japan the decision had been taken to abandon these entries and to concentrate upon the 250cc class.

The race began sensationally with Ito in the lead at the end of the first lap at a speed from a standing start of 95.93 mph with Godfrey in second place and Jim Redman on the Honda third. On the second lap, Godfrey had sparking plug trouble and was forced to call at the pits. In hurrying to regain lost places, he crashed heavily near Milntown, sustaining injuries which effectively ended his racing career. On the third lap, Ito slowed, allowing Redman to take the lead, and in that order they finished, Redman winning by the incredibly slender margin of 0.27 seconds! Hasegawa finished fourth. Truly a wonderful TT debut for the RD56. At Assen in Holland, Ito was again second to Redman with Sunako fourth.

The following weekend at Spa in Belgium, Ito scored Yamaha's first win in a European Championship Grand Prix, Redman being sidelined with a broken collar bone, and none of the other Honda riders being able to catch the flying Yamahas. Ito won with ease, raising the lap record to 117.82 mph and Sunako was second, 15 seconds behind. With that extremely convincing demonstration of what they could achieve, the Yamaha team once again returned to Japan. In November they raced again at Suzuka, an event that was of crucial importance for Jim Redman and Honda, for incredibly he was trailing in the World Championship to Italian rider Tarquinio Provini on the single-cylinder Morini! Unfortunately for Provini, the best he could achieve was fourth, and thus he lost the Championship to Redman, who won the race, by 0.4 seconds, from Ito's Yamaha! Third, with a sick engine, was Phil Read, who had flown out to Japan at the factory's request for his first ride for Yamaha. He was to join them for the 1964 season.

1963 had been a wonderful year for Yamaha, during which they had done all that could have been expected. They had never anticipated beating the massive Honda organization with its experienced European riders, but they had come close to doing so and had given Honda many a fright.

It was all the more gratifying that this had been achieved by Yamaha's own Race Development section working to Makayasu Nakamura's ideas, step by step, in a scientific fashion. No doubt Ernst Degner's defection to Suzuki at the end of 1961 had increased the common fund of understanding of the problems of racing two-strokes, but Yamaha had been on the right path since 1961.

The machinery for 1964 was altered only in detail, but none the less, power was up to close on 50 hp. At Clermont Ferrand, Read won easily when Jim Redman's Honda uncharacteristically had valve spring problems. It was at this stage that Fumio Ito, so long Yamaha's star rider, abruptly disappeared from the racing scene. He had been in poor health early in the year and though he went with the team to the Isle of Man he did not practice. He was flown out at Yamaha's expense to convalesce with an extended holiday in Miami. I have not been able to discover his subsequent movements. At the TT Read was forced to change a plug, and in trying to make up lost places, he lapped at 99.42 mph on lap four to take the lead ahead of Redman, but the Yamaha's crankshaft broke on the last lap. At Assen, Read finished second to Redman. At Solitude in West Germany, a course to which he was a stranger, Read beat Redman, and at the Sachsenring in East Germany the result was the same. The final round was at Monza, and here Honda shook the world of road racing by wheeling out a *six-cylinder* machine for Jim Redman!

It was a bad moment for Yamaha. The 'six' was sensationally fast, far faster than the Yamaha, but luck was with Phil Read, and the six went first on to five, then on to four cylinders and Read swept to a win, closely followed by Mike Duff, who made fastest lap at 116.02 mph. The World Championship was Yamaha's!

It was a wonderful achievement – in four scant seasons from celebrating a sixth place in the Lightweight TT to being Champions of the World – but the Race Development department scarcely had time to congratulate themselves in the face of the menace posed by Honda's six. And that it *was* a menace was amply confirmed at Suzuka, when Redman ran rings around the Yamaha twins. Drastic rethinking was called for. It took the form of the remarkable four-cylinder RDO5. During 1964 a 125cc twin, the RA97 had been built with bore and stroke of 40 × 41mm. Apart from an eight-speed gearbox, it was almost literally a scaled-down version of the RD56, and produced close to 30 hp at 13,000 rpm. This was raced only once, at Assen, when Phil Read finished a good second to Redman's Honda four. For the 1965 season it was converted to water-cooling. If the RD section could make a 125cc twin, then they could make a 250cc four.

But despite confident assertions by the Press that such a four-cylinder machine would appear at Daytona in March, it was very much in the future, and for most of 1965 Phil Read and Mike Duff depended upon the twins. At Daytona, Read and Duff took an easy win and second place against negligible opposition, after which they and the bikes flew to Europe. It is a measure of the RD section's confidence in the machinery that there was to be no massive back-up support. A team of mechanics was sent over for the TT and the Dutch and Belgian Grands Prix, but for the rest of the season there was only one Japanese mechanic to attend to vital maintenance between races! At the opening European round in Germany, Jim Redman was unlucky enough to fall heavily in the 350cc race, breaking his arm and thus eliminating himself from the 250cc race, which was once again a walk-over for

The RD05 looks as though it would be a pig to ride, and it certainly proved so in the early days.

Read and Duff. Read won the Spanish Grand Prix in Redman's absence, but the Honda rider was back in action for Rouen, and demonstrated the six's superior speed before the gearbox failed. Another win for Read.

At the TT Read made history with a standing start lap of 100.01 mph, but on the next lap his engine failed, letting Jim Redman into first place and Bill Ivy, who had joined Read and Duff for the TT into second place, and Mike Duff into third. On the fourth lap, Bill Ivy threw his bike away at Brandywell, and Mike Duff was the only Yamaha finisher, second to Redman.

Read had persuaded Yamaha to overbore an RD56 to 254cc, and with this he finished second in the 350cc race, again to Jim Redman. In the 125cc race, all three Yamaha riders rode the water-cooled RA97s, and Read won the race from Luigi Taveri on the Honda, with Mike Duff third.

The Dutch Grand Prix saw Read beating Redman fair and square, though the positions were reversed both at Spa Francorchamps in Belgium and at the very wet East German Grand Prix. At the Ulster Grand Prix, Jim Redman was literally cruising home in the 350cc race when he hit a patch of oil and crashed, breaking his arm, and eliminating himself from the last few meetings. Once again, the 250cc World Championship was Yamaha's, and Phil Read's.

In early September at Monza, Yamaha wheeled out the worst kept secret of the year, the 250cc Vee-four RD05 for Phil Read to ride.

In the race it proved difficult to start, and Read was last off the grid, but by the ninth lap he had worked his way up to second behind Tarquinio Provini on the four-cylinder Benelli. Then the Yamaha went on to three cylinders, forcing Read to make a pit stop and change plugs. After that he could do no better than to work his way back up to seventh at the race's end. Nevertheless, the Vee-four's speed was unquestionable, and highly promising for 1966.

The RD05 was a machine of ferocious complexity calculated to make any race mechanic's heart sink at the sight of it. The engine in effect consisted of two twins, one lying horizontal, the other at an included angle of about 80 degrees leaning slightly forward from the vertical. There was, of course, central gear drive to a seven- or eight-speed gearbox (depending upon the circuit) with a huge external dry clutch on the right. Each crankcase had its own disc valve and carburettor and there were of course four exhaust pipes, two carried at low level, tucked inside the frame rails, with the two pipes for the upright cylinders facing rearward and carried straight back, outside the frame and fitted with heat shields. A very large radiator for the impeller-assisted cooling was fitted high up under the front of the tank rails. The front forks were exact copies of the Italian Ceriani, with a huge twin-leading-shoe ventilated front brake. The whole engine/gearbox unit was very large and bulky and closely shoehorned into what appeared to be the standard RD56 frame.

Phil Read on the 125cc V-four RA31 in 1968.

In the few races they had contested in 1965, the little water-cooled RA97 twins had gone well – Duff had won the 125cc race at Assen and Read the 125cc TT, beating Taveri's Honda and with Mike Duff third. The RA97s were to race again in 1966, now fitted with nine-speed gearboxes. Only Read and Ivy were to ride the 250cc-Vee fours, Mike Duff being mounted on an updated RD56. Throughout 1956, both Read and Ivy (and on occasion Japanese rider Motohashi) rode twins in British events. This caused considerable ill-feeling amongst the rank-and-file British riders, but the appearance of Yamaha, Honda and Suzuki works machines and riders was a powerful attraction welcomed by promoters and spectators alike.

The first outing of 1966 was as usual at the West German Grand Prix at Hockenheim in May. It was not particularly rewarding for Yamaha, with Read third in the 125cc race and Ivy third in the 250cc. Read had shown that the RD05 was as fast as the six-cylinder Hondas of Redman and Hailwood, but a fall ended his 250cc race. There was no 125cc event at Clermont Ferrand, and again the best that Read could do on the four was third place – Ivy fell early in the race.

The TT series was postponed until September in 1966 because of a seamen's strike, and perhaps just as well for Yamaha, because by June it was painfully obvious that neither the handling nor the braking of the Vee-fours were up to the power of the engines. New brakes with heavy, interrupted firing on the drums were made and at one stage Reynolds Tubes in Birmingham were asked to make a frame and fly it out to Japan for evaluation. By July there was quite serious discussion about reverting to a water-cooled version of the 250cc twin. And at the Finnish Grand Prix, though Read and Ivy rode in the 125cc event, the 250cc bikes were absent, being completely rebuilt in anticipation of the Ulster Grand Prix and the TT – not that Yamaha scored any points in the 250cc class at *either* event! At the Ulster, Yamaha sprang a complete surprise – especially in view of the problems with the RD05 – in the shape of a 125cc Vee-four, an almost exact scaled-down copy of the 250cc machine and known as the RA31. It ran in practice but was not raced. At the TT the RA97 twins were raced and Ivy won with Read second and Mike Duff fourth.

Although Jim Redman had retired after the Belgian Grand Prix, the six-cylinder Honda, now ridden to even greater effect by Mike Hailwood, still had the legs of Yamaha, and it was no surprise when Hailwood won the 250cc World Championship. He had scored an overwhelming 56 points to Read's 34. In the 125cc class, Bill Ivy did relatively better with 40 points to Luigi Tavini's winning total of 44. The RD Section worked hard over the winter of 1966, for though Honda had announced their withdrawal from the 125cc class, they were as keen as ever on the 250cc class and hoped and intended that Mike Hailwood should again win the Championship. Determined to overcome the difficulties they had experienced in 1966, Yamaha redesigned the frame yet again, lower and stiffer, and with a longer swinging arm. Mike Duff was told in February that he could expect no support, all of which would be concentrated on Ivy and Read. It was decided too, that the RA97 twins would be retired and the new 125cc RA31 Vee-4 would be used – much to Bill Ivy's initial dismay, for at the start of the season he had not even seen the four, let alone ridden it! Nevertheless, he was immediately at home on it and won first time out in May at the Spanish Grand Prix. Altogether in 1967 he had no less than eight straight wins and one second place on the 125cc Vee-four – enough points to give him an overwhelming victory in the World Championship.

Yet the 250cc Vee-four, over which so much time and effort had been spent and which was now supposedly developing 70 hp, continued to suffer at the hands of Hailwood and the Honda six.

At the opening round in Spain, Read won the 250cc race, but only after Hailwood had a punctured tyre while 35 seconds in the lead! At Spa-Francorchamps, both Yamaha riders beat Hailwood, but only because he had terminal problems with his gearbox. The 250cc Championship was in the balance right up until the season's end with both Read and Hailwood having scored 50 points up to the Japanese Grand Prix at Fuji. Ironically, neither rider finished, but the Championship was Hailwood's under FIM regulations.

At the start of 1968, Honda withdrew from Grand Prix racing, and Suzuki followed suit. Perhaps Yamaha should have done the same, because their two World Championships in the 125cc and 250cc class in 1968 not only were hollow in view of the lack of credible opposition, but were gained amid an atmosphere of sordid squabbling and backbiting that did nobody's reputation any good. About the only memorable feature of the year's result was Bill Ivy's lap of the Mountain circuit on the 125cc Vee-four at 100.32 mph. After that, his second lap, Bill slowed right down, and the race was won by Phil Read (who had at one stage been 15 seconds in arrears) at 99.12 mph. Engine trouble for an unfortunate Bill Ivy? Not at all! He had been told to let Phil Read win the race, because Yamaha wanted the 125cc World Championship to go to Read and the 250cc to Ivy. But Bill's temperament was such that, believing that he could lap at 100 mph, he did so, and then pulled up, chatted to the crowd, and generally made it offensively clear that he was riding to orders and could have won hands down had he been allowed. Despite this exhibition of pique, relations between Ivy and Read remained good on the surface. Their agreement still held at the Dutch at the end of June and at the Sachsenring in July, but by now Read had a shrewd idea that Yamaha would follow Honda and Suzuki and withdraw from racing at the end of the season.

The split came at the Czechoslovakian round at Brno, when, after Ivy had fallen in the wet 125cc race, heavily bruising himself, Read refused to make allowances and stormed off to win the 250cc race. He then had 36 points in the World Championship to Bill's 38. Exactly when Phil Read decided to break the agreement is not clear, and nor is his reason for so doing. Without doubt he had been irritated by some of Bill's ill-considered remarks to the Press, and he was thinking, too, of the future. Practically the only 'works' riders in 1969 would be with the MV and Benelli factories, and a 250cc World Championship would count for so much more than a 125cc. In Finland, he clinched the 125cc title, and in the 250cc race relentlessly harried Ivy, who fell, cracking a bone in his leg. Read now led the 250cc Championship on points. The 'feud' was now common news and the Press milked it for all it was worth. Ivy continued to be indiscreet and bitter – Read said nothing. At the Ulster Grand Prix, Ivy secretly had an oversize fuel tank made so as to run non-stop. Read found out – and had one made too! Yamaha flew out special exhaust pipes for Ivy's bike, but the outcome was non-committal, because, shadowing Ivy, Read's radiator was punctured by a stone, he lost the cooling water, and the bike seized.

The final race – and the decider – was Monza, and Read won, securing the 250cc World Championship. In an almost unbelievably petty way, which lost him a lot of sympathy, Ivy protested the result on the grounds that Read's front number plate (which had identical dimensions to his own) was not as specified in the regulations, and that Read had used a make of chain other than that specified on the entry form. The protest was treated with the contempt it deserved. Later, to justify his action, Ivy claimed that Read had told him that if he (Ivy) won, he (Read) would protest on the grounds that Ivy was below the FIM's minimum weight for a rider of 132 lb. Whatever Yamaha's intentions may have been over 1969, there is no doubt but that this squalid public feud decided them to withdraw. All the bikes and spares were collected and returned to Japan during November 1968. In that month, one time works rider Hasegawa, now an executive of Yamaha, took a busman's holiday and gave the RD05 its last victory of all at the Macau Grand Prix.

What few works racing Yamahas survive – for example there is only one complete RD56 – belong to the factory, who sometimes loan them to museums in Japan. As far as is known, none escaped into private hands, and certainly none are ever seen at European events.